THE LIBERTY READER

edited and introduced by
David Miller

EDINBURGH UNIVERSITY PRESS

© Paradigm Publishers, 2006

First published in the UK in 2006 by
Edinburgh University Press Ltd
22 George Square, Edinburgh

First published in the USA in 2006 by Paradigm Publishers

Parts of this book were originally published as *Liberty* by Oxford University Press
in 1991

Typeset by Straight Creek Bookmakers, and
printed and bound in the USA

A CIP record for this book is available from the British Library

ISBN 0 7486 2484 8 (hardback)
ISBN 0 7486 2485 6 (paperback)

The right of the contributors to be identified as authors of this work has been
asserted in accordance with the Copyright, Designs and Patents Act 1988.

Contents

INTRODUCTION

David Miller

Liberty, or freedom, is the most potent of political ideas. When we think of liberty, we think of people struggling to throw off the shackles of some outside oppressive force. Sometimes the struggle is a collective one: a whole people is held in chains by a foreign power or a local dictator. Sometimes an individual person fights or protests against a law that prevents him from saying what he wants to say or doing what he wants to do. Sometimes the struggle is more internal—for example, a person might endeavor to rid herself of inhibitions or ways of thinking that prevent her from living the way she really wants. Images of these efforts resonate throughout history: Spartacus leading the slave revolt against the armies of Rome; Latimer and Ridley going to the stake for their religious convictions; Americans in native dress dumping chests of tea into Boston harbour; Thoreau retreating from society to build his cabin in the woods; black Americans boycotting segregated buses in Montgomery, Alabama; Chinese students standing face-to-face with tanks in Tiananmen Square; Berliners hacking down the wall that had divided East from West. In each case it is easy to see who the enemies of liberty are. But it is harder to say what exactly these freedom fighters were fighting for: is it one thing, or several different things? Liberty is an elusive as well as a potent ideal.

The essays collected in this book are all attempts to explain what liberty means and why it is important. Written mainly by philosophers, they deal with questions that may at times seem quite abstract and unrelated to the practical issues that arise in social and political life. Yet they are all driven by the political beliefs of their authors, which lead them to highlight one or another aspect of this complex idea. Indeed it is a good test of a theory of liberty that it can help us make sense of historical struggles such as those referred to previously. There cannot be a purely philosophical analysis of liberty, even though philosophical analysis can help us think more clearly and avoid confusing liberty with other political values such as justice or democracy.[1]

I have chosen essays composed in the last hundred or so years—chosen on grounds of their intellectual quality, but also to reflect a wide range of views about what liberty means and how it can be achieved—but thinking about liberty goes back much further in time. We can better understand these contributions by placing them in the context of longer-standing traditions of thought about liberty. There are three main traditions, which I shall refer to as *families* of ideas, since they do not amount to three cut-and-dried conceptions of freedom, but rather are clusters of ideas held together by a family resemblance among their members. Moreover, as I shall illustrate, there can be fruitful intermarriages where an idea of freedom combines elements from two or even perhaps all three of these lineages.

The first and oldest family, I shall call *republican*. This is the most directly political conception of freedom, since it defines freedom by reference to a certain set of political arrangements. To be a free person is to be a citizen of a free political community. A free political community, in turn, is one that is self-governing. This means, first of all, one that is not subject to rule by foreigners, second, one in which the citizens play an active role in government, so that the laws that are enacted in some sense reflect the wishes of the people. That does not imply strict democracy. There is a long-running family argument about precisely which political arrangements are best suited to preserving liberty, and about the related question concerning the qualifications necessary for a person to be a citizen. The Greek political philosophers, who originated this way of understanding freedom, generally assumed that large classes of people were disqualified from citizenship by nature or by social role—women, slaves, manual labourers. So not everyone was capable of achieving freedom. Again, the repub-

---

[1] The essays are about 'liberty' or 'freedom' (I shall use these terms interchangeably) in the social-cum-political sense and not about freedom in the metaphysical sense of freedom of the will, which is indeed a purely philosophical issue. Whether these two forms of freedom can ultimately be kept separate is itself a disputed question. This topic is touched upon in the contributions by Arendt and Hayek reprinted here (chs. 3 and 4, respectively).

lican tradition as a whole does not exclude the possibility that freedom might exist in, say, a constitutional monarchy, provided that the citizens were properly consulted before legislation was enacted (more radical members of the family would contend that this is too weak a view of citizenship). The opposite of freedom, in this tradition, is despotism—the arbitrary rule of a tyrant who disposes of his subjects' lives and possessions by means that they are powerless to resist.

The second family of views about freedom I shall call *liberal.* Freedom here is a property of individuals and consists in the absence of constraint or interference by others. A person is free to the extent that he is able to do things if he wishes—speak, worship, travel, marry—without these actions being blocked or hindered by the activities of other people. This conception of freedom is also directly related to politics, but in a quite different way from the first. In the liberal view, government secures freedom by protecting each person from the interference of others, but it also threatens freedom by itself imposing laws and directives backed up by the threat of force. So whereas the republican sees freedom as being realized through a certain kind of politics, the liberal tends to see freedom as beginning where politics ends, especially in various forms of private life. The extreme view here is that of the anarchist, who holds that freedom can only be fully realized when the coercive powers of government are destroyed. As we shall see, other members of the liberal family have quite different beliefs about the proper role of government activity—depending in particular on what they see as constraints on or interferences with people's lives—but they all share the view that freedom is a matter of the scope or extent of government rather than of its form or character.

Finally, we have those views of freedom that I shall collectively label *idealist.* Here the focus shifts from the social arrangements within which a person lives to the internal forces that determine how he shall act. A person is free when he is autonomous—when he follows his own authentic desires, or his rational beliefs about how he should live. The struggle for freedom is no longer directly with the external environment, but with elements within the person himself that thwart his desire to realize his own true nature—weaknesses, compulsions, irrational beliefs, and so forth. Now it might at first seem as though this conception of freedom has nothing to do with politics. But a connection is made as soon as the idealist identifies certain political conditions as necessary for freedom in this sense—and in the history of political thought such connections have often been made. However, the political implications of idealist views of freedom are very diverse indeed; members of this family often barely acknowledge one another, let alone debate. Some seem hardly to recognize politics at all, except as a distraction and interference with a life properly led in artistic spontaneity, in meditation, and the like.[2] Others see political arrangements as providing the conditions under which individuals may achieve their own freedom, for instance, by encouraging the cultural diversity that alone makes an authentic choice of lifestyle possible. Yet others see politics as the means whereby people can be disciplined to follow a rational mode of life. It is this last possibility that has preoccupied liberal critics of the idealist conception of freedom. As they see it, ordinary liberal freedoms—of speech, movement, and so on—may be sacrificed in the pursuit of a 'higher' form of freedom, as the state eliminates all those options that it would not be rational for people to choose. Thus, in the liberal view, there is a close connection between idealism as I have defined it here and totalitarianism in politics, whether of the Right (Nazism) or of the Left (Stalinist Communism). This connection is eloquently spelt out in Isaiah Berlin's 'Two Concepts of Liberty', reprinted in this volume (chapter 2). Equally, republicans will claim that, by turning the spotlight inward and conceiving of freedom as a condition of the self, idealists neglect those public institutions that alone safeguard worldly freedom from totalitarian despotism. Hannah Arendt's 'Freedom and Politics', also reprinted here (chapter 3), advances this claim.

Later we shall want to ask how far these charges are justified. Let me now illustrate how a political theorist may interbreed from the different families in the course of working out a particular conception of liberty. Jean Jacques Rousseau drew heavily on the republican tradition in developing a view of liberty under the social contract.[3] A person is free, he argued, when he is subject

---

[2] Diogenes the Cynic, who advocated a life of material self-sufficiency achieved by reducing one's needs as far as possible, stands at the head of this line. His attitude toward politics is captured in the story of his meeting with Alexander. Asked if he required anything, the philosopher asked the king to step aside from his sunlight.

[3] J. J. Rousseau, 'The Social Contract', in *The Social Contract and Discourses*, trans. and ed. G. D. H. Cole, J. H. Brumfitt, and J. C. Hall (London: Dent, 1973).

to laws that he has imposed on himself by participating in the formation of the general will—the collective view of his society about what is just or in the common interest. Here, then, is a republican view of freedom with a strongly democratic twist to it (Rousseau insisted that everyone—or at least every man[4]—must belong to the sovereign body that makes law). But he added to this an idealist claim: when a person is subject to the guidance of the general will, he achieves moral liberty, 'for the mere impulse of appetite is slavery, while obedience to a law which we prescribe to ourselves is liberty'.[5] Here Rousseau identifies freedom with the overcoming of desires that are seen as alien to our true nature. Political liberty under the general will also provides freedom in this higher and more intimate sense.

For a second illustration, consider the political thought of Niccolò Machiavelli. Again we have a thinker who falls broadly into the republican tradition. Machiavelli uses 'liberty' in a bewildering variety of senses, and it is far harder than in the case of Rousseau to pin down his idea with any precision.[6] In one major usage, however, he predicates liberty primarily of the state as a whole and contrasts the self-governing state with a tyranny in which laws are imposed by a prince in defiance of local practice. This is a quintessentially republican understanding of freedom. Yet, at the same time, he often uses the idea in liberal fashion to refer to personal freedom from constraint, as Quentin Skinner has argued in several essays. A person is free when he is able to pursue whatever private ends he may have, secure from interference by political authorities or by other private persons. Now Skinner seems to me to overstate his case when he claims that Machiavelli and others in the republican tradition use 'a *purely* negative view of liberty as the absence of impediments to the realization of our chosen ends',[7] since that overlooks the fact that a person's freedom

[4] Rousseau's exclusion of women from the political realm is discussed in S. M. Okin, *Women in Western Political Thought* (London: Virago, 1980), part III.

[5] Rousseau, *Social Contract*, p. 178.

[6] See the very helpful survey in M. L. Colish, 'The Idea of Liberty in Machiavelli', *Journal of the History of Ideas*, 32 (1971), 323–350.

[7] Skinner, 'The Paradoxes of Political Liberty', in *The Tanner Lectures on Human Values,* VII (Salt Lake City: University of Utah Press, 1986), p. 247, reprinted in D. Miller (ed.), *Liberty* (Oxford: Oxford University Press, 1991), p. 202 (emphasis added). In 'Machiavelli on the Maintenance of Liberty', *Politics* 18 (1983), 3–15, Skinner uses the vocabulary of 'public' and 'personal' liberty to describe Machiavelli's standpoint, which brings out

consists also in his membership in a self-governing state (the first sense of liberty noted previously). But the importance of Skinner's argument is the connection he establishes in these writings between republican institutions and the civic virtue that sustains them and the liberal freedoms that can only be securely enjoyed when such institutions are in place. Rather than having to choose between republican freedom and liberal freedom, perhaps we should see the former as a precondition of the latter.

So by identifying three broad ways of thinking about liberty, I do not mean to suggest that we should favour one and discard the other two. On the contrary, I want eventually to propose that a fully adequate understanding of social and political freedom needs to draw upon the resources of all three families. But next I would like to consider how the threefold contrast I have drawn relates to two more familiar distinctions that have been made in discussing liberty: that between ancient and modern liberty, and that between negative and positive freedom.

The first of these distinctions is due chiefly to the nineteenth-century French liberal Benjamin Constant and his lecture "The Liberty of the Ancients Compared with that of the Moderns."[8] According to Constant, liberty in the states of antiquity—especially ancient Greece—meant political liberty, the liberty to participate in a wide range of collective activities, deliberating in the agora, sitting on juries, and so forth. Among modern European nations, by contrast, liberty has come to mean civil liberty, freedom from arbitrary arrest, freedom of opinion, freedom of occupation and association, and other such individual rights. Constant used this distinction to make two main points. The first was that it was a grave error to attempt to resurrect liberty of the former kind in place of liberty of the latter kind in these modern states, an attempt to which he attributed some of the excesses of the French Revolution. One simple reason for this was that the ancient polities were small, and this allowed political participation to be a

---

(note 7 continued) more adequately the two-sided character of his view of liberty. Skinner is, however, undoubtedly right in his main contention, that the republican writers did not invoke a positive view of freedom if that connotes what I called an idealist view.

[8] B. Constant, "The Liberty of the Ancients Compared with that of the Moderns," in B. Constant, *Political Writings*, ed. B. Fontana (Cambridge, UK: Cambridge University Press, 1988).

meaningful and vivid experience for each person. The second point (sometimes overlooked by those wanting to draw straightforward liberal conclusions from Constant) was that a diluted form of ancient liberty—diluted through the interposition of a system of political representation—was nonetheless essential if modern liberty was to be secured. Constant warned his compatriots against being seduced by private enjoyments away from exercising their proper share of political power.

Constant's distinction corresponds almost precisely to the contrast drawn here between republican and liberal ideas of freedom. His thesis therefore raises two key questions: is the liberal view of freedom exclusively a product of the modern period? Has the republican tradition any relevance to modern debates about liberty, or has it now become anachronistic?

As far as the first question is concerned, Constant's claim appears with some qualifications to hold good. Although (as he himself concedes) the ancient city-states, and especially Athens, did in practice grant their citizens a measure of civil liberty, this was not the attribute that they primarily thought of and valued when they spoke of liberty. Freedom meant for them a social status, first and foremost the position of someone who was not a slave, but beyond that the status of citizen in a self-governing state.[9] The liberal view first came to the fore at the time of the Renaissance. We have seen already how republican and liberal ideas of freedom coexisted and complemented one another in the works of Machiavelli; Hobbes, writing just over a century later, was able vigorously to repudiate the republican view as involving a blatant confusion between the freedom of the commonwealth and the freedom of the individual.[10] This was an extreme position, and the tradition of republican liberalism continued to flourish for many years to come, but it demonstrates that a conception of freedom as consisting simply in the absence of external constraints was no longer unthinkable. Coming down to our time, this has become the dominant view of liberty in practical politics and in the writing of many liberal theorists.

[9] See the very lucid account in R. Mulgan, 'Liberty in Ancient Greece', in Z. Pelczynski and J. N. Gray (eds.), *Conceptions of Liberty in Political Philosophy* (London: Athlone Press, 1984).

[10] T. Hobbes, *Leviathan,* ed. R. Tuck (Cambridge, UK: Cambridge University Press, 1996), chapter 21.

Turning to the second question, does this imply that the republican view is moribund? Three essays included in this collection argue otherwise, while presenting significantly different accounts of republican freedom. Hannah Arendt (chapter 3) offers a defence of the ancient political ideal of liberty against both the liberal view and the idealist interpretation of liberty as an internal condition of the self. Arendt's argument is that both these latter views represent surrogates adopted by people to whom the authentic experience of freedom was no longer available. Freedom in the true sense, she claims, consists in acting on a public stage in the sight of other men who are then able to remember and so immortalize what was done. Only in such a context is it possible for a person to break out of the cycle of natural causation and achieve something genuinely original. The ancient city-states offered such a context: 'the Greek polis once was precisely that "form of government" which provided men with a space of appearances where they could act, with a kind of theatre where freedom could appear'.[11] Subsequently such 'spaces' have emerged only spasmodically, in particular in such moments of popular revolution as the founding of the American republic, the birth of workers' soviets in Russia, and so on.[12]

What is striking about such a view—apart from its pessimism about the chances of *sustaining* freedom in the modern world—is the way in which modern concerns have been infiltrated back into an account of the Greek polis. Arendt is preoccupied with the question of how genuine originality is possible, how people can break out of the mechanical routines of domestic and economic life. She finds the escape route in politics, but in doing so she distorts the latter activity to the point where it is barely recognizable. Arendt's political actor seems more like an actor in the literal sense than a participant in the making of decisions; the act is what counts—the delivery of the memorable speech, and so forth—not the practical outcome in the form of a law or policy that affects the community thereafter. We may find this a dangerously narcissistic view—and Arendt's view of the political process strangely insubstantial, in that she wants to exclude all consideration of the community's material interests from the agenda. But the main thing we can learn from Arendt is how difficult it is to defend a republican posi-

---

[11] H. Arendt, 'Freedom and Politics'; p. 65.
[12] See H. Arendt, *On Revolution* (Harmondsworth, UK: Penguin, 1973).

tion in the modern age without introducing, openly or covertly, an idea of freedom as a property of individuals, drawn from either the liberal or the idealist tradition.

Philip Pettit (chapter 11) responds to Constant's challenge in a different way. He accuses Constant of having loaded the scales against republicanism by ignoring the republican conception of freedom as nondomination. This conception indeed sees freedom as a property of individuals, but in contrast to the narrow liberal view of Hobbes, for instance, freedom is taken to mean the absence of *arbitrary* interference, not noninterference per se. This radically changes the relationship between liberty and law, in particular. A properly functioning legal system will protect freedom rather than infringe upon it, because although law sets limits to what people can do, it does not interfere arbitrarily in their lives; moreover it safeguards them against other individuals who may seek to dominate them. Pettit claims that republican freedom so understood is an idea fully relevant to modern conditions. It can be used, for instance, to justify redistributive policies of the kind associated with the welfare state, on the grounds that such policies protect individuals from domination, by their employers and others.

Freedom as nondomination bridges the gap between the republican and liberal traditions. But does it water down republicanism to the point where it becomes indistinguishable from a thoughtful liberalism? Whereas Arendt makes political action central to the life of the free individual, Pettit relegates it to the margins. He relies chiefly on constitutional constraints to prevent government itself from becoming an agent of domination. Quentin Skinner (chapter 12), although he shares Pettit's critique of liberty as the absence of interference, gives the alternative, republican, view—freedom as not being dependent on the will of another—a more strongly political reading. To be free is not simply to live under the rule of law, but to be an active citizen ready to challenge your government if it begins to act contrary to the best interests of the people. This, Skinner stresses, is not a 'positive' or what I am calling an idealist view of freedom. There is no suggestion that the good life for human beings is the life of politics. But political engagement is necessary if rights and liberties are to be protected against kings and others who would usurp them.

I have suggested that freedom can best be understood by reference to three families of views: republican, liberal, and idealist. But several authors prefer to use a twofold distinction between negative and posi-

rty, most famously Isaiah Berlin in his essay 'Two Concepts of
y' (chapter 2). How does Berlin distinguish these two senses of
m? Negative liberty is said to consist in the absence of obstruction or interference by other people. There are certain ambiguities
in Berlin's account of what constitutes obstruction or interference,
which I shall return to later, but the concept itself clearly corresponds
to what I have called the liberal view of freedom. Berlin's positive
sense of freedom, however, is far less clearly specified. When he first
introduces it, he identifies it as self-mastery: a person is free when he
controls his own life, rather than being an instrument of someone
else's will. As the concept is developed, however, it comes to embrace
a number of quite different doctrines, of which three in particular
may usefully be isolated:

1. Freedom as the power or capacity to act in certain ways, as contrasted with the mere absence of interference.
2. Freedom as rational self-direction, the condition in which a person's
   life is governed by rational desires as opposed to the desires that she
   just as a matter of fact has.
3. Freedom as collective self-determination, the condition where each
   person plays his part in controlling his social environment through
   democratic institutions.

It should be apparent that the third of these 'positive' views of freedom corresponds to what I have called republican freedom, and
the second to what I have called idealist freedom. Berlin is quite
correct to distinguish these ideas from the 'negative' conception of
freedom favoured by liberals, but it may not be illuminating to lump
them together as versions of a single 'positive' concept. In Berlin's
defence it should be said that some advocates of 'positive' freedom
do amalgamate various different elements in a single conception.
We can see this happening, for instance, in the essay by T. H. Green
that opens this collection.

Green defines freedom as 'a positive power or capacity of doing or
enjoying something worth doing or enjoying, and that, too, something
that we do or enjoy in common with others'.[13] He contrasts this with
mere freedom from restraint or, compulsion, which he regards as
worthless by comparison. Notice that Green's definition contains

---

[13] T. H. Green, 'Liberal Legislation and Freedom of Contract', p. 21.

three elements that in principle can be separated. First there is the claim that true freedom involves the capacity to do things, not the mere absence of restraint. Second there is the moral element: the things we do must be worth doing, which for Green meant that they had moral value. Third there is the social element: freedom must be enjoyed 'in common with others', which meant not only that one person cannot enjoy freedom at the cost of imposing restrictions on other people, but also that when I act freely I make some positive contribution to the well-being of others. None of these elements entails the others: you could define freedom as a power without bringing in any moral evaluation of how the power was used; you could claim that a person is only free when he does something valuable without implying that freedom must be a common possession, and so on.

The internal complexity of Green's 'positive' conception of freedom seems to bear out Berlin's wide-ranging critique of the notion. But we should perhaps pause to ask why Green thought it necessary to pack so much into the definition. Green wanted to wean liberals away from laissez-faire policies, encapsulated in the doctrine that freedom of contract was a sacred thing, not to be interfered with by government legislation. In particular, he favoured factory legislation to protect the health and safety of workers, legislation to protect the position of agricultural tenants who were being exploited by landlords, and tighter controls on the public sale of liquor, including the option of complete prohibition if the residents of a particular locality voted for it. On the face of it, these measures involved restricting people's freedom in the ordinary, negative sense; but, Green argued, they could be seen as means of promoting freedom in its true, positive sense. The first element in Green's definition catered for the workers and the tenants, who while enjoying the formal freedom to make whatever contracts they liked with their employers and landlords, respectively, were in fact powerless to do anything other than accept disadvantageous terms. By narrowing down the range of permissible contracts, legislation would increase their power to achieve a decent standard of life. The second element in the definition catered for the drunkards, whose consumption of liquor did not amount to 'something worth doing or enjoying', whereas constraint in this respect would liberate them for more worthwhile activities. The third element catered for both groups, since Green claimed that employers' and landlords' freedom of contract was presently enjoyed at the expense of workers and tenants, while the freedom to drink imposed costs on the rest of society, especially on the family of the drunkard. Thus Green's portmanteau definition of freedom admirably served the political case he wanted to make, but at the cost of introducing confusion as to how exactly the 'positive' sense of freedom is supposed to differ from the 'negative'.

If we return to Berlin, we can see that the heart of his objection to 'positive' liberty lies in his opposition to the idealist view of freedom as rational self-direction. It is this view that, he believes, easily becomes transformed into a recipe for controlling and manipulating people so that they come to serve the ends that some authority has decreed to be rational—a belief for which there is plainly considerable historical warrant.[14] Apart from that, Berlin's main plea is that freedom in the negative or liberal sense should not be confused with other ideals that have also been called by that name. He does not, for instance, oppose the ideal of national self-determination—indeed he sympathizes with it.[15] Nor does he deny that it is naturally and properly seen as an ideal of liberty. His point is that liberty in this sense is neither conceptually nor as a matter of fact identical with negative liberty. A nation may govern itself collectively, yet impose severe restrictions on the freedom of action of its members. This point is both true and important.[16]

Berlin's essay raises several questions requiring further discussion. One is whether it is possible to draw a valid conceptual distinction between negative and positive freedom, as Berlin attempts to do. A second is how best to define the negative view: if we say that negative (or liberal) freedom consists in the absence of external interference or constraint, what, more precisely, should count as interference or constraint? A third is whether a fully adequate understanding of human freedom does not require us to include some elements of the 'positive', or what I have been calling the idealist, conception. I shall look at each of these questions in turn.

[14] See Berlin, 'Two Concepts of Liberty', ss. 2 and 3.

[15] I have discussed Berlin's attitude to nationalism in 'Crooked Timber or Bent Twig? Isaiah Berlin's Nationalism', *Political Studies,* 53 (2005), 100–123.

[16] Like Constant, with whom he has much in common, Berlin has been presented as a simpleminded devotee of negative liberty. Apart from anything else, this conflicts with his general doctrine that liberty in this sense is only one among many values, none of which has absolute priority over the rest. The claim he wishes to make is that the safeguarding of a certain minimum area of negative liberty is essential to human well-being, and that this minimum should not be snatched from us on the pretext that no real loss of liberty is involved since 'true' or 'positive' freedom is being

On the conceptual question, the most powerful response to Berlin is to be found in G. C. MacCallum's essay 'Negative and Positive Freedom' (chapter 5). MacCallum argues that there is only one concept of liberty, embodied in the formula 'X (an agent) is free from Y (preventing condition) to do or become Z'.[17] Disputes about the nature of liberty, MacCallum claims, are disputes about the proper range of the three variables, X, Y, and Z. Thus whereas for 'negative' conceptions the X variable covers ordinary flesh and blood people with their preferences, beliefs, and so forth, for 'positive' conceptions X may cover 'real' selves—persons with the preferences and beliefs they would have if they were fully rational, for instance. MacCallum offers us a way of thinking about different views of freedom that many have found helpful; in particular, he shows that the contrast between negative and positive views cannot be captured by the verbal difference between 'freedom from' and 'freedom to', as Berlin occasionally suggests. Yet we may still wonder whether MacCallum's formula is really neutral as between the three broad ways of thinking about freedom we have identified—republican, liberal, and idealist—or whether it is not specifically tailored to the liberal family of ideas.[18] And we should also ask whether, even if all statements about freedom can be made to fit MacCallum's formula, this is sufficient to establish the existence of a single idea of liberty. The three traditions appear to embody very different basic assumptions about human beings and what gives meaning to their lives: is it not more illuminating to say that, because of this, we have here three contrasting ways of understanding liberty?

Turning now to the question of what, in the negative view, should count as an interference with, or constraint on, freedom, we find that Berlin is neither clear nor consistent in what he says. At one point he speaks of freedom as consisting in the absence of coercion, 'the deliberate interference of other human beings within the area in which I could otherwise act'; at another of human beings 'making

---

(*note 16 continued*) promoted. This is made especially clear in the introduction to I. Berlin, *Liberty,* ed. H. Hardy (Oxford, UK: Oxford University Press, 2002).

[17] See also the somewhat similar analysis in J. Feinberg, 'The Idea of a Free Man', in J. Feinberg, *Rights, Justice, and the Bounds of Liberty* (Princeton, NJ: Princeton University Press, 1980).

[18] For criticism of MacCallum on this point, see T. Baldwin, 'MacCallum and the Two Concepts of Freedom', *Ratio* 26 (1984), 125–142; J. N. Gray, 'On Negative and Positive Liberty', in Z. Pelczynski and J. N. Gray (eds.), *Conceptions of Liberty in Political Philosophy* (London: Athlone Press, 1984).

arrangements' that prevent me from achieving my aims; at yet another of 'the part that I believe to be played by other human beings, directly or indirectly, with or without the intention of doing so, in frustrating my wishes'.[19] These formulations concur in asserting that constraints on freedom must be attributable to human agency (as opposed to natural obstacles such as the force of gravity), but they diverge over whether freedom can only be restricted by the deliberate acts of other human beings and also over whether there must be a direct connection between the act and the restriction for it to count as such. Equally, Berlin is ambiguous as to whether economic obstacles—lack of resources, say—should count as limitations on negative freedom, or whether only laws, coercive threats, and other such actively imposed obstacles should qualify.[20]

These are important issues for a defender of the liberal view of freedom. For illumination we may turn to the papers by Hayek, Steiner, Cohen, and myself, which present clear, but contrasting, accounts of what negative liberty consists in.

Hayek (chapter 4) develops the idea that freedom consists in the absence of deliberate interference by other people. His is a classical liberal view of freedom, and, although like Berlin he insists on keeping the negative concept separate from republican and idealist views of liberty, his most important objective is to defeat the belief that a person's freedom depends on the material resources available to him—a belief that might justify economic redistribution as a means of increasing the freedom of the poor. He defines freedom as the absence of coercion, and coercion as a state of affairs in which one person is made into the instrument of another's will. For Hayek, this implies that rules of law—general, abstract rules laid down in advance of the particular activities they are meant to regulate—are not coercive, for such laws do not direct behaviour but are merely conditions that a person takes into account when deciding how to act. Thus in Hayek's view a liberal political order, composed entirely of such rules, imposes no limits at all on negative liberty in the proper sense of that term.

[19] These phrases all occur within the space of a single paragraph in Berlin, 'Two Concepts of Liberty', pp. 34–35.

[20] Berlin's formulations cannot be made wholly consistent with one another, but they may be reconciled to some degree through his claim that our understanding of freedom will depend upon our beliefs about the causes of the obstacles that lie in our path; what we count as constraint, in other words, will depend upon our social theory, which tells us which aspects of our environment are to be regarded as human artifacts and which as natural conditions.

There are a number of problems with Hayek's analysis. It is often difficult to see what justifies his drawing the boundaries in the places that he does. Why, for instance, analyze freedom simply in terms of coercion in the first place? Someone who physically restrains me— shackles me to a wall, for instance—surely impedes my freedom just as much as another who makes me perform some action by issuing a threat, the paradigm case of coercion. There are difficulties, too, with the claim that rules of law do not coerce those who are subject to them—Hayek's argument here seems to rest on a conceptual error.[21] A number of libertarian critics have pointed out that Hayek's claim about liberty and the rule of law overlooks the possibility that a law might be general and abstract and yet highly restrictive of the behaviour of those subject to it—consider, for instance, the American prohibition laws.[22] Finally, Hayek appears to put the cat among the pigeons when he concedes that in certain circumstances economic power might be used in a coercive manner.[23] Once the possibility has been conceded, why restrict the circumstances as narrowly as Hayek does, confining them to extreme cases where an individual enjoys a monopoly of a vital resource? Why not admit that the distribution of resources is always going to be relevant to the distribution of negative liberty in a society?

Both Steiner and Cohen would endorse this last suggestion.[24] Steiner's paper (chapter 6) presents a conception of negative liberty that is in many respects the direct opposite of Hayek's. It defines freedom as 'the personal possession of physical objects' and denies that coercive threats interfere with freedom, since, Steiner argues, such threats make courses of action less desirable without making them impossible to follow. This view descends directly from Hobbes, who, as we saw earlier, was the first to present an unequivocally liberal or negative concept of freedom. Hobbes defined liberty as the

---

[21] See D. Miller, *Market, State, and Community: Theoretical Foundations of Market Socialism* (Oxford, UK: Clarendon Press, 1989), chapter 1, s. 2, and C. Kukathas, *Hayek and Modern Liberalism* (Oxford, UK: Clarendon Press, 1989), chapter 4, s. 4, for two slightly different diagnoses of where the error lies.

[22] See especially R. Hamowy, 'Freedom and the Rule of Law in F. A. Hayek', *Il politico* 36 (1971), 349–377; J. N. Gray, 'Hayek on Liberty, Rights and Justice', *Ethics* 92 (1981–1982), 73–84.

[23] See his discussion of the water monopolist in *The Constitution of Liberty* (London: Routledge and Kegan Paul, 1960), chapter 9, s. 3, reprinted here as 'Freedom and Coercion', chapter 4, s. 2.3.

[24] As would P. Jones, 'Freedom and the Redistribution of Resources', *Journal of Social Policy* 11 (1982), 217–238, and Miller, *Market, State, and Community*, chapter 1.

absence of external impediments to motion, and Steiner likewise argues that B only impinges on A's freedom when he renders one or more of A's actions impossible by controlling the physical space in which it could occur.

This conception of liberty has a number of advantages deriving from the clear and robust notion of constraint that it embodies. We can establish whether a person is at liberty to perform some action without making any assumptions about their psychology—for example, about the deterrent effect on them of legal sanctions or threats of other kinds. We are never placed in the somewhat awkward position of having to say that a person was not free to do what they have actually done, as we are by more conventional negative conceptions.[25] And Steiner's view allows us to compute the extent of a person's liberty simply by summing up the objects he controls,[26] thus avoiding the difficulties faced by Berlin, for instance, in making such a computation,[27] and which critics of the negative view such as Charles Taylor seize upon as a way of dislodging it.[28]

Corresponding to these advantages, however, are some major drawbacks. The impossibility criterion seems too restrictive a way of characterizing *human* freedom. What if someone prevents me from embarking upon a course of action by threatening my life if I proceed with it? Is my freedom not diminished here, even though I do of course still make a choice in complying with the threat? And is it not equally strange to conclude, as Steiner does, that the total amount of freedom present in a society can never be increased or decreased, but only distributed in different ways? The physicalist approach advocated by Steiner appears in the end to detach the concept of liberty too radically from assumptions about human aims and purposes that normally give point to that concept.

Cohen (chapter 8) agrees with Steiner that the distribution of freedom in a society depends upon the distribution of property, but he rejects the implication that the sum total of freedom is fixed. In

---

[25] For instance, given that there is a law prohibiting bodily assault backed up by substantial penalties, we would normally say that people are not free to assault one another; nevertheless some attacks do take place, and we are then in the position of having to say that the assailants did what they were not free to do.

[26] See further H. Steiner, 'How Free: Computing Personal Liberty', in A. Phillips Griffiths (ed.), *Of Liberty* (Cambridge, UK: Cambridge University Press, 1983).

[27] As he concedes in 'Two Concepts of Liberty', chapter 2, n. 17.

[28] I shall shortly come to discuss Taylor's argument.

particular, he considers the possibility that a certain form of socialism would extend freedom more widely than the private property system characteristic of capitalism. One of the incidental virtues of Cohen's paper is that it demonstrates how an argument for socialism can be mounted simply in terms of the negative or liberal notion of freedom.[29] It is sometimes alleged that socialists must have recourse to a 'positive' view of liberty; Cohen's paper proves otherwise.

We have still not found a satisfactory way of distinguishing between restrictions of (negative) freedom and other kinds of obstructions that may prevent us from acting as we would like. In the paper reprinted as chapter 9, I argue that the distinction can only be made by introducing the notion of moral responsibility; constraints on freedom are those obstacles for which other human beings can be held morally responsible, either because they have created them, deliberately or negligently, or because they have failed to remove them, despite being under an obligation to do so. Thus poverty or disease will be seen as restricting the freedom of those who suffer from them *if* we believe that someone else—the government, say—has an obligation to remove these evils. If this analysis is correct, it suggests one reason why people who share the liberal view of freedom continue to argue so much about its political implications—in particular whether it supports a capitalist or a socialist economic system: they cannot agree about the limits of social obligation, and therefore about whether human agents should be held responsible for the persistence of poverty and other such disabling conditions.

But can we say everything we want to say about individual freedom using only some version of the negative idea? Two essays included here suggest otherwise. Charles Taylor (chapter 7) agrees with Berlin that there is a contrast between the negative and positive senses of freedom, but he believes that we cannot do without some form of the positive concept. In particular, he claims that we cannot make sense of judgments about the relative degrees of freedom enjoyed

[29] I should stress, therefore, that when I label this view of freedom 'liberal', I do not intend the label to be interpreted in any narrow, party-political sense. Many socialists have used the negative conception, as have many conservatives. Political disputes about liberty can take many forms without thereby becoming disagreements about the concept itself: disputes about what should count as 'constraint', disputes about how much liberty different classes of people should enjoy, disputes about how valuable liberty is in comparison to other social goods (justice, authority, etc.). Berlin also recognizes this point (see *Liberty*, Introduction, pp. 38–39).

in different societies without evaluating the *significance* of actions to those who perform them. He also defends the central idealist claim that a person who does not act on his most significant desires is to that extent unfree, and so it matters in assessing freedom not only what opportunities people have but also what they actually choose to do. However, the political implications of this position are not traced through; Taylor does not tell us who decides which desires are most significant or what we might be justified in doing about people who act on a distorted view of their own desires.

Compare the position taken by John Stuart Mill in his essay 'On Liberty'.[30] Mill wanted to defend negative liberty, in particular by invoking the principle that the state had no right to interfere with what he called 'self-regarding' conduct. Like Taylor, however, Mill was keenly aware that people might fail to recognize and act upon their most significant aims in life, and to that extent we can say that there are strong idealist (or 'positive') elements in Mill's conception of liberty. But since he at the same time believed that each person had to discover his own best path in life, there was no practical conflict: protecting negative liberty in the form of each person's right to their private space gave the best chance for liberty in the form of self-determination to flourish.[31] This suggests that shifting from a liberal view of freedom as the absence of external constraints to a more complex position that includes 'positive' or idealist elements, as Taylor does, does not mean abandoning liberalism as a general political creed.

A stronger challenge to liberalism is posed by Nancy Hirschmann's feminist view of freedom in chapter 10. Hirschmann argues that reflecting on practical cases in which women's freedom is at issue reveals that neither negative nor positive conceptions, as normally understood, are adequate to explain how women are made unfree by patriarchal societies. External constraints and women's own self-consciousness interact to create barriers that women cannot cross. But at the same time we cannot postulate an 'authentic' female self in opposition to the socially constructed selves that we find around us. Instead we need to identify circumstances under which women will

[30] J. S. Mill, 'On Liberty', in J. S. Mill, *Utilitarianism; On Liberty; Representative Government*, ed. A. D. Lindsay (London: Dent, 1964).

[31] This claim is, of course, challengeable. For criticism, see Berlin, chapter 2, s. i, and S. Mendus, 'Liberty and Autonomy', *Proceedings of the Aristotelian Society* 87 (1986–1987), 207–220.

be best able to define themselves and decide how to live. Hirschmann argues that women-only groups provide the necessary contexts. Thus she rejects the liberal idea that the coexistence in a society of many different ideas and forms of life is in general sufficient by itself to enable individuals to become autonomous. Because patriarchy has penetrated so deeply into women's consciousness, only a retreat into separatist groups can accomplish this.

Critics will argue that Hirschmann's conception of freedom is open to the same objections as other idealist views. Separatist activity of the kind she describes will in fact give rise to 'correct' and 'incorrect' ways of being a woman, rather than to genuine autonomy. If women are socially constructed all the way down, then entry into *autocoscienza* groups will construct them differently, but no more authentically. Certainly standard negative freedoms of thought, expression, and association seem essential as a background against which women's search for personal autonomy can proceed.

What, then, should we conclude about the meaning of liberty after reading the essays contained in this book? First, that liberty is a complex achievement, and to understand it properly we need to draw on the resources of each of three main traditions we have identified. Freedom can be lost because you cannot achieve political self-determination but are governed by unaccountable rulers or by outsiders; it can be lost because your options are narrowed down by oppressive laws, by lawless threats, or by lack of resources; or it can be lost because although you have options, you cannot choose autonomously which you will pursue, because you are confused, or a slave to tradition. Conversely, to be genuinely free, a person must live under social and political arrangements that she has helped to make; she must enjoy an extensive sphere of activity within which she is not subject to constraint; and she must decide for herself how she is to live, not borrow her ideas from others. Now there can be no guarantee that achieving freedom on any of these dimensions will also bring freedom on the others. But there is some cause for optimism. We have seen how republican freedom as self-government can contribute to the protection of liberal freedom as the absence of constraint. Equally, having a wide sphere within which a person can act without constraint is at least a necessary condition for that person's becoming autonomous. It may not be a sufficient condition because, as Mill pointed out, even where people are negatively free to choose their own pattern of life, they may be too dominated by custom, too afraid to step into the unknown, to make use of that freedom. What else is needed? Philosophers disagree about this question, but cultural diversity, in the sense of having many different belief systems and ways of living present in your society, seems important.[32] Choice becomes inescapable when there is no dominant view about how you are to conduct your life.

I began by citing some historical examples of people fighting for freedom and asked the question whether there was a single goal that united them. The answer, we now see, is that liberty has more than one dimension, and so over the course of history the quest for freedom has inevitably taken different forms. Moreover, philosophers disagree about which aspect of liberty is most significant, some stressing political freedom as self-government, others the importance to individuals of having spheres of free action, yet others the inner quest for authenticity. But my final suggestion is that we should resist the idea that only one of these dimensions constitutes the 'real' meaning of freedom. Liberty is not a single thing, but a precious (and always precarious) human achievement of considerable intricacy.

ACKNOWLEDGMENTS

This book is a revised and expanded version of an anthology first published by Oxford University Press, with additional essays and an updated bibliography. I should like to thank Geoffrey Smith for his advice on the original introduction and Julia Skorupska and Zofia Stemplowska for their invaluable help in selecting texts and preparing the new bibliography.

---

[32] See S. I. Benn, *A Theory of Freedom* (Cambridge, UK: Cambridge University Press, 1988) and J. Raz, *The Morality of Freedom* (Oxford, UK: Clarendon Press, 1986), part v. for arguments to this effect.

ONE

LIBERAL LEGISLATION AND FREEDOM OF CONTRACT

T. H. Green

Delivered as a lecture to the Leicester Liberal Association in January 1881.
Green began the lecture by pointing out that liberals, who in the early part of the
19th century had favoured complete freedom of contract, had in recent years
supported legislation limiting that freedom in the interests of the more
vulnerable party. He referred to factory legislation and to compulsory schooling.
After explaining, in the first section reprinted here, how these interferences with
freedom of contract could be seen as contributing to freedom in the true sense, he
considered two further applications of the same principle: the regulation of
agricultural tenancies (omitted here) and measures to control the liquor trade
(included).

We shall probably all agree that freedom, rightly understood, is the greatest of blessings; that its attainment is the true end of all our effort as citizens. But when we thus speak of freedom, we should consider carefully what we mean by it. We do not mean merely freedom from restraint or compulsion. We do not mean merely freedom to do as we like irrespectively of what it is that we like. We do not mean a freedom that can be enjoyed by one man or one set of men at the cost of a loss of freedom to others. When we speak of freedom as something to be so highly prized, we mean a positive power or capacity of doing or enjoying something worth doing or enjoying, and that, too, something that we do or enjoy in common with others. We mean by it a power which each man exercises through the help or security given him by his fellow-men, and which he in turn helps to secure for them. When we measure

T. H. Green, 'Liberal Legislation and Freedom of Contract', abridged from
Works of T. H. Green, III (Longmans, Green & Co., 1888), 370–7, 382–6.

the progress of a society by its growth in freedom, we measure it by the increasing development and exercise on the whole of those powers of contributing to social good with which we believe the members of the society to be endowed; in short, by the greater power on the part of the citizens as a body to make the most and best of themselves. Thus, though of course there can be no freedom among men who act not willingly but under compulsion, yet on the other hand the mere removal of compulsion, the mere enabling a man to do as he likes, is in itself no contribution to true freedom. In one sense no man is so well able to do as he likes as the wandering savage. He has no master. There is no one to say him nay. Yet we do not count him really free, because the freedom of savagery is not strength, but weakness. The actual powers of the noblest savage do not admit of comparison with those of the humblest citizen of a law-abiding state. He is not the slave of man, but he is the slave of nature. Of compulsion by natural necessity he has plenty of experience, though of restraint by society none at all. Nor can he deliver himself from that compulsion except by submitting to this restraint. So to submit is the first step in true freedom, because the first step towards the full exercise of the faculties with which man is endowed. But we rightly refuse to recognise the highest development on the part of an exceptional individual or exceptional class, as an advance towards the true freedom of man, if it is founded on a refusal of the same opportunity to other men. The powers of the human mind have probably never attained such force and keenness, the proof of what society can do for the individual has never been so strikingly exhibited, as among the small groups of men who possessed civil privileges in the small republics of antiquity. The whole framework of our political ideas, to say nothing of our philosophy, is derived from them. But in them this extraordinary efflorescence of the privileged class was accompanied by the slavery of the multitude. That slavery was the condition on which it depended, and for that reason it was doomed to decay. There is no clearer ordinance of that supreme reason, often dark to us, which governs the course of man's affairs, than that no body of men should in the long run be able to strengthen itself at the cost of others' weakness. The civilization and freedom of the ancient world were short-lived because they were partial and exceptional. If the ideal of true freedom is the maximum of power for all members of human society alike to make the best of themselves, we are right in refusing to ascribe the glory of freedom to a state in which the apparent elevation of the few is founded on the degradation of the many, and in ranking modern society, founded as it is on free industry, with all its confusion and ignorant licence and waste of effort, above the most splendid of ancient republics.

If I have given a true account of that freedom which forms the goal of social effort, we shall see that freedom of contract, freedom in all the forms of doing what one will with one's own, is valuable only as a means to an end. That end is what I call freedom in the positive sense: in other words, the liberation of the powers of all men equally for contributions to a common good. No one has a right to do what he will with his own in such a way as to contravene this end. It is only through the guarantee which society gives him that he has property at all, or, strictly speaking, any right to his possessions. This guarantee is founded on a sense of common interest. Everyone has an interest in securing to everyone else the free use and enjoyment and disposal of his possessions, so long as that freedom on the part of one does not interfere with a like freedom on the part of others, because such freedom contributes to that equal development of the faculties of all which is the highest good for all. This is the true and the only justification of rights of property. Rights of property, however, have been and are claimed which cannot be thus justified. We are all now agreed that men cannot rightly be the property of men. The institution of property being only justifiable as a means to the free exercise of the social capabilities of all, there can be no true right to property of a kind which debars one class of men from such free exercise altogether. We condemn slavery no less when it arises out of a voluntary agreement on the part of the enslaved person. A contract by which anyone agreed for a certain consideration to become the slave of another we should reckon a void contract. Here, then, is a limitation upon freedom of contract which we all recognize as rightful. No contract is valid in which human persons, willingly or unwillingly, are dealt with as commodities, because such contracts of necessity defeat the end for which alone society enforces contracts at all.

Are there no other contracts which, less obviously perhaps but really, are open to the same objection? In the first place, let us consider contracts affecting labour. Labour, the economist tells us, is a commodity exchangeable like other commodities. This is in a certain sense true, but it is a commodity which attaches in a particular manner to the person of man. Hence restrictions may need to be placed on the sale of this commodity which would be unnecessary in other cases, in order to prevent labour from being sold under conditions which make it impossible for the person selling it ever to become a free contributor to social good in any form. This is most plainly the case when a man bargains to work under conditions fatal to health, e.g. in an unventilated factory. Every injury to the health of the individual is, so far as it goes, a public injury. It is an impediment to the general freedom; so much deduction from our power, as members of society, to make the best of ourselves. Society is, therefore, plainly within its right when it limits freedom of contract for the sale of labour, so far as is done by our laws for the sanitary regulations of factories, workshops, and mines. It is equally within its right in prohibiting the labour of women and young persons beyond certain hours. If they work beyond those hours, the result is demonstrably physical deterioration; which, as demonstrably, carries with it a lowering of the moral forces of society. For the sake of that general freedom of its members to make the best of themselves, which it is the object of civil society to secure, a prohibition should be put by law, which is the deliberate voice of society, on all such contracts of service as in a general way yield such a result. The purchase or hire of unwholesome dwellings is properly forbidden on the same principle. Its application to compulsory education may not be quite so obvious, but it will appear on a little reflection. Without a command of certain elementary arts and knowledge, the individual in modern society is as effectually crippled as by the loss of a limb or a broken constitution. He is not free to develop his faculties. With a view to securing such freedom among its members it is as certainly within the province of the state to prevent children from growing up in that kind of ignorance which practically excludes them from a free career in life, as it is within its province to require the sort of building and drainage necessary for public health.

Our modern legislation then with reference to labour, and education, and health, involving as it does manifold interference with freedom of contract, is justified on the ground that it is the business of the state, not indeed directly to promote moral goodness, for that, from the very nature of moral goodness, it cannot do, but to maintain the conditions without which a free exercise of the human faculties is impossible. It does not indeed follow that it is advisable for the state to do all which it is justified in doing. We are often warned nowadays against the danger of over-legislation; or as I heard it put in a speech of the present home secretary[1] in days when he was sowing his political wild oats, of 'grandmotherly government'. There may be good ground for the warning, but at any rate we should be quite clear what we mean by it. The outcry against state interference is often raised by men whose real objection is not to state interference but to centralization, to the constant aggression of the central executive upon local authorities. As I have already pointed out, compulsion at the discretion of some elected municipal board proceeds just as much from the state as does compulsion exercised by a government office in London. No doubt, much needless friction is avoided, much is gained in the way of elasticity and adjustment to circumstances, by the independent local administration of general laws; and most of us would agree that of late there has been a dangerous tendency to override municipal discretion by the hard and fast rules of London 'departments'. But centralization is one thing: over-legislation, or the improper exercise of the power of the state, quite another. It is one question whether of late the central government has been unduly trenching on local government, and another question whether the law of the state, either as administered by central or by provincial authorities, has been unduly interfering with the discretion of individuals. We may object most strongly to advancing centralization, and yet wish that the law should put rather more than less restraint on

[1] Sir William Vernon-Harcourt.

those liberties of the individual which are a social nuisance. But there are some political speculators whose objection is not merely to centralization, but to the extended action of law altogether. They think that the individual ought to be left much more to himself than has of late been the case. Might not our people, they ask, have been trusted to learn in time for themselves to eschew unhealthy dwellings, to refuse dangerous and degrading employment, to get their children the schooling necessary for making their way in the world? Would they not for their own comfort, if not from more chivalrous feeling, keep their wives and daughters from overwork? Or, failing this, ought not women, like men, to learn to protect themselves? Might not all the rules, in short, which legislation of the kind we have been discussing is intended to attain, have been attained without it; not so quickly, perhaps, but without tampering so dangerously with the independence and self-reliance of the people?

Now, we shall probably all agree that a society in which the public health was duly protected, and necessary education duly provided for, by the spontaneous action of individuals, was in a higher condition than one in which the compulsion of law was needed to secure these ends. But we must take men as we find them. Until such a condition of society is reached, it is the business of the state to take the best security it can for the young citizens' growing up in such health and with so much knowledge as is necessary for their real freedom. In so doing it need not at all interfere with the independence and self-reliance of those whom it requires to do what they would otherwise do for themselves. The man who, of his own right feeling, saves his wife from overwork and sends his children to school, suffers no moral degradation from a law which, if he did not do this for himself, would seek to make him do it. Such a man does not feel the law as constraint at all. To him it is simply a powerful friend. It gives him security for that being done efficiently which, with the best wishes, he might have much trouble in getting done efficiently if left to himself. No doubt it relieves him from some of the responsibility which would otherwise fall to him as head of a family, but, if he is what we are supposing him to be, in proportion as he is relieved of responsibilities in one direction he will assume them in another. The security which the state gives him for the safe housing and sufficient schooling of his family will only make him the more careful from their well-being in other respects, which he is left to look after for himself. We need have no fear, then, of such legislation having an ill effect on those who, without the law, would have seen to that being done, though probably less efficiently, which the law requires to be done. But it was not their case that the laws we are considering were especially meant to meet. It was the overworked women, the ill-housed and untaught families, for whose benefit they were intended. And the question is whether without these laws the suffering classes could have been delivered quickly or slowly from the condition they were in. Could the enlightened self-interest or benevolence of individuals, working under a system of unlimited freedom of contract, have ever brought them into a state compatible with the free development of the human faculties? No one considering the facts can have any doubt as to the answer to this question. Left to itself, or to the operation of casual benevolence, a degraded population perpetuates and increases itself. Read any of the authorized accounts, given before royal or parliamentary commissions, of the state of the labourers, especially of the women and children, as they were in our great industries before the law was first brought to bear on them, and before freedom of contract was first interfered with in them. Ask yourself what chance there was of a generation, born and bred under such conditions, ever contracting itself out of them. Given a certain standard of moral and material well-being, people may be trusted not to sell their labour, or the labour of their children, on terms which would not allow that standard to be maintained. But with large masses of our population, until the laws we have been considering took effect, there was no such standard. There was nothing on their part, in the way either of self-respect or established demand for comforts, to prevent them from working and living, or from putting their children to work and live, in a way in which no one who is to be a healthy and free citizen can work and live. No doubt there were many high-minded employers who did their best for their workpeople before the days of state-interference, but they could not prevent less scrupulous hirers of labour from hiring it on the cheapest terms. It is true that cheap labour is in the long run dear labour, but it is so only in the long run, and eager traders do not think of the long run. If labour is to be had under conditions incompatible with the health or decent housing or education of the labourer, there will always be plenty of people to buy it under those conditions, careless of the burden in the shape of rates and taxes which they may be laying up for posterity. Either the standard of well-being on the part of the sellers of labour must prevent them from selling their labour under those conditions, or the law must prevent it. With a population such as ours was forty years ago, and still largely is, the law must prevent it and continue the prevention for some generations, before the sellers will be in a state to prevent it for themselves. . . .

I have left myself little time to speak of the principles on which some of us hold that, in the matter of intoxicating drinks, a further limitation of freedom of contract is needed in the interest of general freedom. I say a further limitation, because there is no such thing as a free sale of these drinks at present. Men are not at liberty to buy and sell them when they will, where they will, and as they will. But our present licensing system, while it creates a class of monopolists especially interested in resisting any effectual restraint of the liquor traffic, does little to lessen the facilities for obtaining strong drink. Indeed the principle upon which licences have been generally given has been avowedly to make it easy to get drink. The restriction of the hours of sale is no doubt a real check so far as it goes, but it remains the case that everyone who has a weakness for drink has the temptation staring him in the face during all hours but those when he ought to be in bed. The effect of the present system, in short, is to prevent the drink-shops from coming unpleasantly near the houses of well-to-do people, and to crowd them upon the quarters occupied by the poorer classes, who have practically no power of keeping the nuisance from them. Now it is clear that the only remedy which the law can afford for this state of things must take the form either of more stringent rules of licensing, or of a power entrusted to the householders in each district of excluding the sale of intoxicants altogether from among them.

I do not propose to discuss the comparative merits of these methods of procedure. One does not exclude the other. They may very well be combined. One may be best suited for one kind of population, the other for another kind. But either, to be effectual, must involve a large interference with the liberty of the individual to do as he likes in the matter of buying and selling alcohol. It is the justifiability of that interference that I wish briefly to consider.

We justify it on the simple ground of the recognized right on the part of society to prevent men from doing as they like, if, in the exercise of their peculiar tastes in doing as they like, they create a social nuisance. There is no right to freedom in the purchase and sale of a particular commodity, if the general result of allowing such freedom is to detract from freedom in the higher sense, from the general power of men to make the best of themselves. Now with anyone who looks calmly at the facts, there can be no doubt that the present habits of drinking in England do lay a heavy burden on the free development of man's powers for social good, a heavier burden probably than arises from all other preventible causes put together. It used to be the fashion to look on drunkenness as a vice which was the concern only of the person who fell into it, so long as it did not lead him to commit an assault on his neighbours. No thoughtful man any longer looks on it in this way. We know that, however decently carried on, the excessive drinking of one man means an injury to others in health, purse, and capability, to which no limits can be placed. Drunkenness in the head of a family means, as a rule, the impoverishment and degradation of all members of the family; and the presence of a drink-shop at the corner of a street means, as a rule, the drunkenness of a certain number of heads of families in that street. Remove the drink-shops, and, as the experience of many happy communities sufficiently shows, you almost, perhaps in time altogether, remove the drunkenness. Here, then, is a wide-spreading social evil, of which society may, if it will, by a restraining law, to a great extent, rid itself, to the infinite enhancement of the positive freedom enjoyed by its members. All that is required for the attainmer' of so blessed a result is so much effort and self-sacrifice on the part of the majority of citizens as is necessary for the enactment and enforcement of the restraining law. The majority of citizens may still be far from prepared for such an effort. That is a point on which I express no opinion. To attempt a restraining law in advance of the social sentiment necessary to give real effect to it, is always a mistake. But to argue that an effectual law in restraint of the drink-traffic would be a wrongful interference with individual liberty is to ignore the essential condition under which alone every particular liberty can rightly be allowed to the individual, the condition, namely, that the allowance of that liberty is not, as a rule, and on the whole, an impediment to social good.

The more reasonable opponents of the restraint for which I plead, would probably argue not so much that it was necessarily wrong in principle, as that it was one of those short cuts to a good end which ultimately defeat their own object. They would take the same line that has been taken by the opponents of state-interference in all its forms. 'Leave the people to themselves,' they would say; 'as their standard of self-respect rises, as they become better housed and better educated, they will gradually shake off the evil habit. The cure so effected may not be so rapid as that brought by a repressive law, but it will be more lasting. Better that it should come more slowly through the spontaneous action of individuals, than more quickly through compulsion.'

But here again we reply that it is dangerous to wait. The slower remedy might be preferable if we were sure that it was a remedy at all, but we have no such assurance. There is strong reason to think the contrary. Every year that the evil is left to itself, it becomes greater. The vested interest in the encouragement of the vice becomes larger, and the persons affected by it more numerous. If any abatement of it has already taken place, we may fairly argue that this is because it has not been altogether left to itself; for the licensing law, as it is, is much more stringent and more stringently administered than it was ten years ago. A drunken population naturally perpetuates and increases itself. Many families, it is true, keep emerging from the conditions which render them specially liable to the evil habit, but on the other hand descent through drunkenness from respectability to squalor is constantly going on. The families of drunkards do not seem to be smaller than those of sober men, though they are shorter-lived; and that the children of a drunkard should escape from drunkenness is what we call almost a miracle. Better education, better housing, more healthy rules of labour, no doubt lessen the temptations to drink for those who have the benefit of these advantages, but meanwhile drunkenness is constantly recruiting the ranks of those who cannot be really educated, who will not be better housed, who make their employments dangerous and unhealthy. An effectual liquor law in short is the necessary complement of our factory acts, our education acts, our public health acts. Without it the full measure of their usefulness will never be attained. They were all opposed in their turn by the same arguments that are now used against a restraint of the facilities for drinking. Sometimes it was the argument that the state had no business to interfere with the liberties of the individual. Sometimes it was the dilatory plea that the better nature of man would in time assert itself, and that meanwhile it would be lowered by compulsion. Happily a sense of the facts and necessities of the case got the better of the delusive cry of liberty. Act after act was passed preventing master and workman, parent and child, house-builder and householder, from doing as they pleased, with the result of a great addition to the real freedom of society. The spirit of self-reliance and independence was not weakened by those acts. Rather it received a new development. The dead weight of ignorance and unhealthy surroundings, with which it would otherwise have had to struggle, being partially removed by law, it was more free to exert itself for higher objects. When we ask for a stringent liquor law, which should even go to the length of allowing the householders of a district to exclude the drink traffic altogether, we are only asking for a continuation of the same work, a continuation necessary to its complete success. It is a poor sophistry to tell us that it is a moral cowardice to seek to remove by law a temptation which everyone ought to be able to resist for himself. It is not the part of a considerate self-reliance to remain in presence of a temptation merely for the sake of being tempted. When all temptations are removed which law can remove, there will still be room enough, nay, much more room, for the play of our moral energies. The temptation to excessive drinking is one which upon sufficient evidence we hold that the law can at least greatly diminish. If it can, it ought to do so. This then, along with the effectual liberation of the soil, is the next great conquest which our democracy, on behalf of its own true freedom, has to make. The danger of legislation, either in the interests of a privileged class or for the promotion of particular religious opinions, we may fairly assume to be over. The popular jealousy of law, once justifiable enough, is therefore out of date. The citizens of England now make its law. We ask them by law to put a restraint on themselves in the matter of strong drink. We ask them further to limit, or even altogether to give up, the not very precious liberty of buying and selling alcohol, in order that they may become more free to exercise the faculties and improve the talents which God has given them.

TWO

TWO CONCEPTS OF LIBERTY

Isaiah Berlin

This is an abridgement of Berlin's inaugural lecture as Chichele Professor of Social and Political Theory in the University of Oxford, delivered in 1958. It comprises sections I and II of the full text, in which Berlin outlines the 'negative' and 'positive' notions of freedom, respectively, and section V, in which he criticizes the doctrine that freedom consists in conformity to those arrangements that all enlightened persons must regard as rational. Of the omitted sections, section III discusses the stoic idea that freedom consists in eliminating desires that cannot be satisfied; section IV presents the view that freedom consists in rational self-direction; section VI argues that freedom and collective self-determination cannot be assimilated into one another; section VII proposes that freedom and democracy are likewise distinct, and potentially conflicting, ideals; and section VIII expounds Berlin's underlying belief that human beings have many diverse fundamental goals that cannot all be harmoniously realized.

I

To coerce a man is to deprive him of freedom—freedom from what? Almost every moralist in human history has praised freedom. Like happiness and goodness, like nature and reality, it is a term whose meaning is so porous that there is little interpretation that it seems able to resist. I do not propose to discuss either the history of this protean word or the more than two hundred senses of it

Abridged from Isaiah Berlin, 'Two Concepts of Liberty', in I. Berlin, *Liberty*, ed. Henry Hardy (Oxford, UK: Oxford University Press, 2002), pp. 168–181, 191–200. Reproduced with permission of Curtis Brown Group Ltd., London, on behalf of the Isaiah Berlin Literary Trust. Copyright © Isaiah Berlin, 1958, 1969, 1997.

recorded by historians of ideas. I propose to examine no more than two of these senses—but they are central ones, with a great deal of human history behind them, and, I dare say, still to come. The first of these political senses of freedom or liberty (I shall use both words to mean the same), which (following much precedent) I shall call the 'negative' sense, is involved in the answer to the question 'What is the area within which the subject—a person or group of persons—is or should be left to do or be what he is able to do or be, without interference by other persons?' The second, which I shall call the 'positive' sense, is involved in the answer to the question 'What, or who, is the source of control or interference that can determine someone to do, or be, this rather than that?' The two questions are clearly different, even though the answers to them may overlap.

The Notion of Negative Freedom

I am normally said to be free to the degree to which no man or body of men interferes with my activity. Political liberty in this sense is simply the area within which a man can act unobstructed by others. If I am prevented by others from doing what I could otherwise do, I am to that degree unfree; and if this area is contracted by other men beyond a certain minimum, I can be described as being coerced, or, it may be, enslaved. Coercion is not, however, a term that covers every form of inability. If I say that I am unable to jump more than ten feet in the air, or cannot read because I am blind, or cannot understand the darker pages of Hegel, it would be eccentric to say that I am to that degree enslaved or coerced. Coercion implies the deliberate interference of other human beings within the area in which I could otherwise act. You lack political liberty or freedom only if you are prevented from attaining a goal by human beings.[1] Mere incapacity to attain a goal is not lack of political freedom.[2] This is brought out by the use of such modern expressions as 'economic freedom' and its counterpart, 'economic slavery'. It is argued, very plausibly, that

---

[1] I do not, of course, mean to imply the truth of the converse.

[2] Helvetius made this point very clearly: 'The free man is the man who is not in irons, not imprisoned in a gaol, nor terrorised like a slave by the fear of punishment'. It is not lack of freedom not to fly like an eagle or swim like a whale. *De l'esprit*, first discourse, chapter 4.

if a man is too poor to afford something on which there is no legal ban—a loaf of bread, a journey round the world, recourse to the law courts—he is as little free to have it as he would be if it were forbidden him by law. If my poverty were a kind of disease which prevented me from buying bread, or paying for the journey round the world or getting my case heard, as lameness prevents me from running, this inability would not naturally be described as a lack of freedom, least of all political freedom. It is only because I believe that my inability to get a given thing is due to the fact that other human beings have made arrangements whereby I am, whereas others are not, prevented from having enough money with which to pay for it, that I think myself a victim of coercion or slavery. In other words, this use of the term depends on a particular social and economic theory about the causes of my poverty or weakness. If my lack of material means is due to my lack of mental or physical capacity, then I begin to speak of being deprived of freedom (and not simply about poverty) only if I accept the theory.[3] If, in addition, I believe that I am being kept in want by a specific arrangement which I consider unjust or unfair, I speak of economic slavery or oppression. The nature of things does not madden us, only ill will does, said Rousseau.[4] The criterion of oppression is the part that I believe to be played by other human beings, directly or indirectly, with or without the intention of doing so, in frustrating my wishes. By being free in this sense I mean not being interfered with by others. The wider the area of non-interference the wider my freedom.

This is what the classical English political philosophers meant when they used this word.[5] They disagreed about how wide the area could or should be. They supposed that it could not, as things were, be unlimited, because if it were, it would entail a state in which all men could boundlessly interfere with all other men;

[3] The Marxist conception of social laws is, of course, the best-known version of this theory, but it forms a large element in some Christian and utilitarian, and all socialist, doctrines.

[4] *Émile,* book 2: vol. 4, p. 320, in *Oeuvres complètes,* ed. Bernard Gagnebin and others (Paris, 1959–95).

[5] 'A free man', said Hobbes, 'is he that … is not hindered to do what he has a will to'. *Leviathan,* chapter 21: p. 146 in Richard Tuck's edition (Cambridge, 1991). Law is always a fetter, even if it protects you from being bound in chains that are heavier than those of the law, say some more repressive law or custom, or arbitrary despotism or chaos. Bentham says much the same.

and this kind of 'natural' freedom would lead to social chaos in which men's minimum needs would not be satisfied; or else the liberties of the weak would be suppressed by the strong. Because they perceived that human purposes and activities do not automatically harmonise with one another, and because (whatever their official doctrines) they put high value on other goals, such as justice, or happiness, or culture, or security, or varying degrees of equality, they were prepared to curtail freedom in the interests of other values and, indeed, of freedom itself. For, without this, it was impossible to create the kind of association that they thought desirable. Consequently, it is assumed by these thinkers that the area of men's free action must be limited by law. But equally it is assumed, especially by such libertarians as Locke and Mill in England, and Constant and Tocqueville in France, that there ought to exist a certain minimum area of personal freedom which must on no account be violated; for if it is overstepped, the individual will find himself in an area too narrow for even that minimum development of his natural faculties which alone makes it possible to pursue, and even to conceive, the various ends which men hold good or right or sacred. It follows that a frontier must be drawn between the area of private life and that of public authority. Where it is to be drawn is a matter of argument, indeed of haggling. Men are largely interdependent, and no man's activity is so completely private as never to obstruct the lives of others in any way. 'Freedom for the pike is death for the minnows';[6] the liberty of some must depend on the restraint of others. Freedom for an Oxford don, others have been known to add, is a very different thing from freedom for an Egyptian peasant.

This proposition derives its force from something that is both true and important, but the phrase itself remains a piece of political claptrap. It is true that to offer political rights, or safeguards against intervention by the State, to men who are half-naked, illiterate, underfed, and diseased is to mock their condition; they need medical help or education before they can understand, or make use of, an increase in their freedom. What is freedom to those who cannot make use of it? Without adequate conditions for the use of freedom, what is the value of freedom? First things come first:

---

[6] R. H. Tawney, *Equality* (1931), 3rd ed. (London, 1938), chapter 5, section 2, 'Equality and Liberty', p. 208 (not in previous editions).

there are situations in which—to use a saying satirically attributed to the nihilists by Dostoevsky—boots are superior to Pushkin; individual freedom is not everyone's primary need. For freedom is not the mere absence of frustration of whatever kind; this would inflate the meaning of the word until it meant too much or too little. The Egyptian peasant needs clothes or medicine before, and more than, personal liberty, but the minimum freedom that he needs today, and the greater degree of freedom that he may need tomorrow, is not some species of freedom peculiar to him, but identical with that of professors, artists, and millionaires.

What troubles the consciences of Western liberals is, I think, the belief, not that the freedom that men seek differs according to their social or economic conditions, but that the minority who possess it have gained it by exploiting, or, at least, averting their gaze from, the vast majority who do not. They believe, with good reason, that if individual liberty is an ultimate end for human beings, none should be deprived of it by others; least of all that some should enjoy it at the expense of others. Equality of liberty; not to treat others as I should not wish them to treat me; repayment of my debt to those who alone have made possible my liberty or prosperity or enlightenment; justice, in its simplest and most universal sense—these are the foundations of liberal morality. Liberty is not the only goal of men. I can, like the Russian critic Belinsky, say that if others are to be deprived of it—if my brothers are to remain in poverty, squalor, and chains—then I do not want it for myself, I reject it with both hands and infinitely prefer to share their fate. But nothing is gained by a confusion of terms. To avoid glaring inequality or widespread misery I am ready to sacrifice some, or all, of my freedom: I may do so willingly and freely; but it is freedom that I am giving up for the sake of justice or equality or the love of my fellow men. I should be guilt-stricken, and rightly so, if I were not, in some circumstances, ready to make this sacrifice. But a sacrifice is not an increase in what is being sacrificed, namely freedom, however great the moral need or the compensation for it. Everything is what it is: liberty is liberty, not equality or fairness or justice or culture, or human happiness or a quiet conscience. If the liberty of myself or my class or nation depends on the misery of a number of other human beings, the system which promotes this is unjust and immoral. But if I curtail or lose my freedom in order to lessen the shame of such inequality, and do not thereby materially increase the individual liberty of others, an absolute loss of liberty occurs. This may be compensated for by a gain in justice or in happiness or in peace, but the loss remains, and it is a confusion of values to say that although my 'liberal', individual freedom may go by the board, some other kind of freedom—'social' or 'economic'—is increased. Yet it remains true that the freedom of some must at times be curtailed to secure the freedom of others. Upon what principle should this be done? If freedom is a sacred, untouchable value, there can be no such principle. One or other of these conflicting rules or principles must, at any rate in practice, yield: not always for reasons which can be clearly stated, let alone generalised into rules or universal maxims. Still, a practical compromise has to be found.

Philosophers with an optimistic view of human nature and a belief in the possibility of harmonising human interests, such as Locke or Adam Smith or, in some moods, Mill, believed that social harmony and progress were compatible with reserving a large area for private life over which neither the State nor any other authority must be allowed to trespass. Hobbes, and those who agreed with him, especially conservative or reactionary thinkers, argued that if men were to be prevented from destroying one another and making social life a jungle or a wilderness, greater safeguards must be instituted to keep them in their places; he wished correspondingly to increase the area of centralised control and decrease that of the individual. But both sides agreed that some portion of human existence must remain independent of the sphere of social control. To invade that preserve, however small, would be despotism. The most eloquent of all defenders of freedom and privacy, Benjamin Constant, who had not forgotten the Jacobin dictatorship, declared that at the very least the liberty of religion, opinion, expression, property must be guaranteed against arbitrary invasion. Jefferson, Burke, Paine, Mill compiled different catalogues of individual liberties, but the argument for keeping authority at bay is always substantially the same. We must preserve a minimum area of personal freedom if we are not to 'degrade or deny our nature'.[7] We cannot remain absolutely free,

---

[7] Constant, *Principes de politique,* chapter 1: p. 318, in Benjamin Constant, *Écrits politiques,* ed. Marcel Gauchet (Paris, 1997).

and must give up some of our liberty to preserve the rest. But total self-surrender is self-defeating. What then must the minimum be? That which a man cannot give up without offending against the essence of his human nature. What is this essence? What are the standards which it entails? This has been, and perhaps always will be, a matter of infinite debate. But whatever the principle in terms of which the area of non-interference is to be drawn, whether it is that of natural law or natural rights, or of utility, or the pronouncements of a categorical imperative, or the sanctity of the social contract, or any other concept with which men have sought to clarify and justify their convictions, liberty in this sense means liberty *from;* absence of interference beyond the shifting, but always recognisable, frontier. 'The only freedom which deserves the name, is that of pursuing our own good in our own way', said the most celebrated of its champions.[8] If this is so, is compulsion ever justified? Mill had no doubt that it was. Since justice demands that all individuals be entitled to a minimum of freedom, all other individuals were of necessity to be restrained, if need be by force, from depriving anyone of it. Indeed, the whole function of law was the prevention of just such collisions: the State was reduced to what Lassalle contemptuously described as the functions of a night-watchman or traffic policeman.

What made the protection of individual liberty so sacred to Mill? In his famous essay he declares that, unless the individual is left to live as he wishes in 'the part [of his conduct] which merely concerns himself',[9] civilisation cannot advance; the truth will not, for lack of a free market in ideas, come to light; there will be no scope for spontaneity, originality, genius, for mental energy, for moral courage. Society will be crushed by the weight of 'collective mediocrity'.[10] Whatever is rich and diversified will be crushed by the weight of custom, by men's constant tendency to conformity, which breeds only 'withered' capacities, 'pinched and hidebound', 'cramped and dwarfed' human beings. 'Pagan self-assertion' is as worthy as 'Christian self-denial'.[11] 'All errors which [a man] is

---

[8] J. S. Mill, 'On Liberty', chapter 1: vol. 18, p. 226, in *Collected Works of John Stuart Mill*, ed. J. M. Robson and others (Toronto/London, 1963–91).

[9] Ibid., p. 224.

[10] Ibid., chapter 3, p. 268.

[11] Ibid., pp. 265–266. The last two phrases are from John Sterling's essay on Simonides: vol 1, p. 190, in his *Essays and Tales*, ed. Julius Charles Hare (London, 1848).

likely to commit against advice and warning, are far outweighed by the evil of allowing others to constrain him to what they deem his good'.[12] The defence of liberty consists in the 'negative' goal of warding off interference. To threaten a man with persecution unless he submits to a life in which he exercises no choices of his goals; to block before him every door but one, no matter how noble the prospect upon which it opens, or how benevolent the motives of those who arrange this, is to sin against the truth that he is a man, a being with a life of his own to live. This is liberty as it has been conceived by liberals in the modern world from the days of Erasmus (some would say of Occam) to our own. Every plea for civil liberties and individual rights, every protest against exploitation and humiliation, against the encroachment of public authority, or the mass hypnosis of custom or organised propaganda, springs from this individualistic, and much disputed, conception of man.

Three facts about this position may be noted. In the first place Mill confuses two distinct notions. One is that all coercion is, in so far as it frustrates human desires, bad as such, although it may have to be applied to prevent other, greater evils; while non-interference, which is the opposite of coercion, is good as such, although it is not the only good. This is the 'negative' conception of liberty in its classical form. The other is that men should seek to discover the truth, or to develop a certain type of character of which Mill approved—critical, original, imaginative, independent, non-conforming to the point of eccentricity, and so on—and that truth can be found, and such character can be bred, only in conditions of freedom. Both these are liberal views, but they are not identical, and the connection between them is, at best, empirical. No one would argue that truth or freedom of self-expression could flourish where dogma crushes all thought. But the evidence of history tends to show (as, indeed, was argued by James Stephen in his formidable attack on Mill in his *Liberty, Equality, Fraternity*) that integrity, love of truth, and fiery individualism grow at least as often in severely disciplined communities, among, for example, the puritan Calvinists of Scotland or New England, or under military discipline, as in more tolerant or indifferent societies; and if this is so, Mill's argument for liberty as a necessary condi-

---

[12] Mill, chapter 4, p. 277.

tion for the growth of human genius falls to the ground. If his two goals proved incompatible, Mill would be faced with a cruel dilemma, quite apart from the further difficulties created by the inconsistency of his doctrines with strict utilitarianism, even in his own humane version of it.[13]

In the second place, the doctrine is comparatively modern. There seems to be scarcely any discussion of individual liberty as a conscious political ideal (as opposed to its actual existence) in the ancient world. Condorcet had already remarked that the notion of individual rights was absent from the legal conceptions of the Romans and Greeks; this seems to hold equally of the Jewish, Chinese, and all other ancient civilisations that have since come to light.[14] The domination of this ideal has been the exception rather than the rule, even in the recent history of the West. Nor has liberty in this sense often formed a rallying cry for the great masses of mankind. The desire not to be impinged upon, to be left to oneself, has been a mark of high civilisation on the part of both individuals and communities. The sense of privacy itself, of the area of personal relationships as something sacred in its own right, derives from a conception of freedom which, for all its religious roots, is scarcely older, in its developed state, than the Renaissance or the Reformation.[15] Yet its decline would mark the death of a civilisation, of an entire moral outlook.

The third characteristic of this notion of liberty is of greater importance. It is that liberty in this sense is not incompatible with some kinds of autocracy, or at any rate with the absence of self-government. Liberty in this sense is principally concerned with the area of control, not with its source. Just as a democracy may, in fact, deprive

---

[13] This is but another illustration of the natural tendency of all but a very few thinkers to believe that all the things they hold good must be intimately connected, or at least compatible, with one another. The history of thought, like the history of nations, is strewn with examples of inconsistent, or at least disparate, elements artificially yoked together in a despotic system, or held together by the danger of some common enemy. In due course the danger passes, and conflicts between the allies arise, which often disrupt the system, sometimes to the great benefit of mankind.

[14] See the valuable discussion of this in Michel Villey, *Leçons d'histoire de la philosophie du droit* (Paris, 1957), chapter 14, which traces the embryo of the notion of subjective rights to Occam (see p. 272).

[15] Christian (and Jewish or Muslim) belief in the absolute authority of divine or natural laws, or in the equality of all men in the sight of God, is very different from belief in freedom to live as one prefers.

the individual citizen of a great many liberties which he might have in some other form of society, so it is perfectly conceivable that a liberal-minded despot would allow his subjects a large measure of personal freedom. The despot who leaves his subjects a wide area of liberty may be unjust, or encourage the wildest inequalities, care little for order, or virtue, or knowledge; but provided he does not curb their liberty, or at least curbs it less than many other regimes, he meets with Mill's specification.[16]

Freedom in this sense is not, at any rate logically, connected with democracy or self-government. Self-government may, on the whole, provide a better guarantee of the preservation of civil liberties than other regimes, and has been defended as such by libertarians. But there is no necessary connection between individual liberty and democratic rule. The answer to the question 'Who governs me?' is logically distinct from the question 'How far does government interfere with me?' It is in this difference that the great contrast between the two concepts of negative and positive liberty, in the end, consists.[17] For the 'positive' sense of

---

[16] Indeed, it is arguable that in the Prussia of Frederick the Great or in the Austria of Joseph II men of imagination, originality and creative genius, and, indeed, minorities of all kinds, were less persecuted and felt the pressure, both of institutions and custom, less heavy upon them than in many an earlier or later democracy.

[17] 'Negative liberty' is something the extent of which, in a given case, it is difficult to estimate. It might, prima facie, seem to depend simply on the power to choose between at any rate two alternatives. Nevertheless, not all choices are equally free, or free at all. If in a totalitarian State I betray my friend under threat of torture, perhaps even if I act from fear of losing my job, I can reasonably say that I did not act freely. Nevertheless, I did, of course, make a choice, and could, at any rate in theory, have chosen to be killed or tortured or imprisoned. The mere existence of alternatives is not, therefore, enough to make my action free (although it may be voluntary) in the normal sense of the word. The extent of my freedom seems to depend on (a) how many possibilities are open to me (although the method of counting these can never be more than impressionistic; possibilities of action are not discrete entities like apples, which can be exhaustively enumerated); (b) how easy or difficult each of these possibilities is to actualise; (c) how important in my plan of life, given my character and circumstances, these possibilities are when compared with each other; (d) how far they are closed and opened by deliberate human acts; (e) what value not merely the agent, but the general sentiment of the society in which he lives, puts on the various possibilities. All these magnitudes must be 'integrated', and a conclusion, necessarily never precise, or indisputable, drawn from this process. It may well be that there are many incommensurable kinds and degrees of freedom, and that they cannot be drawn up on any single scale

liberty comes to light if we try to answer the question, not 'What am I free to do or be?', but 'By whom am I ruled?' or 'Who is to say what I am, and what I am not, to be or do?' The connection between democracy and individual liberty is a good deal more tenuous than it seemed to many advocates of both. The desire to be governed by myself, or at any rate to participate in the process by which my life is to be controlled, may be as deep a wish as that for a free area for action, and perhaps historically older. But it is not a desire for the same thing. So different is it, indeed, as to have led in the end to the great clash of ideologies that dominates our world. For it is this, the 'positive' conception of liberty, not freedom from, but freedom to—to lead one prescribed form of life—which the adherents of the 'negative' notion represent as being, at times, no better than a specious disguise for brutal tyranny.

2

The Notion of Positive Freedom

The 'positive' sense of the word 'liberty' derives from the wish on the part of the individual to be his own master. I wish my life and decisions to depend on myself, not on external forces of whatever kind. I wish to be the instrument of my own, not of other men's, acts of will. I wish to be a subject, not an object; to be moved by reasons, by conscious purposes, which are my own, not by causes which affect me, as it were, from outside. I wish to be somebody, not nobody; a doer—deciding, not being decided for, self-directed

(note 17 continued) of magnitude. Moreover, in the case of societies, we are faced by such (logically absurd) questions as, 'Would arrangement X increase the liberty of Mr A more than it would that of Messrs B, C, and D between them, added together?' The same difficulties arise in applying utilitarian criteria. Nevertheless, provided we do not demand precise measurement, we can give valid reasons for saying that the average subject of the King of Sweden is, on the whole, a good deal freer today [1958] than the average citizen of Spain or Albania. Total patterns of life must be compared directly as wholes, although the method by which we make the comparison, and the truth of the conclusions, are difficult or impossible to demonstrate. But the vagueness of the concepts, and the multiplicity of the criteria involved, are attributes of the subject matter itself, not of our imperfect methods of measurement, or of incapacity for precise thought.

and not acted upon by external nature or by other men as if I were a thing, or an animal, or a slave incapable of playing a human role, that is, of conceiving goals and policies of my own and realising them. This is at least part of what I mean when I say that I am rational, and that it is my reason that distinguishes me as a human being from the rest of the world. I wish, above all, to be conscious of myself as a thinking, willing, active being, bearing responsibility for my choices and able to explain them by reference to my own ideas and purposes. I feel free to the degree that I believe this to be true, and enslaved to the degree that I am made to realise that it is not.

The freedom which consists in being one's own master, and the freedom which consists in not being prevented from choosing as I do by other men, may, on the face of it, seem concepts at no great logical distance from each other—no more than negative and positive ways of saying much the same thing. Yet the 'positive' and 'negative' notions of freedom historically developed in divergent directions, not always by logically reputable steps, until, in the end, they came into direct conflict with each other.

One way of making this clear is in terms of the independent momentum which the, initially perhaps quite harmless, metaphor of self-mastery acquired. 'I am my own master'; 'I am slave to no man'; but may I not (as Platonists or Hegelians tend to say) be a slave to nature? Or to my own 'unbridled' passions? Are these not so many species of the identical genus 'slave'—some political or legal, others moral or spiritual? Have not men had the experience of liberating themselves from spiritual slavery, or slavery to nature, and do they not in the course of it become aware, on the one hand, of a self which dominates, and, on the other, of something in them which is brought to heel? This dominant self is then variously identified with reason, with my 'higher nature', with the self which calculates and aims at what will satisfy it in the long run, with my 'real', or 'ideal', or 'autonomous' self, or with my self 'at its best'; which is then contrasted with irrational impulse, uncontrolled desires, my 'lower' nature, the pursuit of immediate pleasures, my 'empirical' or 'heteronomous' self, swept by every gust of desire and passion, needing to be rigidly disciplined if it is ever to rise to the full height of its 'real' nature. Presently the two selves may be represented as divided by an even larger gap; the real self may be conceived as something wider than the individual (as the term is normally understood), as a social 'whole' of which the individual is an element or aspect: a tribe, a race, a Church, a State, the great society of the living and the dead and the yet unborn. This entity is then identified as being the 'true' self which, by imposing its collective, or 'organic', single will upon its recalcitrant 'members', achieves its own, and therefore their, 'higher' freedom. The perils of using organic metaphors to justify the coercion of some men by others in order to raise them to a 'higher' level of freedom have often been pointed out. But what gives such plausibility as it has to this kind of language is that we recognise that it is possible, and at times justifiable, to coerce men in the name of some goal (let us say, justice or public health) which they would, if they were more enlightened, themselves pursue, but do not, because they are blind or ignorant or corrupt. This renders it easy for me to conceive of myself as coercing others for their own sake, in their, not my, interest. I am then claiming that I know what they truly need better than they know it themselves. What, at most, this entails is that they would not resist me if they were rational and as wise as I and understood their interests as I do. But I may go on to claim a good deal more than this. I may declare that they are actually aiming at what in their benighted state they consciously resist, because there exists within them an occult entity—their latent rational will, or their 'true' purpose—and that this entity, although it is belied by all that they overtly feel and do and say, is their 'real' self, of which the poor empirical self in space and time may know nothing or little; and that this inner spirit is the only self that deserves to have its wishes taken into account.[18] Once I take this view, I am in a position to ignore the actual wishes of men or societies, to bully, oppress, torture them in the name, and on behalf, of their 'real' selves, in the secure knowledge that whatever is the true goal of man (happiness, performance of duty, wisdom, a just society, self-fulfilment) must

[18] '[T]he ideal of true freedom is the maximum of power for all members of human society alike to make the best of themselves', said T. H. Green in 1881: *Lectures on the Principles of Political Obligation and Other Writings,* ed. Paul Harris and John Morrow (Cambridge, 1986), p. 200. Apart from the confusion of freedom with equality, this entails that if a man chose some immediate pleasure—which (in whose view?) would not enable him to make the best of himself (what self?)—what he was exercising was not 'true' freedom: and if deprived of it, he would not lose anything that mattered. Green was a genuine liberal: but many a tyrant could use this formula to justify his worst acts of oppression.

be identical with his freedom—the free choice of his 'true', albeit often submerged and inarticulate, self.

This paradox has been often exposed. It is one thing to say that I know what is good for X, while he himself does not; and even to ignore his wishes for its—and his—sake; and a very different one to say that he has *eo ipso* chosen it, not indeed consciously, not as he seems in everyday life, but in his role as a rational self which his empirical self may not know—the 'real' self which discerns the good, and cannot help choosing it once it is revealed. This monstrous impersonation, which consists in equating what X would choose if he were something he is not, or at least not yet, with what X actually seeks and chooses, is at the heart of all political theories of self-realisation. It is one thing to say that I may be coerced for my own good, which I am too blind to see: this may, on occasion, be for my benefit; indeed it may enlarge the scope of my liberty. It is another to say that if it is my good, then I am not being coerced, for I have willed it, whether I know this or not, and am free (or 'truly' free) even while my poor earthly body and foolish mind bitterly reject it, and struggle with the greatest desperation against those who seek, however benevolently, to impose it.

This magical transformation, or sleight of hand (for which William James so justly mocked the Hegelians), can no doubt be perpetrated just as easily with the 'negative' concept of freedom, where the self that should not be interfered with is no longer the individual with his actual wishes and needs as they are normally conceived, but the 'real' man within, identified with the pursuit of some ideal purpose not dreamed of by his empirical self. And, as in the case of the 'positively' free self, this entity may be inflated into some super-personal entity—a State, a class, a nation, or the march of history itself, regarded as a more 'real' subject of attributes than the empirical self. But the 'positive' conception of freedom as self-mastery, with its suggestion of a man divided against himself, has in fact, and as a matter of history, of doctrine, and of practice, lent itself more easily to this splitting of personality into two: the transcendent, dominant controller, and the empirical bundle of desires and passions to be disciplined and brought to heel. It is this historical fact that has been influential. This demonstrates (if demonstration of so obvious a truth is needed) that conceptions of freedom directly derive from views of what constitutes a self, a person, a man. Enough manipulation of the definition of man, and freedom can be made to mean whatever the manipulator wishes. Recent history has made it only too clear that the issue is not merely academic.

The consequences of distinguishing between two selves will become even clearer if one considers the two major forms which the desire to be self-directed—directed by one's 'true' self—has historically taken: the first, that of self-abnegation in order to attain independence; the second, that of self-realisation, or total self-identification with a specific principle or ideal in order to attain the selfsame end....

5

The Temple of Sarastro

Those who believed in freedom as rational self-direction were bound, sooner or later, to consider how this was to be applied not merely to a man's inner life, but to his relations with other members of his society. Even the most individualistic among them—and Rousseau, Kant, and Fichte certainly began as individualists—came at some point to ask themselves whether a rational life not only for the individual, but also for society, was possible, and if so, how it was to be achieved. I wish to be free to live as my rational will (my 'real self') commands, but so must others be. How am I to avoid collisions with their wills? Where is the frontier that lies between my (rationally determined) rights and the identical rights of others? For if I am rational, I cannot deny that what is right for me must, for the same reasons, be right for others who are rational like me. A rational (or free) State would be a State governed by such laws as all rational men would freely accept; that is to say, such laws as they would themselves have enacted had they been asked what, as rational beings, they demanded; hence the frontiers would be such as all rational men would consider to be the right frontiers for rational beings.

But who, in fact, was to determine what these frontiers were? Thinkers of this type argued that if moral and political problems were genuine—as surely they were—they must in principle be soluble; that is to say, there must exist one and only one true solution to any problem. All truths could in principle be discovered by any rational thinker, and demonstrated so clearly that all other rational men could not but accept them; indeed, this was already to a large extent the case in the new natural sciences. On this assumption the problem of political liberty was soluble by establishing a just order that would give to each man all the freedom to which a rational being was entitled. My claim to unfettered freedom can prima facie at times not be reconciled with your equally unqualified claim; but the rational solution of one problem cannot collide with the equally true solution of another, for two truths cannot logically be incompatible; therefore a just order must in principle be discoverable—an order of which the rules make possible correct solutions to all possible problems that could arise in it. This ideal, harmonious state of affairs was sometimes imagined as a Garden of Eden before the Fall of Man, an Eden from which we were expelled, but for which we were still filled with longing; or as a golden age still before us, in which men, having become rational, will no longer be 'other-directed', nor 'alienate' or frustrate one another. In existing societies justice and equality are ideals which still call for some measure of coercion, because the premature lifting of social controls might lead to the oppression of the weaker and the stupider by the stronger or abler or more energetic and unscrupulous. But it is only irrationality on the part of men (according to this doctrine) that leads them to wish to oppress or exploit or humiliate one another. Rational men will respect the principle of reason in each other, and lack all desire to fight or dominate one another. The desire to dominate is itself a symptom of irrationality, and can be explained and cured by rational methods. Spinoza offers one kind of explanation and remedy, Hegel another, Marx a third. Some of these theories may perhaps, to some degree, supplement each other, others are not combinable. But they all assume that in a society of perfectly rational beings the lust for domination over men will be absent or ineffective. The existence of, or cravings for, oppression will be the first symptom that the true solution to the problems of social life has not been reached.

This can be put in another way. Freedom is self-mastery, the elimination of obstacles to my will, whatever these obstacles may be—the resistance of nature, of my ungoverned passions, of irrational institutions, of the opposing wills or behaviour of others. Nature I can, at least in principle, always mould by technical means, and shape to my will. But how am I to treat recalcitrant human beings? I must, if I can, impose my will on them too, 'mould' them to my pattern, cast parts for them in my play. But will this not mean that I alone am free, while they are slaves? They will be so if my plan has nothing to do with their wishes or values, only with my own. But if my plan is fully rational, it will allow for the full development of their 'true' natures, the realisation of their capacities for rational decisions, for 'making the best of themselves'—as a part of the realisation of my own 'true' self. All true solutions to all genuine problems must be compatible: more than this, they must fit into a single whole; for this is what is meant by calling them all rational and the universe harmonious. Each man has his specific character, abilities, aspirations, ends. If I grasp both what these ends and natures are, and how they all relate to one another, I can, at least in principle, if I have the knowledge and the strength, satisfy them all, so long as the nature and the purposes in question are rational. Rationality is knowing things and people for what they are: I must not use stones to make violins, nor try to make born violin-players play flutes. If the universe is governed by reason, then there will be no need for coercion; a correctly planned life for all will coincide with full freedom—the freedom of rational self-direction—for all. This will be so if, and only if, the plan is the true plan—the one unique pattern which alone fulfils the claims of reason. Its laws will be the rules which reason prescribes: they will only seem irksome to those whose reason is dormant, who do not understand the true 'needs' of their own 'real' selves. So long as each player recognises and plays the part set him by reason—the faculty that understands his true nature and discerns his true ends—there can be no conflict. Each man will be a liberated, self-directed actor in the cosmic drama. Thus Spinoza tells us that children, although they are coerced, are not slaves, because they obey orders given in their own interests, and that the subject of a true commonwealth is no slave, because the common interests must include his own.[19] Similarly, Locke says 'Where there is no law there is no freedom', because rational law is a direction to a man's 'proper interests' or 'general good'; and adds that since law of this kind is what 'hedges

---

[19] *Tractatus Theologico-Politicus,* chapter 16: p. 137 in Benedict de Spinoza, *The Political Works,* ed. A. G. Wernham (Oxford, 1958).

us in only from bogs and precipices' it 'ill deserves the name of confinement',[20] and speaks of desires to escape from it as being irrational, forms of 'licence', as 'brutish',[21] and so on. Montesquieu, forgetting his liberal moments, speaks of political liberty as being not permission to do what we want, or even what the law allows, but only 'the power of doing what we ought to will',[22] which Kant virtually repeats. Burke proclaims the individual's 'right' to be restrained in his own interest, because 'the presumed consent of every rational creature is in unison with the predisposed order of things'.[23]

The common assumption of these thinkers (and of many a schoolman before them and Jacobin and Communist after them) is that the rational ends of our 'true' natures must coincide, or be made to coincide, however violently our poor, ignorant, desire-ridden, passionate, empirical selves may cry out against this process. Freedom is not freedom to do what is irrational, or stupid, or wrong. To force empirical selves into the right pattern is no tyranny, but liberation.[24] Rousseau tells me that if I freely surrender all the parts of my life to society, I create an entity which, because it has been built by an equality of sacrifice of all its members, cannot wish to hurt any one of them; in such a society, we are informed, it can be in nobody's interest to damage anyone else. 'In giving myself to all, I give myself to none',[25] and get back as

---

[20] *Two Treatises of Government,* second treatise, § 57.

[21] Ibid., §§ 6, 163.

[22] *De L'esprit des lois,* book II, chapter 3: p. 205, in *Oeuvres complètes de Montesquieu,* ed. A. Masson (Paris, 1950–55), vol. I A.

[23] *Appeal from the Old to the New Whigs* (1791): pp. 93–94, in *The Works of the Right Honourable Edmund Burke* (World's Classics edition), vol. 5 (London, 1907).

[24] On this Bentham seems to me to have said the last word: 'The liberty of doing evil, is it not liberty? If it is not liberty, what is it then? ... Do we not say that liberty should be taken away from fools, and wicked persons, because they abuse it?' *The Works of Jeremy Bentham,* ed. John Bowring (Edinburgh, 1843), vol. I, p. 301. Compare with this the view of the Jacobins in the same period, discussed by Crane Brinton in 'Political Ideas in the Jacobin Clubs', *Political Science Quarterly* 43 (1928), 249–264, esp. 257: 'no man is free in doing evil. To prevent him is to free him'. This view is echoed in almost identical terms by British Idealists at the end of the following century.

[25] *Social Contract,* book 1, chapter 6: vol. 3, p. 361, in *Oeuvres complètes,* ed. Bernard Gagnebin and others (Paris, 1959–95).

much as I lose, with enough new force to preserve my new gains. Kant tells us that when 'the individual has entirely abandoned his wild, lawless freedom, to find it again, unimpaired, in a state of dependence according to law', that alone is true freedom, 'for this dependence is the work of my own will acting as a lawgiver'.[26] Liberty, so far from being incompatible with authority, becomes virtually identical with it. This is the thought and language of all the declarations of the rights of man in the eighteenth century, and of all those who look upon society as a design constructed according to the rational laws of the wise lawgiver, or of nature, or of history, or of the Supreme Being. Bentham, almost alone, doggedly went on repeating that the business of laws was not to liberate but to restrain: every law is an infraction of liberty[27]—even if such infraction leads to an increase of the sum of liberty.

If the underlying assumptions had been correct—if the method of solving social problems resembled the way in which solutions to the problems of the natural sciences are found, and if reason were what rationalists said that it was—all this would perhaps follow. In the ideal case, liberty coincides with law: autonomy with authority. A law which forbids me to do what I could not, as a sane being, conceivably wish to do is not a restraint of my freedom. In the ideal society, composed of wholly responsible beings, rules, because I should scarcely be conscious of them, would gradually wither away. Only one social movement was bold enough to render this assumption quite explicit and accept its consequences—that of the Anarchists. But all forms of liberalism founded on a rationalist metaphysics are less or more watered-down versions of this creed.

In due course, the thinkers who bent their energies to the solution of the problem on these lines came to be faced with the question of how in practice men were to be made rational in this way. Clearly they must be educated. For the uneducated are irrational, heteronomous, and need to be coerced, if only to make life tolerable for the rational if they are to live in the same society and not be compelled to withdraw to a desert or some Olympian height. But the uneducated cannot be expected to understand or co-operate with the purposes of their educators. Education, says

[26] *Metaphysische Anfangsgründe der Rechtslehre* in *Kant's gesammelte Schriften* (Berlin, 1900–), vol. 6, p. 316, line 2.

[27] Op. cit., ibid.: 'every law is contrary to liberty'.

Fichte, must inevitably work in such a way that 'you will later recognise the reasons for what I am doing now'.[28] Children cannot be expected to understand why they are compelled to go to school, nor the ignorant—that is, for the moment, the majority of mankind—why they are made to obey the laws that will presently make them rational. 'Compulsion is also a kind of education'.[29] You learn the great virtue of obedience to superior persons. If you cannot understand your own interests as a rational being, I cannot be expected to consult you, or abide by your wishes, in the course of making you rational. I must, in the end, force you to be protected against smallpox, even though you may not wish it. Even Mill is prepared to say that I may forcibly prevent a man from crossing a bridge if there is not time to warn him that it is about to collapse, for I know, or am justified in assuming, that he cannot wish to fall into the water. Fichte knows what the uneducated German of his time wishes to be or do better than he can possibly know this for himself. The sage knows you better than you know yourself, for you are the victim of your passions, a slave living a heteronomous life, purblind, unable to understand your true goals. You want to be a human being. It is the aim of the State to satisfy your wish. 'Compulsion is justified by education for future insight'.[30] The reason within me, if it is to triumph, must eliminate and suppress my 'lower' instincts, my passions and desires, which render me a slave; similarly (the fatal transition from individual to social concepts is almost imperceptible) the higher elements in society—the better educated, the more rational, those who 'possess the highest insight of their time and people'[31]—may exercise compulsion to rationalise the irrational section of society. For—so Hegel, Bradley, Bosanquet have often assured us—by obeying the rational man we obey ourselves: not indeed as we are, sunk in our ignorance and our passions, weak creatures afflicted by diseases that need a healer, wards who require a guardian, but as we could be if we were rational; as we could be even now, if only we would listen to the rational element which is, *ex hypothesi,* within every human being who deserves the name.

---

[28] *Johann Gottlieb Fichte's sämmtliche Werke,* ed. I. H. Fichte (Berlin, 1845–46), vol. 7, p. 576.

[29] Ibid., p. 574.

[30] Ibid., p. 578.

[31] Ibid., p. 576.

The philosophers of 'Objective Reason', from the tough, rigidly centralised, 'organic' State of Fichte, to the mild and humane liberalism of T. H. Green, certainly supposed themselves to be fulfilling, and not resisting, the rational demands which, however inchoate, were to be found in the breast of every sentient being.

But I may reject such democratic optimism, and turning away from the teleological determinism of the Hegelians towards some more voluntarist philosophy, conceive the idea of imposing on my society—for its own betterment—a plan of my own, which in my rational wisdom I have elaborated; and which, unless I act on my own, perhaps against the permanent wishes of the vast majority of my fellow citizens, may never come to fruition at all. Or, abandoning the concept of reason altogether, I may conceive myself as an inspired artist, who moulds men into patterns in the light of his unique vision, as painters combine colours or composers sounds; humanity is the raw material upon which I impose my creative will; even though men suffer and die in the process, they are lifted by it to a height to which they could never have risen without my coercive—but creative—violation of their lives. This is the argument used by every dictator, inquisitor, and bully who seeks some moral, or even aesthetic, justification for his conduct. I must do for men (or with them) what they cannot do for themselves, and I cannot ask their permission or consent, because they are in no condition to know what is best for them; indeed, what they will permit and accept may mean a life of contemptible mediocrity, or perhaps even their ruin and suicide. Let me quote from the true progenitor of the heroic doctrine, Fichte, once again: 'No one has ... rights against reason'. 'Man is afraid of subordinating his subjectivity to the laws of reason. He prefers tradition or arbitrariness'.[32] Nevertheless, subordinated he must be.[33] Fichte puts forward the claims of what he called reason; Napoleon, or Carlyle, or romantic authoritarians may worship other values, and see in their establishment by force the only path to 'true' freedom.

[32] Ibid., pp. 578, 580.
[33] 'To compel men to adopt the right form of government, to impose Right on them by force, is not only the right, but the sacred duty of every man who has both the insight and the power to do so'. Ibid., vol. 4, p. 436.

The same attitude was pointedly expressed by August Comte, who asked why, if we do not allow free thinking in chemistry or biology, we should allow it in morals or politics.[34] Why indeed? If it makes sense to speak of political truths—assertions of social ends which all men, because they are men, must, once they are discovered, agree to be such; and if, as Comte believed, scientific method will in due course reveal them; then what case is there for freedom of opinion or action—at least as an end in itself, and not merely as a stimulating intellectual climate—either for individuals or for groups? Why should any conduct be tolerated that is not authorised by appropriate experts? Comte put bluntly what had been implicit in the rationalist theory of politics from its ancient Greek beginnings. There can, in principle, be only one correct way of life; the wise lead it spontaneously, that is why they are called wise. The unwise must be dragged towards it by all the social means in the power of the wise; for why should demonstrable error be suffered to survive and breed? The immature and untutored must be made to say to themselves: 'Only the truth liberates, and the only way in which I can learn the truth is by doing blindly today what you, who know it, order me, or coerce me, to do, in the certain knowledge that only thus will I arrive at your clear vision, and be free like you'.

We have wandered indeed from our liberal beginnings. This argument, employed by Fichte in his latest phase, and after him by other defenders of authority, from Victorian schoolmasters and colonial administrators to the latest nationalist or Communist dictator, is precisely what the Stoic and Kantian morality protests against most bitterly in the name of the reason of the free individual following his own inner light. In this way the rationalist argument, with its assumption of the single true solution, has led by steps which, if not logically valid, are historically and psychologically intelligible from an ethical doctrine of individual responsibility and individual self-perfection to an authoritarian State obedient to the directives of an élite of Platonic guardians.

What can have led to so strange a reversal—the transformation of Kant's severe individualism into something close to a pure totalitarian doctrine on the part of thinkers some of whom claimed to be his disciples? This question is not of merely historical inter-

---

[34] See *Plan des travaux scientifiques nécessaires pour réorganiser la société* (1822): p. 53, in August Comte, *Appendice général du système de politique positive* (Paris, 1854), published as part of vol. 4 of *Système de politique positive* (Paris 1851–54).

est, for not a few contemporary liberals have gone through the same peculiar evolution. It is true that Kant insisted, following Rousseau, that a capacity for rational self-direction belonged to all men; that there could be no experts in moral matters, since morality was a matter not of specialised knowledge (as the Utilitarians and *philosophes* had maintained), but of the correct use of a universal human faculty; and consequently that what made men free was not acting in certain self-improving ways, which they could be coerced to do, but knowing why they ought to do so, which nobody could do for, or on behalf of, anyone else. But even Kant, when he came to deal with political issues, conceded that no law, provided that it was such that I should, if I were asked, approve it as a rational being, could possibly deprive me of any portion of my rational freedom. With this the door was opened wide to the rule of experts. I cannot consult all men about all enactments all the time. The government cannot be a continuous plebiscite. Moreover, some men are not as well attuned to the voice of their own reason as others: some seem singularly deaf. If I am a legislator or a ruler, I must assume that if the law I impose is rational (and I can consult only my own reason) it will automatically be approved by all the members of my society so far as they are rational beings. For if they disapprove, they must, *pro tanto*, be irrational; then they will need to be repressed by reason: whether their own or mine cannot matter, for the pronouncements of reason must be the same in all minds. I issue my orders and, if you resist, take it upon myself to repress the irrational element in you which opposes reason. My task would be easier if you repressed it in yourself; I try to educate you to do so. But I am responsible for public welfare, I cannot wait until all men are wholly rational. Kant may protest that the essence of the subject's freedom is that he, and he alone, has given himself the order to obey. But this is a counsel of perfection. If you fail to discipline yourself, I must do so for you; and you cannot complain of lack of freedom, for the fact that Kant's rational judge has sent you to prison is evidence that you have not listened to your own inner reason, that, like a child, a savage, an idiot, you are either not ripe for self-direction, or permanently incapable of it.[35]

[35] Kant came nearest to asserting the 'negative' ideal of liberty when (in one of his political treatises) he declared that 'The greatest problem of the human race, to the solution of which it is compelled by nature, is the establishment of a civil society universally administering right according to law. It is only in a society

If this leads to despotism, albeit by the best or the wisest—to Sarastro's temple in *The Magic Flute*—but still despotism, which turns out to be identical with freedom, can it be that there is something amiss in the premises of the argument? That the basic assumptions are themselves somewhere at fault? Let me state them once more: first, that all men have one true purpose, and one only, that of rational self-direction; second, that the ends of all rational beings must of necessity fit into a single universal, harmonious pattern, which some men may be able to discern more clearly than others; third, that all conflict, and consequently all tragedy, is due solely to the clash of reason with the irrational or the insufficiently rational—the immature and undeveloped elements in life, whether individual or communal—and that such clashes are, in principle, avoidable, and for wholly rational beings

(note 35 continued) which possesses the greatest liberty ... and also the most exact determination and guarantee of the limits of [the] liberty [of each individual] in order that it may co-exist with the liberty of others—that the highest purpose of nature, which is the development of all her capacities, can be attained in the case of mankind'. *'Idee zu einer allgemeinen Geschichte in weltburgerlicher Absicht'* (1784), in *Kant's gesammelte Schriften* (Berlin, 1900–), vol. 8, p. 22, line 6. Apart from the teleological implications, this formulation does not at first appear very different from orthodox liberalism. The crucial point, however, is how to determine the criterion for the 'exact determination and guarantee of the limits' of individual liberty. Most modern liberals, at their most consistent, want a situation in which as many individuals as possible can realise as many of their ends as possible, without assessment of the value of these ends as such, save in so far as they may frustrate the purposes of others. They wish the frontiers between individuals or groups of men to be drawn solely with a view to preventing collisions between human purposes, all of which must be considered to be equally ultimate, uncriticisable ends in themselves. Kant, and the rationalists of his type, do not regard all ends as of equal value. For them the limits of liberty are determined by applying the rules of 'reason', which is much more than the mere generality of rules as such, and is a faculty that creates or reveals a purpose identical in, and for, all men. In the name of reason anything that is non-rational may be condemned, so that the various personal reasons which their individual imaginations and idiosyncrasies lead men to pursue—for example, aesthetic and other non-rational kinds of self-fulfilment—may, at least in theory, be ruthlessly suppressed to make way for the demands of reason. The authority of reason and of the duties it lays upon men is identified with individual freedom, on the assumption that only rational ends can be the 'true' objects of a 'free' man's 'real' nature.

I have never, I must own, understood what 'reason' means in this context; and here merely wish to point out that the a priori assumptions of this philosophical psychology are not compatible with empiricism: that is to say, with any doctrine founded on knowledge derived from experience of what men are and seek.

impossible; finally, that when all men have been made rational, they will obey the rational laws of their own natures, which are one and the same in them all, and so be at once wholly law-abiding and wholly free. Can it be that Socrates and the creators of the central Western tradition in ethics and politics who followed him have been mistaken, for more than two millennia, that virtue is not knowledge, nor freedom identical with either? That despite the fact that it rules the lives of more men than ever before in its long history, not one of the basic assumptions of this famous view is demonstrable, or, perhaps, even true?

THREE

FREEDOM AND POLITICS

Hannah Arendt

To discuss the relation of freedom to politics in the brief time of a lecture can be justified only because a book would be nearly as inadequate. Whether we know it or not, the question of politics is always present when we speak of the problem of freedom; and we can hardly touch a single political issue without, implicitly or explicitly, touching upon an issue of man's liberty. For freedom, which is only seldom—in times of crisis or revolution—the direct aim of political action, is actually the reason why men live together in political organization at all; without it, political life as such would be meaningless. The *raison d'être* of politics is freedom, and its field of experience is action.

We shall see later that freedom and free will (a human faculty the philosophers have defined and redefined for centuries) are by no means the same. Even less is it identical with inner freedom, this inward space into which men may escape from external coercion and *feel* free. Whatever the legitimacy of this feeling may be and however eloquently it might have been described in late antiquity, it is historically a late phenomenon, and it was originally the result of an estrangement from the world in which certain worldly experiences were transformed into experiences within one's own self. The experiences of inner freedom are derivative in that they always presuppose a retreat from the world, where

This lecture was first published in the *Chicago Review*, 14 (1) (Spring 1960), 18–46. Expanded versions later appeared as 'Freedom and Politics', in A. Hunold (ed.), *Freedom and Serfdom* (Dordrecht: D. Reidel, 1961), and as 'What is Freedom?', in H. Arendt, *Between Past and Future* (New York: Viking Press, 2nd edn., 1968).

freedom was denied, into an inwardness to which no other has access. This inward space where the self is sheltered against the world must not be mistaken for the heart or the mind, both of which exist and function only in interrelationship with the world. Not the heart and not the mind, but inwardness as a place of absolute freedom within one's own self was discovered in late antiquity by those who had no place of their own in the world and hence lacked a worldly condition which, from early antiquity to almost the middle of the nineteenth century, was unanimously held to be a prerequisite for freedom.[1]

Hence, in spite of the great influence which the concept of an inner, non-political freedom has exerted upon the tradition

[1] The derivative character of the concept of inner freedom, as of the experiences underlying the theory that 'the appropriate region of human liberty' is the 'inward domain of consciousness' (John Stuart Mill), appears more clearly if we go back to the origins. Not the modern individual with its desire to unfold, to develop, and to expand, with its justified fear lest society get the better of its individuality, with its emphatic insistence 'on the importance of genius' and originality, but the philosophers of late antiquity are representative in this respect. Thus, the most persuasive arguments for the absolute superiority of inner freedom can still be found in an essay of Epictetus, the slave-philosopher, 'On Freedom' (*Dissertationes*, Book IV. 1). Epictetus begins by stating that free is who lives as he wishes (s. 1), a definition which oddly echoes a sentence from Aristotle's *Politics* in which the statement 'Freedom means the doing what a man likes' is put in the mouth of those who do not know what freedom is (1310^a 25 f.). Epictetus then goes on to show that a man is free, if he limits himself to what is in his power, if he does not reach into a realm where he can be hindered (s. 75). The 'science of living' (s. 118) consists in knowing how to distinguish between the alien world over which man has no power and the self of which he may dispose as he sees fit (ss. 81 and 83). In this interpretation, freedom and politics have parted for good. If the only possible obstacle to freedom is man's own self or rather his inability to restrain his self's desires, then he needs no politics and no political organization in order to be free. He can be a slave in the world and still be free. The political background of this theory is clearly indicated by the role which the ideas of power, domination, and property play in it. According to ancient understanding, man could liberate himself from necessity only through power over other men, and he could be free only if he owned a place, a home in the world. Epictetus transposed these worldly relationships into relationships within man's own self, whereby he discovered that no power is so absolute as that which man yields over himself, and that the inward space where man struggles and subdues himself is more entirely his own, namely more securely shielded from outside interference, than any worldly home could ever be.

of thought, it seems safe to say that man would know nothing of inner freedom if he had not first experienced a condition of being free among others as a worldly tangible reality. We first become aware of freedom or its opposite in our intercourse with others, not in intercourse with ourselves. Before it became an attribute of thought or a quality of the will, freedom was understood to be the free man's status which enabled him to move, to get away from home, to go out into the world and meet other people in deed and word. This freedom clearly was preceded by liberation: in order to be free, man must have liberated himself from the necessities of life. But the status of freedom did not follow automatically upon the act of liberation. Freedom needed in addition to mere liberation the company of other men who were in the same state, and it needed a common public space to meet them—a politically organized world, in other words, into which each of the free-men could insert himself by word and deed.

Obviously, not every form of human intercourse and not every kind of community is characterized by freedom. Where men live together but do not form a body politic—as, for example, in tribal societies or in the privacy of the household—the factor ruling their actions and behaviour is not freedom but the necessities of life and concern for its preservation. Moreover, wherever the man-made world does not become the scene for action and speech—as in despotically ruled communities which banish their subjects into the narrowness of the home and thus prevent the rise of a public realm—freedom has no worldly reality. Without a politically guaranteed public realm, freedom lacks the worldly space to make its appearance. To be sure it may still dwell in men's hearts as desire or will or hope or yearning; but the human heart, as we all know, is a very dark place and whatever goes on in its obscurity can hardly be called a demonstrable fact. Freedom as a demonstrable fact and politics coincide and are related to each other like two sides of the same matter.

Yet, it is precisely this coincidence of politics and freedom which we cannot take for granted in the light of our present political experiences. The rise of totalitarianism, its claim to having subordinated all spheres of life to the demands of politics and its consistent non-recognition of civil rights, above all the rights of privacy, makes us doubt not only the coincidence of politics and freedom but their very compatibility. We are inclined to believe that freedom begins where politics ends, because we have seen that freedom has disappeared when so-called political considerations overruled everything else. Was not the liberal credo, 'the less politics the more freedom', right after all? Is it not true that the smaller the space occupied by the political, the larger the domain left to freedom? Indeed, do we not rightly measure the extent of freedom in any given community by the free scope it grants to apparently non-political activities, free economic enterprise or freedom of teaching, of religion, of cultural and intellectual activities? Is it not true, as we all somehow believe, that politics is compatible with freedom only because and in so far as it guarantees a possible freedom *from* politics?

This definition of political liberty as a potential freedom from politics is not urged upon us merely by our most recent experiences; it has played a large role in the history of political theory. We need go no farther than the political thinkers of the seventeenth and eighteenth centuries who more often than not simply identified political freedom with security. The highest purpose of politics, 'the end of government', was the guarantee of security; security, in turn, made freedom possible, and the word freedom designated a quintessence of activities which occurred outside the political realm. Even Montesquieu, though he had not only a different, but a much higher opinion of the essence of politics than Hobbes or Spinoza, could still occasionally equate political freedom with security.[2] The rise of the political and social sciences in the nineteenth and twentieth centuries has even widened the breach between freedom and politics; for government which, since the beginning of the modern age, had been identified with the total domain of the political, was now considered to be the appointed protector not so much of freedom as of the life process, the interests of society and its individuals. Security remained the decisive criterion, but not the individual's security against 'violent death' as in Hobbes (where the

[2] See *Esprit des lois*, xii. 2: 'La liberté philosophique consiste dans l'exercice de la volonté . . . La liberté politique consiste dans la sûreté.'

condition of all liberty is freedom from fear), but a security which should permit an undisturbed development of the life process of society as a whole. The life process is not bound up with freedom but follows its own inherent necessity; and it can be called free only in the sense that we speak of a freely flowing stream. Here freedom is not even the non-political aim of politics, but a marginal phenomenon—which somehow forms the boundary government should not overstep unless life itself and its immediate interests and necessities are at stake.

Thus not only we, who have reasons of our own to distrust politics for the sake of freedom, but the entire modern age has separated freedom and politics. I could descend even deeper into the past and evoke older memories and traditions. The pre-modern secular concept of freedom certainly was emphatic in its insistence on separating the subjects' freedom from any direct share in government; the people's 'liberty and freedom consisted in having the government of those laws by which their life and their goods may be most their own'—as Charles I summed it up in his speech from the scaffold. It was not out of a desire for freedom that people eventually demanded their share in government or admission to the political realm, but out of mistrust in those who held power over their life and goods. The Christian concept of political freedom, moreover, arose out of the early Christians' suspicion and hostility against the public realm as such, from whose concerns they demanded to be absolved in order to be free. And does not this Christian definition of freedom as freedom from politics only repeat what we know so well from ancient philosophy, namely, the philosopher's demand of σχολή, of 'leisure', or rather of abstention from politics which since Plato and Aristotle was held to be a prerequisite for the βίος θεωρητικός, the philosopher's 'contemplative life', only that now the Christians demanded for all, for 'the many', what the philosophers had asked for only 'the few'.

Despite the enormous weight of this tradition and despite the perhaps even more telling urgency of our own experiences, both pressing into the same direction of a divorce of freedom from politics, I think you all believed you heard not more than an old truism when I first said that the *raison d'être* of politics is freedom and that this freedom is primarily experienced in action. In the following, we shall do no more than reflect on this old truism.

2

Freedom as related to politics is not a phenomenon of the will. We deal here not with the *liberum arbitrium*, a freedom of choice that arbitrates and decides between two given things, one good and one evil, as, for example, Richard III determined to be a villain. Rather it is, to remain with Shakespeare, the freedom of Brutus: 'That this shall be or we will fall for it', that is, the freedom to call something into being which did not exist before, which was not given, not even as an object of cognition or imagination, and which therefore strictly speaking could not be known. What guides this act is not a future aim whose desirability the intellect has grasped before the will wills it, whereby the intellect calls upon the will since only the will can dictate action—to paraphrase a characteristic description of this process by Duns Scotus: 'Intellectus apprehendit agibile antequam voluntas illud velit; sed non apprehendit determinate hoc esse agendum quod apprehendere dicitur dictare' (Oxon. IV, d. 46, qu. 1, no. 10.). Action, to be sure, has an aim, but this aim varies and depends upon the changing circumstances of the world; to recognize the aim is not a matter of freedom, but of right or wrong judgement. Will, seen as a distinct and separate human faculty, follows judgement, i.e. cognition of the right aim, and then commands its execution. The power to command, to dictate action, is not a matter of freedom, but a question of strength or weakness.

Action in so far as it is free is neither under the guidance of the intellect nor under the dictate of the will, although it needs both for the execution of any particular goal. Action springs from something altogether different which (following Montesquieu's famous analysis of forms of government) I shall call a principle. Principles can inspire, but they cannot prescribe a particular result in the sense which is required for carrying out a programme. Unlike the judgement of the intellect which precedes action, and unlike the command of the will which initiates it, the inspiring principle becomes fully manifest only in the performing act itself, which, however, does not exhaust its validity. The principle of an action, in distinction from its goal, can be repeated time and again; it is inexhaustible and remains manifest as long as the action lasts, but no longer. Such principles are honour or glory, love of equality, which Montesquieu called virtue, or distinction or excellence—the Greek ἀεὶ ἀριστεύειν ('always strive to do your best and to be the best of all')—and also fear or distrust or hatred. Freedom or its opposite appear in the world whenever such principles are actualized; the appearance of freedom, like the manifestation of principles, coincides with the performing act. Men *are* free—as distinguished from their possessing the gift for freedom—as long as they act, neither before nor after; for to *be* free and to act are the same.

Freedom as inherent in action is perhaps best illustrated by Machiavelli's concept of *virtù*, the excellence with which man answers the opportunities the world opens up before him in the guise of *fortuna*, and which is neither Roman *virtus* nor our virtue. It is perhaps best translated by 'virtuosity', that is, an excellence we attribute to the performing arts (as distinguished from the creative arts of making), where the accomplishment lies in the performance itself and not in an end product which outlasts the activity that brought it into existence and becomes independent of it. The virtuoso-ship of Machiavelli's *virtù* somehow reminds us of the Greek notion of virtue, ἀρετή, or 'excellence', although Machiavelli hardly knew that the Greeks always used metaphors like flute playing, dancing, healing, and seafaring to distinguish political from other activities, that is, that they drew their analogies from those arts in which virtuosity of performance is decisive.

Since all acting contains an element of virtuosity, and because virtuosity is the excellence we ascribe to the performing arts, politics has often been defined as an art. This, of course, is not a definition but a metaphor, and the metaphor becomes completely false if one falls into the common error of regarding the state or government as a work of art, as a kind of collective masterpiece. In the sense of the creative arts, which bring forth something tangible and reify human thought to such an extent that the produced thing possesses an existence of its own, politics is the exact opposite of art—which incidentally does not mean that it is a science. Political institutions, no matter how well or how badly designed, depend for continued existence upon acting men; their conservation is achieved by the same means that brought them into being. Independent existence marks the work of art as a product of making; utter dependence upon further acts to keep it in existence marks the state as a product of action.

The point here is not whether the creative artist is free in the process of creation, but that the creative process is not displayed in public and not destined to appear in the world. Hence, the element of freedom, certainly present in the creative arts, remains hidden; it is not the free creative process which finally appears and matters for the world, but the work of art itself, the end product of the process. The performing arts, on the contrary, have indeed a certain affinity with politics. Performing artists—dancers, play-artists, musicians, and the like—need an audience to show their virtuosity, just as acting men need the presence of others before whom they can appear; both need a publicly organized space for their 'work' and both depend upon others for the performance itself. Such a space of appearances is not to be taken for granted wherever men live together in a community. The Greek polis once was precisely that 'form of government' which provided men with a space of appearances where they could act, with a kind of theatre where freedom could appear.

I hope you will find it neither arbitrary nor far-fetched if I use the word 'political' in the sense of the Greek polis. Not only etymologically and not only for the learned does the very word, which in all European languages still derives from the historically unique organization of the Greek city-state, echo the experiences of the community which first discovered the essence and the realm of the political. It is indeed difficult and even misleading to talk about politics and its innermost principles without drawing to some extent upon the experiences of Greek and Roman antiquity, and this for no other reason than that men have never, either before or after, thought so highly of political activity and bestowed so much dignity upon its realm. As regards our present concern, the relation of freedom to politics, there is the additional reason that only ancient political communities were founded for the express purpose to serve the free—those who were neither slaves, subject to coercion by others, nor labourers, driven and urged on by the necessities of life. If, then, we understand the political in the sense of the polis, its end or *raison d'être* would be to establish and keep in existence a space where freedom as virtuosity can appear. This is the realm where freedom is a worldly reality, tangible in words which can be heard, in deeds which can be seen, and in events which are talked about and turned into stories before they are remembered and incorporated into the great storybook of human history. Whatever occurs in this space of appearances is political by definition, even when it is not a direct product of action. What remains outside it, such as the great feats of barbarian empires, may be impressive and noteworthy, but it is not political, strictly speaking.

These conceptions of freedom and politics and their mutual relation seem so strange because we usually understand freedom either as free will or free thought, while, on the other hand, we impute to politics the concern for the maintenance of life and safeguarding of its interests. Yet even we, preoccupied as we apparently are with the concern for life, still know that courage is among the cardinal political virtues. Courage is a big word, and I do not mean the daring of adventure which gladly risks life for the sake of being as thoroughly and intensely alive as one can be only in the face of danger and death. Temerity is no less concerned with life than cowardice. Courage, which we still believe to be indispensable for political action, and which Churchill once called 'the first of human qualities, because it is the quality which guarantees all others', does not gratify our individual sense of vitality but is demanded of us by the very nature of the public realm. For this world of ours, because it existed before us and is meant to outlast our lives in it, simply cannot afford to give primary concern to individual lives and the interests connected with them; as such the public realm stands in the sharpest possible contrast to our private domain where, in the protection of family and home, everything serves and must serve the security of the life process. It requires courage even to leave the protective security of our four walls and enter the public realm, not because of particular dangers which may or may not lie in wait for us, but because we have arrived in a realm where the concern for life has lost its validity. Courage liberates men from their worry about life for the freedom of the world. Courage is indispensable because in politics not life but the world is at stake, a world about which we have to decide how it is going to look and to sound and in what shape we want it to outlast us.

' Those therefore who, in spite of all theories, still think of freedom when they hear the word 'politics', will not believe that the political is only the sum total of private interests and that therefore it is the task of politics to check and balance their conflicts; nor are they likely to hold that the role of government is similar to that of a paterfamilias. In both instances, politics is incompatible with freedom. Freedom is the *raison d'être* of politics only if it designs a realm which is public and therefore not merely distinguished from, but even opposed to, the private realm and its interests.

3

Obviously, this notion of an interdependence of freedom and politics stands in contradiction to the social theories of the modern age. Unfortunately, it does not follow that we need only to revert to older pre-modern traditions and theories. Indeed, the greatest difficulty in reaching an understanding of the relation of freedom to politics arises from the fact that a simple return to tradition, and especially to what we are wont to call the great tradition, does not help us. Neither the philosophical concept of freedom as it first arose in late antiquity, where freedom became a phenomenon of thought by which man could, as it were, reason himself out of the world, nor the Christian and modern notion of free will have any ground in political experience. Our philosophical tradition is almost unanimous in holding that freedom begins where men have left the realm of political life inhabited by the many, and that it is not experienced in association with others but in intercourse with oneself—whether in the form of an inner dialogue which, since Socrates, we call thinking, or a conflict within myself, the inner strife between what I would and what I do, whose murderous dialectics disclosed first to Paul and then to Augustine the equivocalities and impotence of the human heart.

For the history of the problem of freedom, Christian tradition has indeed become the decisive factor. We almost automatically equate freedom with free will, that is, with a faculty virtually unknown to classical antiquity. For will, as Christianity discovered it, had so little in common with the well-known capacities to desire and intend that it claimed attention only after it had come into conflict with them. If freedom were actually nothing but a phenomenon of the will, we would have to conclude that the ancients did not know freedom. This, of course, is absurd, but if one wished to assert it he could argue that the idea of freedom played no role in the works of the great philosophers prior to Augustine. The reason for this striking fact is that, in Greek as well as Roman antiquity, freedom was an exclusively political concept, indeed the quintessence of the city-state and of citizenship. Our philosophical tradition, beginning with Parmenides and Plato, was founded explicitly in opposition to this polis and this citizenship. The way of life chosen by the philosopher was understood in opposition to the βίος πολιτικός, the political way of life. Freedom, therefore, the very centre of politics as the Greeks understood it, was an idea which almost by definition could not enter the framework of Greek philosophy. Only when the early Christians, and especially Paul, discovered a kind of freedom which had no relation to politics, could the concept of freedom enter the history of philosophy. Freedom became one of the chief problems of philosophy when it was experienced as something occurring in the intercourse between me with myself, and outside of the intercourse between men. Free will and freedom became synonymous notions,[3] and the presence of freedom was

---

[3] Leibniz only sums up and articulates the Christian tradition when he writes: 'Die Frage, ob unserem Willen Freiheit zukommt, bedeutet eigentlich nichts anderes, al ob ihm "Willen" zukommt. Die Ausdrücke "frei" und "willensgemäss" besagen dasselbe.' (*Schriften zur Metaphysik*, i, Bemerkungen zu dem cartesischen Prinzipien. Zu Artikel 39.)

experienced in complete solitude 'where no man might hinder the hot contention wherein I had engaged with myself', the deadly conflict which took place in the 'inner dwelling' of the soul and the dark 'chamber of the heart' (Augustine, *Confessiones*, book VIII, ch. 8).

In view of the extraordinary potential power inherent in the will—will and will-power are indeed almost identical notions[4]— we tend to forget the historical fact that the phenomenon of the will originally did not manifest itself as I-will-and-I-can, but, on the contrary, in a conflict between the two, in the experience that what I would I do not. What was unknown to antiquity was precisely that I-will and I-can are not the same—'*non hoc est velle, quod posse*' (Augustine, loc. cit.). For the I-will-and-I-can was of course very familiar to the ancients. We need only remember how much Plato insisted that only those who know how to rule themselves had the right to rule others and be freed from the obligation of obedience. And it is true that self-control has remained one of the specifically political virtues, if only because it is an outstanding phenomenon of virtuosity where I-will and I-can must be so well attuned that they practically coincide.

Had ancient philosophy known of a possible conflict between what I can and what I will, it would certainly have understood the phenomenon of freedom as an inherent quality of the I-can, or it might conceivably have defined it as the coincidence of I-will and I-can; it certainly would not have thought of it as an attribute of the I-will or I-would. This assertion is no empty speculation; if we wish to check it we need only to read Montesquieu, whose thought followed so closely the political thought of the ancients, and who therefore was so deeply aware of the inadequacy of the Christian and the philosophers' concept of freedom for political purposes.

---

[4] Augustine, in the famous chapters about will in his *Confessions*, stresses already the great power inherent in will: 'Imperat . . . et paretur statim', 'it commands . . . and is immediately obeyed'; the 'monstrosity' that man might command himself and not be obeyed arises from the fact that 'to will' and 'to command' are the same—'in tantum imperat in quantum vult, et in tantum non fit quod imperat, in quantum non vult'. ('In so far as the mind commands, the mind wills, and in so far the thing commanded is not done, it wills not,' book VIII, ch. 9).

He expressly distinguished between philosophical and political freedom, and the difference consisted in that philosophy demands no more of freedom than the exercise of the will (*l'exercice de la volonté*), independent of circumstances and of attainment of the goals the will has set. Political freedom, on the contrary, consists in being able to do what one ought to will ('*la liberté ne peut consister qu'à pouvoir faire ce que l'on doit vouloir*') (*Esprit des lois*, XII. 2 and XI. 3). For Montesquieu as for the ancients it was obvious that an agent could no longer be called free when he lacked the capacity to do—whereby it is irrelevant whether this failure is caused by exterior or by interior circumstances.

I chose the example of self-control because to us this is clearly a phenomenon of will and of will-power. The Greeks, more than any other people, have reflected on moderation and the necessity to tame the steeds of the soul, and yet they never became aware of the will as a distinct faculty, separate from other human capacities. Historically, men first discovered the will when they experienced its impotence and not its power, when they said with Paul: 'for to will is present with me; but how to perform that which is good I find not'. It is the same will of which Augustine complained that it seemed 'no monstrousness [for it] partly to will, partly to nill'; and although he points out that this is 'a disease of the mind', he also admits that this disease is, as it were, natural for a mind possessed of a will, 'For the will commands that there will be a will, it commands not something else but itself . . . Were the will entire, it would not even command itself to be, because it would already be.' In other words, if man has a will at all, it must always appear as though there were two wills present in the same man, fighting with each other for power over his mind (*Confessiones*, VIII. 9). Hence, the will is both powerful and impotent, free and unfree.

When we speak of impotence and the limits set to will-power, we usually think of man's powerlessness with respect to the surrounding world. It is, therefore, of some importance to notice that in these early testimonies the will was not defeated by some overwhelming force of nature or circumstances; the contention which its appearance raised was neither the conflict between the one against the many nor the strife between body and mind. On the contrary, the relation of mind to body was for Augustine even the outstanding example for the enormous power inherent in the will: 'The mind commands the body, and the body obeys instantly; the mind commands itself, and is resisted' (*ibid.*). The body represents in this context the exterior world and is by no means identical with one's self. It is within one's self, in the 'interior dwelling' (*interior domus*), where Epictetus still believed man to be an absolute master, that the conflict between man and himself broke out and the will was defeated. Christian will-power was discovered as an organ of self-liberation and immediately found wanting. It is as though the I-will immediately paralysed the I-can, as though the moment men *willed* freedom, they lost their capacity to be free. In the deadly conflict with worldly desires and intentions from which will-power was supposed to liberate the self, the most willing seemed able to achieve was oppression. Because of the will's impotence, its incapacity to generate genuine power, its constant defeat in the struggle with the self, in which the power of the I-can exhausted itself, the will-to-power turned at once into a will-to-oppression. I can only hint here at the fatal consequences for political theory of this equation of freedom with the human capacity to will; it was one of the causes why even today we almost automatically equate power with oppression or at least rule over others.

However that may be, what we usually understand by will and will-power has grown out of this conflict between a willing and a performing self, out of the experience of an I-will-and-can*not*, which means that the I-will, no matter what is willed, remains subject to the self, strikes back at it, spurs it on, incites it further, or is ruined by it. How far the will-to-power may reach out, and even if somebody possessed by it begins to conquer the whole world, the I-will can never rid itself of the self; it always remains bound to it and, indeed, under its bondage. This bondage to the self distinguishes the I-will from the I-think, which also is carried on between me and myself but in whose dialogue the self is not the subject of the activity of thought. The fact that the I-will has become so power-thirsty, that will and will-to-power have become practically identical, is perhaps due to its having been first experienced in its impotence. Tyranny at any rate, the only form of government which arises directly out of the I-will, owes its greedy cruelty to an egotism utterly absent from the utopian tyrannies of reason with which the philosophers wished to coerce men and which they conceived on the model of the I-think.

I have said that the philosophers first began to show an interest in the problem of freedom when freedom was no longer experienced in acting and associating with others but in willing and the intercourse with one's self, when, briefly, freedom had become free will. Since then, freedom has been a philosophical problem of the first order; as such it was applied to the political realm and thus has become a political problem as well. Because of the philosophic shift from action to will-power, from freedom as a state of being manifest in action to the *liberum arbitrium*, the ideal of freedom ceased to be virtuosity in the sense we mentioned before and became sovereignty, the ideal of a free will, independent from others and eventually prevailing against them. The philosophic ancestry of our current political notion of freedom is still quite manifest in eighteenth-century political writers, when, for instance, Thomas Paine insisted that 'to be free it is sufficient [for man] that he wills it', a word which Lafayette applied to the nation state: 'pour qu'une nation soit libre, il suffit qu'elle veuille l'être.'[5] Politically, this identification of freedom with sovereignty is perhaps the most pernicious and dangerous consequence of the philosophical equation of freedom and free will. For it leads either to a denial of human freedom—namely if it is realized that whatever men may be, they are never sovereign—or to the insight that the freedom of one man or a group or a body politic can only be purchased at the price of the freedom, i.e. the sovereignty, of all others. Within the conceptual framework of traditional philosophy, it is indeed very difficult to understand how freedom and non-sovereignty

---

[5] Among modern political theorists, Carl Schmitt has remained the most consistent and the most able defender of the notion of sovereignty. He recognizes clearly that the root of sovereignty is the will: Sovereign is who wills and commands. See especially his *Verfassungslere* (Munich, 1928), 7 ff., 146.

can exist together or, to put it another way, how freedom could have been given to men under the condition of non-sovereignty. Actually, it is as unrealistic to deny freedom because of the fact of human non-sovereignty as it is dangerous to believe that one can be free—as an individual or as a group—only if one is sovereign. The famous sovereignty of political bodies has always been an illusion which, moreover, can be maintained only by the instruments of violence, that is, with essentially non-political means. Under human conditions, which are determined by the fact that not man but men live on the earth, freedom and sovereignty are so little identical that they cannot even exist simultaneously. Where men wish to be sovereign, as individuals or as organized groups, they must submit to the oppression of the will, be this the individual will with which I force myself or the 'general will' of an organized group. If men wish to be free, it is precisely sovereignty they must renounce.

4

Since the whole problem of freedom arises for us in the horizon of Christian traditions on the one hand and of an originally anti-political philosophic tradition on the other, we find it difficult to realize that there may exist a freedom which is not an attribute of the will but an accessory of doing and acting. Let us therefore go back once more to antiquity, i.e., to its political and pre-philosophical traditions, certainly not for the sake of erudition and not even because of the continuity of our traditions, but merely because a freedom experienced in the process of acting and nothing else—though, of course, mankind never lost this experience altogether—has never again been articulated with the same classical clarity.

This articulation is ultimately rooted in the curious fact that both the Greek and the Latin language possess two verbs to designate what we uniformly call 'to act'. The two Greek words are ἄρχειν: to begin, to lead, and, finally, to rule, and πράττειν: to carry something through. The corresponding Latin verbs are *agere*: to set something in motion, and *gerere*, which is hard to translate and somehow means the enduring and supporting continuation of past acts which result in the *res gestae*, the deeds and events we call historical. In both instances, action occurs in two different stages; its first stage is a beginning by which something new comes into the world. The Greek word ἄρχειν which covers beginning, leading, and even ruling, that is, the outstanding qualities of the free man, bears witness to an experience in which being free and the capacity to begin something new coincided. Freedom, as we would say today, was experienced in spontaneity. The manifold meaning of ἄρχειν indicates the following: only those could begin something new who were already rulers (i.e. household heads who ruled over slaves and family) and had thus liberated themselves from the necessities of life for enterprises in distant lands or citizenship in the polis; in either case, they no longer ruled, but were rulers among rulers, moving among their peers whose help they enlisted as their leaders in order to begin something new, to start a new enterprise; for only with the help of others could the ἄρχων, the ruler, beginner, and leader, really act, πράττειν, carry through whatever he had started to do.

In Latin, to be free and to begin are also interconnected, though in a different way. Roman freedom was a legacy bequeathed by the founders of Rome to the Roman people; their freedom was tied to the beginning their forefathers had established by founding the City, whose affairs the descendants had to manage, whose consequences they had to bear, and whose foundations they had to 'augment'. All these together are the *res gestae* of the Roman republic. Roman historiography therefore, essentially as political as Greek historiography, never was content with the mere narration of great deeds and events; unlike Thucydides or Herodotus, the Roman historians always felt bound to the beginning of Roman history, because this beginning contained the authentic element of Roman freedom and thus made their history political; whatever they had to relate, they started *ad urbe condita*, with the foundation of the City, the guarantee of Roman freedom.

I have already mentioned that the ancient concept of freedom played no role in Greek philosophy precisely because of its exclusively political origin. Roman writers, it is true rebelled occasionally against the anti-political tendencies of the Socratic school, but their strange lack of philosophic talent apparently prevented their finding a theoretical concept of freedom which could have been adequate to their own experiences and to the great institutions of liberty present in the Roman *res republica*. If the history of ideas were as consistent as its historians sometimes imagine, we should have even less hope to find a valid political idea of freedom in Augustine, the great Christian thinker who in fact introduced Paul's free will, along with its perplexities, into the history of philosophy. Yet we find in Augustine not only the discussion of freedom as *liberum arbitrium*, though this discussion became decisive for the tradition, but also an entirely differently conceived notion which characteristically appears in his only political treatise, in *De civitate Dei*. In the *City of God*, Augustine, as is only natural, speaks more from the background of specifically Roman experiences than in any of his other writings, and freedom is conceived there, not as an inner human disposition, but as a character of human existence in the world. Man does not possess freedom so much as he, or better his coming into the world, is equated with the appearance of freedom in the universe; man is free because he is a beginning and was so created after the universe had already come into existence: '[Initium]ut esset, creatus est homo, ante quem nemo fuit' (book xii, ch. 20). In the birth of each man this initial beginning is reaffirmed, because in each instance something new comes into an already existing world which will continue to exist after each individual's death. Because he *is* a beginning, man can begin; to be human and to be free are one and the same. God created man in order to introduce into the world the faculty of beginning: freedom.

The strong anti-political tendencies of early Christianity are so familiar that the notion that a Christian thinker was the first to formulate the philosophical implications of the ancient political idea of freedom strikes us as almost paradoxical. The only explanation seems to be that Augustine was a Roman as well as a Christian, and that in this part of his work he formulated the central political experience of Roman antiquity, which was that freedom *qua* beginning became manifest in the act of foundation. Yet, I am convinced that this impression would considerably change if the sayings of Jesus of Nazareth were taken more seriously in their philosophic implications. We find in these parts of the New Testament an extraordinary understanding of freedom and particularly of the power inherent in human freedom; but the human capacity which corresponds to this power, which, in the words of the gospel, is capable of removing mountains, is not will but faith. The work of faith, actually its product, is what the gospels called 'miracles', a word with many meanings in the New Testament and difficult to understand. We can neglect the difficulties here and refer only to those passages where miracles are clearly not supernatural events—although all miracles, those performed by men no less than those performed by a divine agent, interrupt a natural series of events or automatic processes in whose context they constitute the wholly unexpected.

If it is true that action and beginning are essentially the same, it follows that a capacity for performing miracles must likewise be within the range of human faculties. This sounds stranger than it actually is. It is in the nature of every new beginning that it breaks into the world wholly unexpected and unforeseen, at least from the viewpoint of the processes it interrupts. Every event, the moment it comes to pass, strikes us with surprise as though it were a miracle. It may well be a prejudice to consider miracles merely in religious contexts as supernatural, wholly inexplicable occurrences. It may be better not to forget that, after all, our whole existence rests, as it were, on a chain of miracles, the coming into being of the earth, the development of organic life on it, the evolution of mankind out of the animal species. For from the viewpoint of processes in the universe and their statistically overwhelming probabilities, the coming into being of the earth is an 'infinite improbability', as the natural scientists would say, a miracle as we might call it. The same is true for the formation of organic life out of inorganic processes or for the evolution of man out of the processes of organic life. Each of these events appears to us like a miracle the moment we look at it from the viewpoint of the processes it interrupted. This viewpoint, moreover, is by no means arbitrary or sophisticated; it is, on the contrary, most natural and indeed, in ordinary life, almost commonplace.

I chose this example to illustrate that what we call 'real' in ordinary experience has come into existence through the advent of infinite improbabilities. Of course, it has its limitations and cannot simply be applied to the realm of human affairs. For there we are confronted with historical processes where one event follows the others, with the result that the miracle of accident and infinite improbability occurs so frequently that it seems strange to speak of miracles at all. However, the reason for this frequency is merely that historical processes are created and constantly interrupted by human initiative. If one considers historical processes only as processes, devoid of human initiative, then every new beginning in it [history], for better or worse, becomes so infinitely unlikely as to be well-nigh inexplicable. Objectively, that is, seen from the outside, the chances that tomorrow will be like yesterday are always overwhelming. Not quite so overwhelming, of course, but very nearly so as the chances are that *no* earth would ever rise out of cosmic occurrences, that *no* life would develop out of inorganic processes, and that *no* man would ever develop out of the evolution of animal life. The decisive difference between the 'infinite improbabilities', on which earthly life and the whole reality of nature rest, and the miraculous character of historical events is obvious; in the realm of human affairs we know the author of these 'miracles'; it is men who perform them, namely, in so far as they have received the twofold gift of freedom and action.

5

From these last considerations, it should be easy to find our way back to contemporary political experiences. It follows from them, that the combined danger of totalitarianism and mass society is not that the former abolishes political freedom and civil rights, and that the latter threatens to engulf all culture, the whole world of durable things, and to abolish the standards of excellence without which no thing can ever be produced—although these dangers are real enough. Beyond them we sense another even more dangerous threat, namely that both totalitarianism and mass society, the one by means of terror and ideology, the other by yielding without violence or doctrine to the general trend toward the socialization of man, are driven to stifle initiative and spontaneity as such, that is, the element of action and freedom present in all activities which are not mere labouring. Of these two, totalitarianism still seems to be more dangerous, because it attempts in all earnest to eliminate the possibility of 'miracles' from the realm of politics, or—in more familiar language—to exclude the possibility of events in order to deliver us entirely to the automatic processes by which we are surrounded anyhow. For our historical and political life takes place in the midst of natural processes which, in turn, take place in the midst of cosmic processes, and we ourselves are driven by very similar forces in so far as we, too, are a part of organic nature. It would be sheer superstition to hope for miracles, for the 'infinitely improbable', in the context of these automatic processes, although even this never can be completely excluded. But it is not in the least superstitious, it is even a counsel of realism, to look for the unforeseeable and unpredictable, to be prepared for and to expect 'miracles', in the political realm where in fact they are always possible. Human freedom is not merely a matter of metaphysics but a matter of fact, no less a reality, indeed, than the automatic processes within and against which action always has to assert itself. For the processes set into motion by action also tend to become automatic—which is why no single act and no single event can ever once and for all deliver and save a man, or a nation, or mankind.

It is in the nature of the automatic processes, to which man is subject and by which he would be ruled absolutely without the miracle of freedom, that they can only spell ruin to human life; once historical processes have become automatic, they are no less ruinous than the life process that drives our organism and which biologically can never lead anywhere but from birth to death. The historical sciences know such cases of petrified and declining civilizations only too well, and they know that the processs of stagnation and decline can last and go on for centuries. Quantitatively, they occupy by far the largest space in recorded history.

In the history of mankind, the periods of being free were always relatively short. In the long epochs of petrification and automatic developments, the faculty of freedom, the sheer capacity to begin, which animates and inspires all human activities, can of course remain intact and produce a great variety of great and beautiful things, none of them political. This is probably why freedom has so frequently been defined as a non-political phenomenon and eventually even as a freedom from politics. Even the current liberal misunderstanding which holds that 'perfect liberty is incompatible with the existence of society', and that freedom is the price the individual has to pay for security, still has its authentic root in a state of affairs in which political life has become petrified and political action impotent to interrupt automatic processes. Under such circumstances, freedom indeed is no longer experienced as a mode of being with its own kind of 'virtue' and virtuosity, but as a supreme gift which only man, of all earthly creatures, seems to have received, of which we can find traces in almost all his activities, but which, nevertheless, can develop fully only where action has created its own worldly space where freedom can appear.

We have always known that freedom as a mode of being, together with the public space where it can unfold its full virtuosity, can be destroyed. Since our acquaintance with totalitarianism, we must fear that not only the state of being free but the sheer gift of freedom, that which man did not make but which was given to him, may be destroyed, too. This fear, based on our knowledge of the newest form of government, and on our suspicion that it may yet prove to be the perfect body politic of a mass society, weighs heavily on us under the present circumstances. For today, more may depend on human freedom than ever before—on man's capacity to turn the scales which are heavily weighed in favour of disaster which always happens automatically and therefore always appears to be irresistible. No less than the continued existence of mankind on earth may depend this time upon man's gift to 'perform miracles', that is, to bring about the infinitely improbable and establish it as reality.

FOUR

FREEDOM AND COERCION

F. A. Hayek

I

1. We are concerned in this book with that condition of men in which coercion of some by others is reduced as much as is possible in society. This state we shall describe throughout as a state of liberty or freedom. These two words have been also used to describe many other good things of life. It would therefore not be very profitable to start by asking what they really mean. It would seem better to state, first, the condition which we shall mean when we use them and then consider the other meanings of the words only in order to define more sharply that which we have adopted.

The state in which a man is not subject to coercion by the arbitrary will of another or others is often also distinguished as 'individual' or 'personal' freedom, and whenever we want to remind the reader that it is in this sense that we are using the word 'freedom', we shall imply that expression. Sometimes the term 'civil liberty' is used in the same sense, but we shall avoid it because it is too liable to be confused with what is called 'political liberty'—an inevitable confusion arising from the fact that 'civil' and 'political' derive, respectively, from Latin and Greek words with the same meaning.

Even our tentative indication of what we shall mean by 'freedom' will have shown that it describes a state which man living among his fellows may hope to approach closely but can hardly expect to realize perfectly. The task of a policy of freedom must therefore be to minimize coercion or its harmful effects, even if it cannot eliminate it completely.

Reprinted by permission of Routledge and the University of Chicago Press from F. A. Hayek, *The Constitution of Liberty* (London: Routledge and Kegan Paul, 1960), Chapter 1, ss. 1–5 and Chapter 9, ss. 1–8. The footnotes, which are largely made up of supporting citations, have been omitted here.

It so happens that the meaning of freedom that we have adopted seems to be the original meaning of the word. Man, or at least European man, enters history divided into free and unfree; and this distinction had a very definite meaning. The freedom of the free may have differed widely, but only in the degree of an independence which the slave did not possess at all. It meant always the possibility of a person's acting according to his own decisions and plans, in contrast to the position of one who was irrevocably subject to the will of another, who by arbitrary decision could coerce him to act or not to act in specific ways. The time-honoured phrase by which this freedom has often been described is therefore 'independence of the arbitrary will of another'.

This oldest meaning of 'freedom' has sometimes been described as its vulgar meaning; but when we consider all the confusion that philosophers have caused by their attempts to refine or improve it, we may do well to accept this description. More important, however, than that it is the original meaning is that it is a distinct meaning and that it describes one thing and one thing only, a state which is desirable for reasons different from those which make us desire other things also called 'freedom'. We shall see that, strictly speaking, these various 'freedoms' are not different species of the same genus but entirely different conditions, often in conflict with one another, which therefore should be kept clearly distinct. Though in some of the other senses it may be legitimate to speak of different kinds of freedom, 'freedoms from' and 'freedoms to', in our sense 'freedom' is one, varying in degree but not in kind.

In this sense 'freedom' refers solely to a relation of men to other men, and the only infringement on it is coercion by men. This means, in particular, that the range of physical possibilities from which a person can choose at a given moment has no direct relevance to freedom. The rock climber on a difficult pitch who sees only one way out to save his life is unquestionably free, though we would hardly say he has any choice. Also, most people will still have enough feeling for the original meaning of the word 'free' to see that if that same climber were to fall into a crevasse and were unable to get out of it, he could only figuratively be called 'unfree', and that to speak of him as being 'deprived of liberty' or of being 'held captive' is to use these terms in a sense different from that in which they apply to social relations.

The question of how many courses of action are open to a person is, of course, very important. But it is a different question from that of how far in acting he can follow his own plans and intentions, to what extent the pattern of his conduct is of his own design, directed toward ends for which he has been persistently striving rather than toward necessities created by others in order to make him do what they want. Whether he is free or not does not depend on the range of choice but on whether he can expect to shape his course of action in accordance with his present intentions, or whether somebody else has power so to manipulate the conditions as to make him act according to that person's will rather than his own. Freedom thus presupposes that the individual has some assured private sphere, that there is some set of circumstances in his environment with which others cannot interfere.

This conception of liberty can be made more precise only after we have examined the related concept of coercion. This we shall do systematically after we have considered why this liberty is so important. But even before we attempt this, we shall endeavour to delineate the character of our concept somewhat more precisely by contrasting it with the other meanings which the word liberty has acquired. They have the one thing in common with the original meaning in that they also describe states which most men regard as desirable; and there are some other connections between the different meanings which account for the same word being used for them. Our immediate task, however, must be to bring out the differences as sharply as possible.

2. The first meaning of 'freedom' with which we must contrast our own use of the term is one generally recognized as distinct. It is what is commonly called 'political freedom', the participation of men in the choice of their government, in the process of legislation, and in the control of administration. It derives from an application of our concept to groups of men as a whole which gives them a sort of collective liberty. But a free people in this sense is not necessarily a people of free men; nor

need one share in this collective freedom to be free as an individual. It can scarcely be contended that the inhabitants of the District of Columbia, or resident aliens in the United States, or persons too young to be entitled to vote do not enjoy full personal liberty because they do not share in political liberty.

It would also be absurd to argue that young people who are just entering into active life are free because they have given their consent to the social order into which they were born: a social order to which they probably know no alternative and which even a whole generation who thought differently from their parents could alter only after they had reached mature age. But this does not, or need not, make them unfree. The connection which is often sought between such consent to the political order and individual liberty is one of the sources of the current confusion about its meaning. Anyone is, of course, entitled to 'identify liberty ... with the process of active participation in public power and public law making'. Only it should be made clear that, if he does so, he is talking about a state other than that with which we are here concerned, and that the common use of the same word to describe these different conditions does not mean that the one is in any sense an equivalent or substitute for the other.

The danger of confusion here is that this use tends to obscure the fact that a person may vote or contract himself into slavery and thus consent to give up freedom in the original sense. It would be difficult to maintain that a man who voluntarily but irrevocably had sold his services for a long period of years to a military organization such as the Foreign Legion remained free thereafter in our sense; or that a Jesuit who lives up to the ideals of the founder of his order and regards himself 'as a corpse which has neither intelligence nor will' could be so described. Perhaps the fact that we have seen millions voting themselves into complete dependence on a tyrant has made our generation understand that to choose one's government is not necessarily to secure freedom. Moreover, it would seem that discussing the value of freedom would be pointless if any regime of which people approved was, by definition, a regime of freedom.

The application of the concept of freedom to a collective

rather than to individuals is clear when we speak of a people's desire to be free from a foreign yoke and to determine its own fate. In this case we use 'freedom' in the sense of absence of coercion of a people as a whole. The advocates of individual freedom have generally sympathized with such aspirations for national freedom, and this led to the constant but uneasy alliance between the liberal and the national movements during the eighteenth century. But though the concept of national freedom is analogous to that of individual freedom, it is not the same; and the striving for the first has not always enhanced the second. It has sometimes led people to prefer a despot of their own race to the liberal government of an alien majority; and it has often provided the pretext for ruthless restrictions of the individual liberty of the members of minorities. Even though the desire for liberty as an individual and the desire for liberty of the group to which the individual belongs may often rest on similar feelings and sentiments, it is still necessary to keep the two conceptions clearly apart.

3. Another different meaning of 'freedom' is that of 'inner' or 'metaphysical' (sometimes also 'subjective') freedom. It is perhaps more closely related to individual freedom and therefore more easily confounded with it. It refers to the extent to which a person is guided in his actions by his own considered will, by his reason or lasting conviction, rather than by momentary impulse or circumstance. But the opposite of 'inner freedom' is not coercion by others but the influence of temporary emotions, or moral or intellectual weakness. If a person does not succeed in doing what, after sober reflection, he decides to do, if his intentions or strength desert him at the decisive moment and he fails to do what he somehow still wishes to do, we may say that he is 'unfree', the 'slave of his passions'. We occasionally also use these terms when we say that ignorance or superstition prevents people from doing what they would do if they were better informed, and we claim that 'knowledge makes free'.

Whether or not a person is able to choose intelligently between alternatives, or to adhere to a resolution he has made, is a problem distinct from whether or not other people will impose their will upon him. They are clearly not without some connection: the same conditions which to some constitute coercion will be to others merely ordinary difficulties which have to be overcome, depending on the strength of will of the people involved. To that extent, 'inner freedom' and 'freedom' in the sense of absence of coercion will together determine how much use a person can make of his knowledge of opportunities. The reason why it is still very important to keep the two apart is the relation which the concept of 'inner freedom' has to the philosophical confusion about what is called the 'freedom of the will'. Few beliefs have done more to discredit the ideal of freedom than the erroneous one that scientific determinism has destroyed the basis for individual responsibility . . . Here we merely want to put the reader on guard against this particular confusion and against the related sophism that we are free only if we do what in some sense we ought to do.

4. Neither of these confusions of individual liberty with different concepts denoted by the same word is as dangerous as its confusion with a third use of the word to which we have already briefly referred: the use of 'liberty' to describe the physical 'ability to do what I want', the power to satisfy our wishes, or the extent of the choice of alternatives open to us. This kind of 'freedom' appears in the dreams of many people in the form of the illusion that they can fly, that they are released from gravity and can move 'free like a bird' to wherever they wish, or that they have the power to alter their environment to their liking.

This metaphorical use of the word has long been common, but until comparatively recent times few people seriously confused this 'freedom from' obstacles, this freedom that means omnipotence, with the individual freedom that any kind of social order can secure. Only since this confusion was deliberately fostered as part of the socialist argument has it become dangerous. Once this identification of freedom with power is admitted, there is no limit to the sophisms by which the attractions of the word 'liberty' can be used to support measures which destroy individual liberty, no end to the tricks by which people can be exhorted in the name of liberty to give up their liberty. It has been with the help of this equivocation that the notion of collective power over circumstances has been substituted for that of individual liberty and that in totalitarian states liberty has been suppressed in the name of liberty.

The transition from the concept of individual liberty to that of liberty as power has been facilitated by the philosophical tradition that uses the word 'restraint' where we have used 'coercion' in defining liberty. Perhaps 'restraint' would in some respects be a more suitable word if it was always remembered that in its strict sense it presupposes the action of a restraining human agent. In this sense, it usefully reminds us that the infringements on liberty consist largely in people's being prevented from doing things, while 'coercion' emphasizes their being made to do particular things. Both aspects are equally important: to be precise, we should probably define liberty as the absence of restraint and constraint. Unfortunately, both these words have come also to be used for influences on human action that do not come from other men; and it is only too easy to pass from defining liberty as the absence of restraint to defining it as the 'absence of obstacles to the realization of our desires' or even more generally as 'the absence of external impediment'. This is equivalent to interpreting it as effective power to do whatever we want.

This reinterpretation of liberty is particularly ominous because it has penetrated deeply into the usage of some of the countries where, in fact, individual freedom is still largely preserved. In the United States it has come to be widely accepted as the foundation for the political philosophy dominant in 'liberal' circles. Such recognized intellectual leaders of the 'progressives' as J. R. Commons and John Dewey have spread an ideology in which 'liberty is power, effective power to do specific things' and the 'demand of liberty is the demand for power', while the absence of coercion is merely 'the negative side of freedom' and 'is to be prized only as a means to Freedom which is power'.

5. This confusion of liberty as power with liberty in its original meaning inevitably leads to the identification of liberty with wealth; and this makes it possible to exploit all the appeal which the word 'liberty' carries in the support for a

demand for the redistribution of wealth. Yet, though freedom and wealth are both good things which most of us desire and though we often need both to obtain what we wish, they still remain different. Whether or not I am my own master and can follow my own choice and whether the possibilities from which I must choose are many or few are two entirely different questions. The courtier living in the lap of luxury but at the beck and call of his prince may be much less free than a poor peasant or artisan, less able to live his own life and to choose his own opportunities for usefulness. Similarly, the general in charge of an army or the director of a large construction project may wield enormous powers which in some respects may be quite uncontrollable, and yet may well be less free, more liable to have to change all his intentions and plans at a word from a superior, less able to change his own life or to decide what to him is most important, than the poorest farmer or shepherd.

If there is to be any clarity in the discussion of liberty, its definition must not depend upon whether or not everybody regards this kind of liberty as a good thing. It is very probable that there are people who do not value the liberty with which we are concerned, who cannot see that they derive great benefits from it, and who will be ready to give it up to gain other advantages; it may even be true that the necessity to act according to one's own plans and decisions may be felt by them to be more of a burden than an advantage. But liberty may be desirable, even though not all persons may take advantage of it. We shall have to consider whether the benefit derived from liberty by the majority is dependent upon their using the opportunities it offers them and whether the case for liberty really rests on most people wanting it for themselves. It may well be that the benefits we receive from the liberty of all do not derive from what most people recognize as its effects; it may even be that liberty exercises its beneficial effects as much through the discipline it imposes on us as through the more visible opportunities it offers. .

Above all, however, we must recognize that we may be free and yet miserable. Liberty does not mean all good things or the absence of all evils. It is true that to be free may mean freedom to starve, to make costly mistakes, or to run mortal risks. In the sense in which we use the term, the penniless vagabond who lives precariously by constant improvisation is indeed freer than the conscripted soldier with all his security and relative comfort. But if liberty may therefore not always seem preferable to other goods, it is a distinctive good that needs a distinctive name. And though 'political liberty' and 'inner liberty' are long-established alternative uses of the term which, with a little care, may be employed without causing confusion, it is questionable whether the use of the word 'liberty' in the sense of 'power' should be tolerated.

In any case, however, the suggestion must be avoided that, because we employ the same word, these 'liberties' are different species of the same genus. This is the source of dangerous nonsense, a verbal trap that leads to the most absurd conclusions. Liberty in the sense of power, political liberty, and inner liberty are not states of the same kind as individual liberty: we cannot, by sacrificing a little of the one in order to get more of the other, on balance gain some common element of freedom. We may well get one good thing in the place of another by such an exchange. But to suggest that there is a common element in them which allows us to speak of the effect that such an exchange has on liberty is sheer obscurantism, the crudest kind of philosophical realism, which assumes that, because we describe these conditions with the same word, there must also be a common element in them. But we want them largely for different reasons, and their presence or absence has different effects. If we have to choose between them, we cannot do so by asking whether liberty will be increased as a whole, but only by deciding which of these different states we value more highly. . . .

2

1. Earlier in our discussion we provisionally defined freedom as the absence of coercion. But coercion is nearly as troublesome a concept as liberty itself, and for much the same reason: we do not clearly distinguish between what other men do to us and the effects on us of physical circumstances. As a

matter of fact, English provides us with two different words to make the necessary distinction: while we can legitimately say that we have been compelled by circumstances to do this or that, we presuppose a human agent if we say that we have been coerced.

Coercion occurs when one man's actions are made to serve another man's will, not for his own but for the other's purpose. It is not that the coerced does not choose at all; if that were the case, we should not speak of his 'acting'. If my hand is guided by physical force to trace my signature or my finger pressed against the trigger of a gun, I have not acted. Such violence, which makes my body someone else's physical tool, is, of course, as bad as coercion proper and must be prevented for the same reason. Coercion implies, however, that I still choose but that my mind is made someone else's tool, because the alternatives before me have been so manipulated that the conduct that the coercer wants me to choose becomes for me the least painful one. Although coerced, it is still I who decide which is the least evil under the circumstances.

Coercion clearly does not include all influences that men can exercise on the action of others. It does not even include all instances in which a person acts or threatens to act in a manner he knows will harm another person and will lead him to change his intentions. A person who blocks my path in the street and causes me to step aside, a person who has borrowed from the library the book I want, or even a person who drives me away by the unpleasant noises he produces cannot properly be said to coerce me. Coercion implies both the threat of inflicting harm and the intention thereby to bring about certain conduct.

Though the coerced still chooses, the alternatives are determined for him by the coercer so that he will choose what the coercer wants. He is not altogether deprived of the use of his capacities; but he is deprived of the possibility of using his knowledge for his own aims. The effective use of a person's intelligence and knowledge in the pursuit of his aims requires that he be able to foresee some of the conditions of his environment and adhere to a plan of action. Most human aims can be achieved only by a chain of connected actions, decided upon as a coherent whole and based on the assumption that the facts will be what they are expected to be. It is because, and in so far as, we can predict events, or at least know probabilities, that we can achieve anything. And though physical circumstances will often be unpredictable, they will not maliciously frustrate our aims. But if the facts which determine our plans are under the sole control of another, our actions will be similarly controlled.

Coercion thus is bad because it prevents a person from using his mental powers to the full and consequently from making the greatest contribution that he is capable of to the community. Though the coerced will still do the best he can do for himself at any given moment, the only comprehensive design that his actions fit into is that of another mind.

2. Political philosophers have discussed power more often than they have coercion because political power usually means power to coerce. But though the great men, from John Milton and Edmund Burke to Lord Acton and Jacob Burckhardt, who have represented power as the archevil, were right in what they meant, it is misleading to speak simply of power in this connection. It is not power as such—the capacity to achieve what one wants—that is bad, but only the power to coerce, to force other men to serve one's will by the threat of inflicting harm. There is no evil in the power wielded by the director of some great enterprise in which men have willingly united of their own will and for their own purposes. It is part of the strength of civilized society that, by such voluntary combination of effort under a unified direction, men can enormously increase their collective power.

It is not power in the sense of an extension of our capacities which corrupts, but the subjection of other human wills to ours, the use of other men against their will for our purposes. It is true that in human relations power and coercion dwell closely together, that great powers possessed by a few may enable them to coerce others, unless those powers are contained by a still greater power; but coercion is neither so necessary nor so common a consequence of power as is generally assumed. Neither the powers of a Henry Ford nor those of the Atomic Energy Commission, neither those of the General of the Salvation Army nor (at least until recently) those of the President of the United States, are powers to coerce particular people for the purposes they choose.

It would be less misleading if occasionally the terms 'force' and 'violence' were used instead of coercion, since the threat of force or violence is the most important form of coercion. But they are not synonymous with coercion, for the threat of physical force is not the only way in which coercion can be exercised. Similarly, 'oppression', which is perhaps as much a true opposite of liberty as coercion, should refer only to a state of continuous acts of coercion.

3. Coercion should be carefully distinguished from the conditions or terms on which our fellow-men are willing to render us specific services or benefits. It is only in very exceptional circumstances that the sole control of a service or resource which is essential to us would confer upon another the power of true coercion. Life in society necessarily means that we are dependent for the satisfaction of most of our needs on the services of some of our fellows; in a free society these mutual services are voluntary, and each can determine to whom he wants to render services and on what terms. The benefits and opportunities which our fellows offer to us will be available only if we satisfy their conditions.

This is as true of social as of economic relations. If a hostess will invite me to her parties only if I conform to certain standards of conduct and dress, or my neighbour converse with me only if I observe conventional manners, this is certainly not coercion. Nor can it be legitimately called 'coercion' if a producer or dealer refuses to supply me with what I want except at his price. This is certainly true in a competitive market, where I can turn to somebody else if the terms of the first offer do not suit me; and it is normally no less true when I face a monopolist. If, for instance, I would very much like to be painted by a famous artist and if he refuses to paint me for less than a very high fee, it would clearly be absurd to say that I am coerced. The same is true of any other commodity or service that I can do without. So long as the services of a particular person are not crucial to my existence or the preservation of what I most value, the conditions he exacts for rendering these services cannot properly be called 'coercion'.

A monopolist could exercise true coercion, however, if he were, say, the owner of a spring in an oasis. Let us say that other persons settled there on the assumption that water would always be available at a reasonable price and then found, perhaps because a second spring dried up, that they had no choice but to do whatever the owner of the spring demanded of them if they were to survive: here would be a clear case of coercion. One could conceive of a few other instances where a monopolist might control an essential commodity on which people were completely dependent. But unless a monopolist is in a position to withhold an indispensable supply, he cannot exercise coercion, however unpleasant his demands may be for those who rely on his services.

It is worth pointing out, in view of what we shall later have to say about the appropriate methods of curbing the coercive power of the state, that whenever there is a danger of a monopolist's acquiring coercive power, the most expedient and effective method of preventing this is probably to require him to treat all customers alike, i.e., to insist that his prices be the same for all and to prohibit all discrimination on his part. This is the same principle by which we have learned to curb the coercive power of the state.

The individual provider of employment cannot normally exercise coercion, any more than can the supplier of a particular commodity or service. So long as he can remove only one opportunity among many to earn a living, so long as he can do no more than cease to pay certain people who cannot hope to earn as much elsewhere as they had done under him, he cannot coerce, though he may cause pain. There are, undeniably, occasions when the condition of employment creates opportunity for true coercion. In periods of acute unemployment the threat of dismissal may be used to enforce actions other than those originally contracted for. And in conditions such as those in a mining town the manager may well exercise an entirely arbitrary and capricious tyranny over a man to whom he has taken a dislike. But such conditions, though not impossible, would, at the worst, be rare exceptions in a prosperous competitive society.

A complete monopoly of employment, such as would exist

in a fully socialist state in which the government was the only employer and the owner of all the instruments of production, would possess unlimited powers of coercion. As Leon Trotsky discovered: 'In a country where the sole employer is the State, opposition means death by slow starvation. The old principle, who does not work shall not eat, has been replaced by a new one: who does not obey shall not eat.'

Except in such instances of monopoly of an essential service, the mere power of withholding a benefit will not produce coercion. The use of such power by another may indeed alter the social landscape to which I have adapted my plans and make it necessary for me to reconsider all my decisions, perhaps to change my whole scheme of life and to worry about many things I had taken for granted. But, though the alternatives before me may be distressingly few and uncertain, and my new plans of a makeshift character, yet it is not some other will that guides my action. I may have to act under great pressure, but I cannot be said to act under coercion. Even if the threat of starvation to me and perhaps to my family impels me to accept a distasteful job at a very low wage, even if I am 'at the mercy' of the only man willing to employ me, I am not coerced by him or anybody else. So long as the act that has placed me in my predicament is not aimed at making me do or not do specific things, so long as the intent of the act that harms me is not to make me serve another person's ends, its effect on my freedom is not different from that of any natural calamity—a fire or a flood that destroys my house or an accident that harms my health.

4. True coercion occurs when armed bands of conquerors make the subject people toil for them, when organized gangsters extort a levy for 'protection', when the knower of an evil secret blackmails his victim, and, of course, when the state threatens to inflict punishment and to employ physical force to make us obey its commands. There are many degrees of coercion, from the extreme case of the dominance of the master over the slave or the tyrant over the subject, where the unlimited power of punishment exacts complete submission to the will of the master, to the instance of the single threat of

inflicting an evil to which the threatened would prefer almost anything else.

Whether or not attempts to coerce a particular person will be successful depends in a large measure on that person's inner strength: the threat of assassination may have less power to turn one man from his aim than the threat of some minor inconvenience in the case of another. But while we may pity the weak or the very sensitive person whom a mere frown may 'compel' to do what he would not do otherwise, we are concerned with coercion that is likely to affect the normal, average person. Though this will usually be some threat of bodily harm to his person or his dear ones, or of damage to a valuable or cherished possession, it need not consist of any use of force or violence. One may frustrate another's every attempt at spontaneous action by placing in his path an infinite variety of minor obstacles: guile and malice may well find the means of coercing the physically stronger. It is not impossible for a horde of cunning boys to drive an unpopular person out of town.

In some degree all close relationships between men, whether they are tied to one another by affection, economic necessity, or physical circumstances (such as on a ship or an expedition), provide opportunities for coercion. The conditions of personal domestic service, like all more intimate relations, undoubtedly offer opportunities for coercion of a peculiarly oppressive kind and are, in consequence, felt as restrictions on personal liberty. And a morose husband, a nagging wife, or a hysterical mother may make life intolerable unless their every mood is obeyed. But here society can do little to protect the individual beyond making such associations with others truly voluntary. Any attempt to regulate these intimate associations further would clearly involve such far-reaching restrictions on choice and conduct as to produce even greater coercion: if people are to be free to choose their associates and intimates, the coercion that arises from voluntary association cannot be the concern of government.

The reader may feel that we have devoted more space than is necessary to the distinction between what can be legitimately called 'coercion' and what cannot and between the more severe forms of coercion, which we should prevent, and the lesser forms, which ought not to be the concern of authority. But, as in the case of liberty, a gradual extension of the concept has almost deprived it of value. Liberty can be so defined as to make it impossible of attainment. Similarly, coercion can be so defined as to make it an all-pervasive and unavoidable phenomenon. We cannot prevent all harm that a person may inflict upon another, or even all the milder forms of coercion to which life in close contact with other men exposes us; but this does not mean that we ought not to try to prevent all the more severe forms of coercion, or that we ought not to define liberty as the absence of such coercion.

5. Since coercion is the control of the essential data of an individual's action by another, it can be prevented only by enabling the individual to secure for himself some private sphere where he is protected against such interference. The assurance that he can count on certain facts not being deliberately shaped by another can be given to him only by some authority that has the necessary power. It is here that coercion of one individual by another can be prevented only by the threat of coercion.

The existence of such an assured free sphere seems to us so much a normal condition of life that we are tempted to define 'coercion' by the use of such terms as 'the interference with legitimate expectations', or 'infringement of rights', or 'arbitrary interference'. But in defining coercion we cannot take for granted the arrangements intended to prevent it. The 'legitimacy' of one's expectations or the 'rights' of the individual are the result of the recognition of such a private sphere. Coercion not only would exist but would be much more common if no such protected sphere existed. Only in a society that has already attempted to prevent coercion by some demarcation of a protected sphere can a concept like 'arbitrary interference' have a definite meaning.

If the recognition of such individual spheres, however, is not itself to become an instrument of coercion, their range and content must not be determined by the deliberate assignment of particular things to particular men. If what was to be included in a man's private sphere were to be determined by the will of any man or group of men, this would simply transfer the power of coercion to that will. Nor would it be desirable to have the particular contents of a man's private sphere fixed once and for all. If people are to make the best use of their knowledge and capacities and foresight, it is desirable that they themselves have some voice in the determination of what will be included in their personal protected sphere.

The solution that men have found for this problem rests on the recognition of general rules governing the conditions under which objects or circumstances become part of the protected sphere of a person or persons. The acceptance of such rules enables each member of a society to shape the content of his protected sphere and all members to recognize what belongs to their sphere and what does not.

We must not think of this sphere as consisting exclusively, or even chiefly, of material things. Although to divide the material objects of our environment into what is mine and what is another's is the principal aim of the rules which delimit the spheres, they also secure for us many other 'rights', such as security in certain uses of things or merely protection against interference with our actions.

6. The recognition of private or several property is thus an essential condition for the prevention of coercion, though by no means the only one. We are rarely in a position to carry out a coherent plan of action unless we are certain of our exclusive control of some material objects; and where we do not control them, it is necessary that we know who does if we are to collaborate with others. The recognition of property is clearly the first step in the delimitation of the private sphere which protects us against coercion; and it has long been recognized that 'a people averse to the institution of private property is without the first element of freedom' and that 'nobody is at liberty to attack several property and to say at the same time that he values civilization. The history of the two cannot be disentangled.' Modern anthropology confirms the fact that 'private property appears very definitely on primitive levels' and that 'the roots of property as a legal principle which determines the physical relationships between man and his environmental setting, natural and artificial, are the very prerequisite of any ordered action in the cultural sense'.

In modern society, however, the essential requisite for the protection of the individual against coercion is not that he possess property but that the material means which enable him to pursue any plan of action should not be all in the exclusive control of one other agent. It is one of the accomplishments of modern society that freedom may be enjoyed by a person with practically no property of his own (beyond personal belongings like clothing—and even these can be rented) and that we can leave the care of the property that serves our needs largely to others. The important point is that the property should be sufficiently dispersed so that the individual is not dependent on particular persons who alone can provide him with what he needs or who alone can employ him.

That other people's property can be serviceable in the achievement of our aims is due mainly to the enforcibility of contracts. The whole network of rights created by contracts is as important a part of our own protected sphere, as much the basis of our plans, as any property of our own. The decisive condition for mutually advantageous collaboration between people, based on voluntary consent rather than coercion, is that there be many people who can serve one's needs, so that nobody has to be dependent on specific persons for the essential conditions of life or the possibility of development in some direction. It is competition made possible by the dispersion of property that deprives the individual owners of particular things of all coercive powers.

In view of a common misunderstanding of a famous maxim, it should be mentioned that we are independent of the will of those whose services we need because they serve us for their own purposes and are normally little interested in the uses we make of their services. We should be very dependent on the beliefs of our fellows if they were prepared to sell their products to us only when they approved of our ends and not for their own advantage. It is largely because in the economic transactions of everyday life we are only impersonal means to our fellows, who help us for their own purposes, that we can count on such help from complete strangers and use it for whatever end we wish.

The rules of property and contract are required to delimit the individual's private sphere wherever the resources or services needed for the pursuit of his aims are scarce and must, in consequence, be under the control of some man or another. But if this is true of most of the benefits we derive from men's efforts, it is not true of all. There are some kinds of services, such as sanitation or roads, which, once they are provided, are normally sufficient for all who want to use them. The provision of such services had long been a recognized field of public effort, and the right to share in them is an important part of the protected sphere of the individual. We need only remember the role that the assured 'access to the King's highway' has played in history to see how important such rights may be for individual liberty.

We cannot enumerate here all the rights or protected interests which serve to secure to the legal person a known sphere of unimpeded action. But, since modern man has become a little insensitive on this point, it ought perhaps to be mentioned that the recognition of a protected individual sphere has in times of freedom normally included a right to privacy and secrecy, the conception that a man's house is his castle and that nobody has a right even to take cognizance of his activities within it.

7. . . . Here we shall consider in a general way how that threat of coercion which is the only means whereby the state can prevent the coercion of one individual by another can be deprived of most of its harmful and objectionable character.

This threat of coercion has a very different effect from that of actual and unavoidable coercion, if it refers only to known circumstances which can be avoided by the potential object of coercion. The great majority of the threats of coercion that a free society must employ are of this avoidable kind. Most of the rules that it enforces, particularly its private law, do not constrain private persons (as distinguished from the servants of the state) to perform specific actions. The sanctions of the law are designed only to prevent a person from doing certain things or to make him perform obligations that he has voluntarily incurred.

Provided that I know beforehand that if I place myself in a particular position, I shall be coerced, and provided that I can avoid putting myself in such a position, I need never be coerced. At least in so far as the rules providing for coercion are not aimed at me personally but are so framed as to apply equally to all people in similar circumstances, they are no different from any of the natural obstacles that affect my plans. In that they tell me what will happen *if* I do this or that, the laws of the state have the same significance for me as the laws of nature; and I can use my knowledge of the laws of the state to achieve my own aims as I use my knowledge of the laws of nature.

8. Of course, in some respects the state uses coercion to make us perform particular actions. The most important of these are taxation and the various compulsory services, especially in the armed forces. Though these are not supposed to be avoidable, they are at least predictable and are enforced irrespective of how the individual would otherwise employ his energies; this deprives them largely of the evil nature of coercion. If the known necessity of paying a certain amount in taxes becomes the basis of all my plans, if a period of military service is a foreseeable part of my career, then I can follow a general plan of life of my own making and am as independent of the will of another person as men have learned to be in society. Though compulsory military service, while it lasts, undoubtedly involves severe coercion, and though a lifelong conscript could not be said ever to be free, a predictable limited period of military service certainly restricts the possibility of shaping one's own life less than would, for instance, a constant threat of arrest resorted to by an arbitrary power to ensure what it regards as good behaviour.

The interference of the coercive power of government with our lives is most disturbing when it is neither avoidable nor predictable. Where such coercion is necessary even in a free society, as when we are called to serve on a jury or to act as special constables, we mitigate the effects by not allowing any person to possess arbitrary power of coercion. Instead, the decision as to who must serve is made to rest on fortuitous processes, such as the drawing of lots. These unpredictable acts of coercion, which follow from unpredictable events but conform to known rules, affect our lives as do other 'acts of God', but do not subject us to the arbitrary will of another person.

FIVE

NEGATIVE AND POSITIVE FREEDOM

Gerald C. MacCallum, Jr.

This paper challenges the view that we may usefully distinguish between two kinds or concepts of political and social freedom—negative and positive. The argument is not that one of these is the only, the 'truest', or the 'most worthwhile' freedom, but rather that the distinction between them has never been made sufficiently clear, is based in part upon a serious confusion, and has drawn attention away from precisely what needs examining if the differences separating philosophers, ideologies, and social movements concerned with freedom are to be understood. The corrective advised is to regard freedom as always one and the same triadic relation, but recognize that various contending parties disagree with each other in what they understand to be the ranges of the term variables. To view the matter in this way is to release oneself from a prevalent but unrewarding concentration on 'kinds' of freedom, and to turn attention toward the truly important issues in this area of social and political philosophy.

I

Controversies generated by appeals to the presence or absence of freedom in societies have been roughly of four closely related kinds—namely (1) about the nature of freedom itself, (2) about the relationships holding between the attainment of freedom and the attainment of other possible social benefits, (3) about the ranking of freedom among such benefits, and (4) about the consequences of this or that policy with respect to realizing or attaining freedom. Disputes of one kind have turned readily into disputes of the other kinds.

Gerald C. MacCallum, Jr., 'Negative and Positive Freedom', reprinted from *The Philosophical Review*, 76 (1967), 312–34 by permission of the publisher.

Of those who agree that freedom is a benefit, most would also agree that it is not the *only* benefit a society may secure its members. Other benefits might include, for example, economic and military security, technological efficiency, and exemplifications of various aesthetic and spiritual values. Once this is admitted, however, disputes of types (2) and (3) are possible. Questions can be raised as to the logical and causal relationships holding between the attainment of freedom and the attainment of these other benefits, and as to whether one could on some occasions reasonably prefer to cultivate or emphasize certain of the latter at the expense of the former. Thus, one may be led to ask: *can* anyone cultivate and emphasize freedom at the cost of realizing these other goals and values (or vice versa) and, secondly, *should* anyone ever do this? In practice, these issues are often masked by or confused with disputes about the consequences of this or that action with respect to realizing the various goals or values.

Further, any of the above disputes may stem from or turn into a dispute about what freedom *is*. The borderlines have never been easy to keep clear. But a reason for this especially worth noting at the start is that disputes about the nature of freedom are certainly historically best understood as a series of attempts by parties opposing each other on very many issues to capture for their own side the favourable attitudes attaching to the notion of freedom. It has commonly been advantageous for partisans to link the presence or absence of freedom as closely as possible to the presence or absence of those other social benefits believed to be secured or denied by the forms of social organization advocated or condemned. Each social benefit is, accordingly, treated as either a result of or a contribution to freedom, and each liability is connected somehow to the absence of freedom. This history of the matter goes far to explain how freedom came to be identified with so many different kinds of social and individual benefits, and why the status of freedom as simply one among a number of social benefits has remained unclear. The resulting flexibility of the notion of freedom, and the resulting enhancement of the value of freedom, have suited the purposes of the polemicist.

It is against this background that one should first see the issues surrounding the distinction between positive and negative freedom as two fundamentally different kinds of freedom. Nevertheless, the difficulties surrounding the distinction should not be attributed solely to the interplay of Machiavellian motives. The disputes, and indeed the distinction itself, have also been influenced by a genuine confusion concerning the concept of freedom. The confusion results from failure to understand fully the conditions under which use of the concept of freedom is intelligible.

2

Whenever the freedom of some agent or agents is in question, it is always freedom from some constraint or restriction on, interference with, or barrier to doing, not doing, becoming, or not becoming something.[1] Such freedom is thus always *of* something (an agent or agents), *from* something, *to* do, not do, become, or not become something; it is a triadic relation. Taking the format '*x* is (is not) free from *y* to do (not do, become, not become) *z*,' *x* ranges over agents, *y* ranges over such 'preventing conditions' as constraints, restrictions, interferences, and barriers, and *z* ranges over actions or conditions of character or circumstance. When reference to one of these three terms is missing in such a discussion of freedom, it should be only because the reference is thought to be understood from the context of the discussion.[2]

Admittedly, the idioms of freedom are such that this is sometimes not obvious. The claim, however, is not about what we say, but rather about the conditions under which what we say is intelligible. And, of course, it is important to notice that the claim is only about what makes talk concerning the

[1] The need to elaborate in this unwieldy way arises from the absence in this paper of any discussion of the verification conditions for claims about freedom. The elaboration is designed to leave open the issues one would want to raise in such a discussion.

[2] Of writers on political and social freedom who have approached this view, the clearest case is Felix Oppenheim in *Dimensions of Freedom* (New York, 1961); but, while viewing social freedom as a triadic relation, he limits the ranges of the term variables so sharply as to cut one off from many issues I wish to reach. Cf. also T. D. Weldon, *The Vocabulary of Politics* (Harmondsworth, 1953), esp. pp. 157 ff.; but see also pp. 70–2.

freedom of agents intelligible. This restriction excludes from consideration, for example, some uses of 'free of' and 'free from'—namely, those not concerned with the freedom of agents, and where, consequently, what is meant may be only 'rid of' or 'without'. Thus, consideration of 'The sky is now free of clouds' is excluded because this expression does not deal with agents at all; but consideration of 'His record is free of blemish' and 'She is free from any vice' is most probably also excluded. Doubt about these latter two hinges on whether these expressions might be thought claims about the freedom of agents; if so, then they are not excluded, but neither are they intelligible *as* claims about the freedom of agents until one is in a position to fill in the elements of the format offered above; if not, then although probably parasitic upon talk about the freedom of agents and thus perhaps viewable as figurative anyway, they fall outside the scope of this investigation.

The claim that freedom, subject to the restriction noted above, is a triadic relation can hardly be substantiated here by exhaustive examination of the idioms of freedom. But the most obviously troublesome cases—namely, those in which one's understanding of the context must in a relevant way carry past the limits of what is explicit in the idiom—may be classified roughly and illustrated as follows:

(*a*) *Cases where agents are not mentioned*: for example, consider any of the wide range of expressions having the form 'free *x*' in which (i) the place of *x* is taken by an expression not clearly referring to an agent—as in 'free society' or 'free will'—or (ii) the place of *x* is taken by an expression clearly not referring to an agent—as in 'free beer'. All such cases can be understood to be concerned with the freedom of agents and, indeed, their intelligibility rests upon their being so understood; they are thus subject to the claims made above. This is fairly obvious in the cases of 'free will' and 'free society'. The intelligibility of the free-will problem is generally and correctly thought to rest at least upon the problem's being concerned with the freedom of persons, even though the criteria for identification of the persons or 'selves' whose freedom is in question have not often been made sufficiently clear.[3] And it is

[3] Indeed, lack of clarity on just this point is probably one of the major sources of confusion in discussions of free will.

beyond question that the expression 'free society', although of course subject to various conflicting analyses with respect to the identity of the agent(s) whose freedom is involved, is thought intelligible only because it is thought to concern the freedom of agents of some sort or other. The expression 'free beer', on the other hand (to take only one of a rich class of cases some of which would have to be managed differently), is ordinarily thought intelligible because thought to refer to beer that *people* are free *from* the ordinary restrictions of the market place *to* drink without paying for it.

For an expression of another grammatical form, consider 'The property is free of (or from) encumbrance.' Although this involves a loose use of 'property', suppose that the term refers to something like a piece of land; the claim then clearly means that *owners* of that land are free *from* certain well-known restrictions (for example, certain types of charges or liabilities consequent upon their ownership of the land) *to* use, enjoy, dispose of the land as they wish.

(*b*) *Cases where it is not clear what corresponds to the second term*: for example, 'freedom of choice', 'freedom to choose as I please'. Here, the range of constraints, restrictions, and so forth is generally clear from the context of the discussion. In political matters, legal constraints or restrictions are most often thought of; but one also sometimes finds, as in Mill's *On Liberty*, concern for constraints and interferences constituted by social pressures. It is sometimes difficult for persons to see social pressures as constraints or interferences; this will be discussed below. It is also notoriously difficult to see causal nexuses as implying constraints or restrictions on the 'will' (the person?) in connection with the free-will problem. But the fact that such difficulties are the focus of so much attention is witness to the importance of getting clear about this term of the relation before such discussions of freedom can be said to be intelligible.

One might think that references to a second term of this sort could always be eliminated by a device such as the following. Instead of saying, for example, (i) 'Smith is free *from* legal restrictions on travel *to* leave the country', one could say (ii) 'Smith is free *to* leave the country *because* there are no legal restrictions on his leaving'. The latter would make freedom appear to be a dyadic, rather than a triadic, relation. But we would be best advised to regard the appearance as illusory, and this may be seen if one thinks a bit about the suggestion or implication of the sentence that nothing hinders or prevents Smith from leaving the country. Difficulties about this might be settled by attaching a qualifier to 'free'—namely, '*legally* free'. Alternatively, one could consider which, of all the things that might still hinder or prevent Smith from leaving the country (for example, has he promised someone to remain? will the responsibilities of his job keep him here? has he enough money to buy passage and, if not, why not?), could count as limitations on his freedom to leave the country; one would then be in a position to determine whether the claim had been misleading or false. In either case, however, the devices adopted would reveal that our understanding of what has been said hinged upon our understanding of the range of obstacles or constraints from which Smith had been claimed to be free.

(*c*) *Cases where it is not clear what corresponds to the third term*: for example, 'freedom from hunger' ('want', 'fear', 'disease', and so forth). One quick but not very satisfactory way of dealing with such expressions is to regard them as figurative, or at least not really concerned with anybody's freedom; thus, being free from hunger would be simply being rid of, or without, hunger—as a sky may be free of clouds (compare the discussion of this above). Alternatively, one might incline toward regarding hunger as a barrier of some sort, and claim that a person free *from* hunger is free *to* be well fed or to do or do well the various things he could not do or do well if hungry. Yet again, and more satisfactorily, one could turn to the context of the initial bit of Rooseveltian rhetoric and there find reason to treat the expression as follows. Suppose that hunger is a feeling and that someone *seeks* hunger; he is on a diet and the hunger feeling reassures him that he is losing weight.[4] Alternatively, suppose that hunger is a bodily condition and that someone seeks it; he is on a Gandhi-style hunger strike. In either case, Roosevelt or his fellow orators might have wanted a world in which these people were free from hunger;

---

[4] I owe this example to Professor James Pratt.

but this surely does not mean that they wanted a world in which people were not hungry despite a wish to be so. They wanted, rather, a world in which people were not victims of hunger they did not seek; that is, they wanted a world without barriers keeping people hungry despite efforts to avoid hunger—a world in which people would be free *from* barriers constituted by various specifiable agricultural, economic, and political conditions *to* get enough food to prevent hunger. This view of 'freedom from hunger' not only makes perfectly good and historically accurate sense out of the expression, but also conforms to the view that freedom is a triadic relation.

In other politically important idioms the *range* of the third term is not always utterly clear. For example, does freedom of religion include freedom *not* to worship? Does freedom of speech include *all* speech no matter what its content, manner of delivery, or the circumstances of its delivery? Such matters, however, raise largely historical questions or questions to be settled by political decision; they do not throw doubt on the need for a third term.

That the intelligibility of talk concerned with the freedom of agents rests in the end upon an understanding of freedom as a triadic relation is what many persons distinguishing between positive and negative freedom apparently fail to see or see clearly enough. Evidence of such failure or, alternatively, invitation to it is found in the simple but conventional characterization of the difference between the two kinds of freedom as the difference between 'freedom from' and 'freedom to'—a characterization suggesting that freedom could be either of two dyadic relations. This characterization, however, cannot distinguish two genuinely different kinds of freedom; it can serve only to emphasize one or the other of two features of *every* case of the freedom of agents. Consequently, anyone who argues that freedom *from* is the 'only' freedom, or that freedom *to* is the 'truest' freedom, or that one is 'more important than' the other, cannot be taken as having said anything both straightforward and sensible about two distinct kinds of freedom. He can, at most, be said to be attending to, or emphasizing the importance of, only one part of what is always present in any case of freedom.

Unfortunately, even if this basis of distinction between

positive and negative freedom as two distinct kinds or concepts of freedom is shown to collapse, one has not gone very far in understanding the issues separating those philosophers or ideologies commonly said to utilize one or the other of them. One has, however, dissipated one of the main confusions blocking understanding of these issues. In recognizing that freedom is always *both* freedom from something and freedom to do or become something, one is provided with a means of making sense out of interminable and poorly defined controversies concerning, for example, when a person really is free, why freedom is important, and on what its importance depends. As these, in turn, are matters on which the distinction between positive and negative freedom has turned, one is given also a means of managing sensibly the writings appearing to accept or to be based upon that distinction.

3

The key to understanding lies in recognition of precisely how differing styles of answer to the question 'When are persons free?' could survive agreement that freedom is a triadic relation. The differences would be rooted in differing views on the ranges of the term variables—that is, on the ('true') identities of the agents whose freedom is in question, on what counts as an obstacle to or interference with the freedom of such agents, or on the range of what such agents might or might not be free to do or become.[5] Although perhaps not always obvious or dramatic, such differences could lead to vastly different accounts of when persons are free. Furthermore, differences on one of these matters might or might not be accompanied by differences on either of the others. There is thus a rich stock of ways in which such accounts might diverge, and a rich stock of possible foci of argument.

It is therefore crucial, when dealing with accounts of when

[5] They might also be rooted in differing views on the verification conditions for claims about freedom. The issue would be important to discuss in a full-scale treatment of freedom but, as already mentioned, it is not discussed in this paper. It plays, at most, an easily eliminable role in the distinction between positive and negative freedom.

persons are free, to insist on getting *quite* clear on what each writer considers to be the ranges of these term variables. Such insistence will reveal where the differences between writers are, and will provide a starting-point for rewarding consideration of what might justify these differences.

The distinction between positive and negative freedom has, however, stood in the way of this approach. It has encouraged us to see differences in accounts of freedom as resulting from differences in concepts of freedom. This in turn has encouraged the wrong sorts of questions. We have been tempted to ask such questions as 'Well, who *is* right? Whose concept of freedom *is* the correct one?' or 'Which *kind* of freedom do we really want after all?' Such questions will not help reveal the fundamental issues separating major writers on freedom from each other, no matter *how* the writers are arranged into 'camps'. It would be far better to insist that the same concept of freedom is operating throughout, and that the differences, rather than being about what *freedom* is, are for example about what persons are, and about what can count as an obstacle to or interference with the freedom of persons so conceived.

The appropriateness of this insistence is easily seen when one examines prevailing characterizations of the differences between 'positive' and 'negative' freedom. Once the alleged difference between 'freedom from' and 'freedom to' has been disallowed (as it must be; see above), the most persuasive of the remaining characterizations appear to be as follows:[6]

1. Writers adhering to the concept of 'negative' freedom hold that only the *presence* of something can render a person unfree; writers adhering to the concept of 'positive' freedom hold that the *absence* of something may also render a person unfree.

2. The former hold that a person is free to do *x* just in case *nothing due to arrangements made by other persons* stops him from doing *x*; the latter adopt no such restriction.

---

[6] Yet other attempts of characterization have been offered—most recently and notably by Sir Isaiah Berlin in *Two Concepts of Liberty* (Oxford, 1958) [repr. with revisions in *Four Essays on Liberty* (Oxford: Oxford University Press, 1969)]. Berlin also offers the second and (more or less) the third of the characterizations cited here.

3. The former hold that the agents whose freedom is in question (for example, 'persons', 'men') are, in effect, identifiable as Anglo-American law would identify 'natural' (as opposed to 'artificial') persons; the latter sometimes hold quite different views as to how these agents are to be identified (see below).

The most obvious thing to be said about these characterizations, of course, is that appeal to them provides at best an excessively crude justification of the conventional classification of writers into opposing camps.[7] When one presses on the alleged points of difference, they have a tendency to break down, or at least to become less dramatic than they at first seemed.[8] As should not be surprising, the patterns of

[7] A fair picture of that classification is provided by Berlin (*Two Concepts*) who cites and quotes from various writers in such a way as to suggest that they are in one camp or the other. Identified in this manner as adherents of 'negative' freedom, one finds Occam, Erasmus, Hobbes, Locke, Bentham, Constant, J. S. Mill, Tocqueville, Jefferson, Burke, Paine. Among adherents of 'positive' freedom one finds Plato, Epictetus, St Ambrose, Montesquieu, Spinoza, Kant, Herder, Rousseau, Hegel, Fichte, Marx, Bukharin, Comte, Carlyle, T. H. Green, Bradley, Bosanquet.

[8] For example, consider No. 1. Perhaps there is something to it, but the following cautionary remarks should be made. (*a*) The so-called adherents of 'negative' freedom might very well accept the *absence* of something as an obstacle to freedom. Consider a man who is not free because, although unguarded, he has been locked in chains. Is he unfree because of the *presence* of the locked chains, or is he unfree because he *lacks* a key? Are adherents of 'negative' freedom prohibited from giving the latter answer? (*b*) Even purported adherents of 'positive' freedom are not always straightforward in their acceptance of the lack of something as an obstacle to freedom. They sometimes swing toward attributing the absence of freedom to the presence of certain conditions causally connected with the lack, absence, or deprivation mentioned initially. For example, it may be said that a person who was unable to qualify for a position owing to lack of training (and thus not free to accept or 'have' it) was prevented from accepting the position by a social, political, economic, or educational 'system' the workings of which resulted in his being bereft of training. Also, in so far as this swing is made, our view of the difference mentioned in No. 2 may become fuzzy; for adherents of 'positive' freedom might be thought at bottom to regard those 'preventing conditions' counting as infringements of freedom as most often if not always circumstances due to human arrangements. This might be true even when, as we shall see is sometimes the case, the focus is on the role of 'irrational passions and appetites'. The presence or undisciplined character of these may be treated as resulting from the operation of certain specifiable

agreement and disagreement on these several points are in fact either too diverse or too indistinct to support any clearly justifiable arrangement of major writers into two camps. The trouble is not merely that some writers do not fit too well where they have been placed; it is rather that writers who are purportedly the very models of membership in one camp or the other (for example, Locke, the Marxists) do not fit very well where they have been placed[9]—thus suggesting that the whole system of dichotomous classification is futile and, even worse, conducive to distortion of important views on freedom.

But, even supposing that there were something to the classification and to the justification for it in terms of the above three points of difference, what then? The differences are of two kinds. They concern (*a*) the ('true') identities of the agents whose freedom is in question, and (*b*) what is to count as an 'obstacle' or 'barrier' to, 'restriction' on, or 'interference' with the freedom of such agents. They are thus clearly about the ranges of two of the three term variables mentioned earlier. It would be a mistake to see them in any other way. We are likely to make this mistake, however, and obscure the path of rewarding argument, if we present them as differences concerning what 'freedom' means.

Consider the following. Suppose that we have been raised in the so-called 'libertarian' tradition (roughly characterized as

social, educational, or moral institutions or arrangements. (Berlin, e.g., seems to acknowledge this with respect to the Marxists. See Berlin, *Two Concepts*, p. 8, n. 1, and the text at this point [ch. 2, n. 3, this volume].) Thus one might in the end be able to say no more than this: that the adherents of 'negative' freedom are on the whole more inclined to require that the *intention* of the arrangements in question have been to coerce, compel, or deprive persons of this or that. The difference here, however, is not very striking.

[9] Locke said: 'liberty . . . is the power a man has to do or forbear doing any particular action according . . . as he himself wills it' (*Essay Concerning Human Understanding*, bk. ii, ch. xxi, s.15). He also said, of law, 'that ill deserves the name of confinement which hedges us in only from bogs and precipices', and 'the end of law is, not to abolish or restrain, but to preserve and enlarge freedom' (*Second Treatise of Government*, s. 57). He also sometimes spoke of a man's consent as though it were the same as the consent of the majority. Why doesn't all this put him in the camp of 'positive' freedom *vis-à-vis* at least points (2) and (3) above? Concerning the Marxists, see n. 8, above.

that of 'negative' freedom). There would be nothing unusual to us, and perhaps even nothing troubling, in conventional accounts of what the adherent of negative freedom treats as the ranges of these variables.

1. He is purported to count persons just as we do—to point to living human bodies and say of each (and only of each), 'There's a person.' Precisely what we ordinarily call persons. (And if he is troubled by non-viable foetuses, and so forth, so are we.)

2. He is purported to mean much what we mean by 'obstacle', and so forth, though this changes with changes in our views of what can be attributed to arrangements made by human beings, and also with variations in the importance we attach to consenting to rules, practices, and so forth.[10]

3. He is purported to have quite 'ordinary' views on what a person may or may not be free to do or become. The actions are sometimes suggested in fairly specific terms—for example, free to have a home, raise a family, 'rise to the top'. But, on the whole, he is purported to talk of persons being free or not free 'to do what they want' or (perhaps) 'to express themselves'.[11] Furthermore, the criteria for determining what a person wants to do are those we customarily use, or perhaps even the most naïve and unsophisticated of them—for example, what a person wants to do is determined by what he *says* he wants to do, or by what he manifestly *tries* to do, or even *does* do.[12]

In contrast, much might trouble us in the accounts of the so-called adherents of 'positive' freedom.

1. They sometimes do not count, as the agent whose

[10] The point of 'consent theories' of political obligation sometimes seems to be to hide from ourselves the fact that a rule of unanimity is an unworkable basis for a system of government and that government does involve coercion. We seem, however, not really to have made up our minds about this.

[11] These last ways of putting it are appreciably different. When a person who would otherwise count as a libertarian speaks of persons as free or not free to express themselves, his position as a libertarian may muddy a bit. One may feel invited to wonder which of the multitudinous wants of a given individual *are* expressive of his nature—that is, which are such that their fulfilment is conducive to the expression of his 'self'.

[12] The possibility of conflicts among these criteria has not been much considered by so-called libertarians.

freedom is being considered, what inheritors of our tradition would unhesitatingly consider to be a 'person'. Instead, they occasionally engage in what has been revealingly but pejoratively called 'the retreat to the inner citadel';[13] the agent in whose freedom they are interested is identified as the 'real' or the 'rational' or the 'moral' person who is somehow sometimes hidden within, or has his seed contained within, the living human body. Sometimes, however, rather than a retreat to such an 'inner citadel', or sometimes in addition to such a retreat, there is an expansion of the limits of 'person' such that the institutions and members, the histories and futures of the communities in which the living human body is found are considered to be inextricable parts of the 'person'.

These expansions or contractions of the criteria for identification of persons may seem unwarranted to us. Whether they are so, however, depends upon the strength of the arguments offered in support of the helpfulness of regarding persons in these ways while discussing freedom. For example, the retreat to the 'inner citadel' may be initiated simply by worries about which, of all the things we want, will give us lasting satisfaction—a view of our interests making it possible to see the surge of impulse or passion as an obstacle to the attainment of what we 'really want'. And the expansion of the limits of the 'self' to include our families, cultures, nations, or races may be launched by awareness that our 'self' is to some extent the product of these associations; by awareness that our identification of our interests may be influenced by our beliefs concerning ways in which our destinies are tied to the destinies of our families, nations, and so forth; by the way we see tugs and stresses upon those associations as tugs and stresses upon us; and by the ways we see ourselves and *identify* ourselves as officeholders in such associations with the rights and obligations of such offices. This expansion, in turn, makes it possible for us to see the infringement of the autonomy of our associations as infringement on our freedom.

Assessing the strengths of the various positions taken on

---

[6] See Berlin, *Two Concepts,* pp. 17 ff. [pp. 44 ff. this volume] (though Berlin significantly admits also that this move can be made by adherents of negative freedom; see p. 19 [p. 46 this volume]).

these matters requires a painstaking investigation and evaluation of the arguments offered—something that can hardly be launched within the confines of this paper. But what should be observed is that this set of seemingly radical departures by adherents of positive freedom from the ways 'we' ordinarily identify persons does not provide us with any reason whatever to claim that a different concept of *freedom* is involved (one might as well say that the shift from 'The apple is to the left of the orange' to 'The seeds of the apple are to the left of the seeds of the orange' changes what 'to the left of' means). Furthermore, that claim would draw attention away from precisely what we should focus on; it would lead us to focus on the wrong concept—namely, 'freedom' instead of 'person'. Only by insisting at least provisionally that all the writers have the same concept of freedom can one see clearly and keep sharply focused the obvious and extremely important differences among them concerning the concept of 'person'.

2. Similarly, adherents of so-called 'positive' freedom purportedly differ from 'us' on what counts as an obstacle. Will *this* difference be revealed adequately if we focus on supposed differences in the concept of 'freedom'? Not likely. Given differences on what a person is, differences in what counts as an obstacle or interference are not surprising, of course, since what could count as an obstacle to the activity of a person identified in one way might not possibly count as an obstacle to persons identified in other ways. But the differences concerning 'obstacle' and so forth are probably not due solely to differences concerning 'person'. If, for example, we so-called adherents of negative freedom, in order to count something as a preventing condition, ordinarily require that it can be shown a result of arrangements made by human beings, and our 'opponents' do not require this, why not? On the whole, perhaps, the latter are saying this: if one is concerned with social, political, and economic policies, and with how these policies can remove or increase human misery, it is quite irrelevant whether difficulties in the way of the policies are or are not *due to* arrangements made by human beings. The only question is whether the difficulties can be removed by human arrangements, and at what cost. This view, seen as an attack upon the 'artificiality' of a borderline

for distinguishing human freedom from other human values, does not seem inherently unreasonable; a close look at the positions and arguments seems called for.[14] But again, the issues and arguments will be misfocused if we fail to see them as about the range of a term variable of a single triadic relation (freedom). Admittedly, we *could* see some aspects of the matter (those where the differences do not follow merely from differences in what is thought to be the agent whose freedom is in question) as amounting to disagreements about what is meant by 'freedom'. But there is no decisive reason for doing so, and this move surely threatens to obscure the socially and politically significant issues raised by the argument suggested above.

3. Concerning treatment of the third term by purported adherents of positive freedom, perhaps enough has already been said to suggest that they tend to emphasize conditions of character rather than actions, and to suggest that, as with 'us' too, the range of character conditions and actions focused on

---

[14] The libertarian position concerning the borderline is well expressed by Berlin in the following passage on the struggle of colonial peoples: 'Is the struggle for higher status, the wish to escape from an inferior position, to be called a struggle for liberty? Is it mere pedantry to confine this word to the main ('negative') senses discussed above, or are we, as I suspect, in danger of calling any adjustment of his social situation favoured by a human being an increase of his liberty, and will this not render this term so vague and distended as to make it virtually useless?' (*Two Concepts*, p. 44 [*Four Essays*, p. 159]). One may surely agree with Berlin that there may be something of a threat here; but one may also agree with him when, in the passage immediately following, he inclines to give back what he has just taken away: 'And yet we cannot simply dismiss this case as a mere confusion of the notion of freedom with those of status, or solidarity, or fraternity, or equality, or some combination of these. For the craving for status is, in certain respects very close to the desire to be an independent agent.' What first needs explaining, of course, is why colonial peoples might believe themselves freer under the rule of local tyrants than under the rule of (possibly) benevolent colonial administrations. Berlin tends to dismiss this as a simple confusion of a desire for freedom with a hankering after status and recognition. What needs more careful evaluation than he gives them are (*a*) the strength of reasons for regarding rule by one's racial and religious peers as self-rule and (*b*) the strength of claims about freedom based on the consequences of consent or authorization for one's capacity to speak of 'self-rule' (cf. Hobbes's famous ch. xvi in *Leviathan*, 'Of Persons and Things Personated'). Cf. n. 10, above.

may influence or be influenced by what is thought to count as agent and by what is thought to count as preventing condition. Thus, though something more definite would have to be said about the matter eventually, at least some contact with the issues previously raised might be expected in arguments about the range of this variable.

It is important to observe here and throughout, however, that close agreement between two writers in their understanding of the range of one of the variables does not make *inevitable* like agreement on the ranges of the others. Indeed, we have gone far enough to see that the kinds of issues arising in determination of the ranges are sufficiently diverse to make such simple correlations unlikely. Precisely this renders attempts to arrange writers on freedom into two opposing camps so distorted and ultimately futile. There is too rich a stock of ways in which accounts of freedom diverge.

If we are to manage these divergences sensibly, we must focus our attention on each of these variables and on differences in views as to their ranges. Until we do this, we will not see clearly the issues which have in fact been raised, and thus will not see clearly what needs arguing. In view of this need, it is both clumsy and misleading to try to sort out writers as adherents of this or that 'kind' or 'concept' of freedom. We would be far better off to insist that they all have the same concept of freedom (as a triadic relation)—thus putting ourselves in a position to notice how, and inquire fruitfully into why, they identify differently what can serve as agent, preventing condition, and action or state of character *vis-à-vis* issues of freedom.

4

If the importance of this approach to discussion of freedom has been generally overlooked, it is because social and political philosophers have, with dreary regularity, made the mistake of trying to answer the unadorned question, 'When are men free?' or, alternatively, 'When are men *really* free?' These questions *invite* confusion and misunderstanding, largely because of their tacit presumption that persons can be free or not free *simpliciter*.

One might suppose that, strictly speaking, a person could be free *simpliciter* only if there were no interference from which he was not free, and nothing that he was not free to do or become. On this view, however, and on acceptance of common views as to what counts as a person, what counts as interference, and what actions or conditions of character may meaningfully be said to be free or not free, all disputes concerning whether or not men in societies are ever free would be inane. Concerning such settings, where the use and threat of coercion are distinctively present, there would *always* be an air of fraud or hocus-pocus about claims that men are free— just like that.

Yet one might hold that men can be free (*simpliciter*) even in society because certain things which ordinarily are counted as interferences or barriers are not actually so, or because certain kinds of behaviour ordinarily thought to be either free or unfree do not, for some reason, 'count'. Thus one might argue that at least in certain (conceivable) societies there is no activity in which men in that society are not free to engage, and no possible restriction or barrier from which they are not free.

The burden of such an argument should now be clear. Everything *from* which a person in that society might ordinarily be considered unfree must be shown not actually an interference or barrier (or not a relevant one), and everything which a person in that society might ordinarily be considered not free to *do* or *become* must be shown irrelevant to the issue of freedom. (Part of the argument in either or both cases might be that the 'true' identity of the person in question is not what it has been thought to be.)

Pitfalls may remain for attempts to evaluate such arguments. For example, one may uncover tendencies to telescope questions concerning the *legitimacy* of interference into questions concerning genuineness *as* interference.[15] One may also find telescoping of questions concerning the *desirability* of

---

[15] Cf. nn. 10 and 14, above.

certain modes of behaviour or character states into questions concerning the *possibility* of being either free or not free to engage in those modes of behaviour or become that kind of person.[16] Nevertheless, a demand for specification of the term variables helps pinpoint such problems, as well as forestalling the confusions obviously encouraged by failure to make the specifications.

Perhaps, however, the claim that certain men are free *simpliciter* is merely elliptical for the claim that they are free in every important respect, or in most important respects, or 'on the whole'. Nevertheless, the point still remains that when this ellipsis is filled in, the reasonableness of asking both 'What are they free from?' and 'What are they free to do or become?' becomes apparent. Only when one gets straightforward answers to these questions is he in any position to judge whether the men *are* free as claimed. Likewise, only then will he be in a position to judge the *value* or *importance* of the freedom(s) in question. It is important to know, for example, whether a man is free from legal restrictions to raise a family. But of course social or economic 'arrangements' may be such that he still could not raise a family if he wanted to. Thus, merely to say that he is free to raise a family, when what is meant is only that he is free from legal restrictions to raise a family, is to invite misunderstanding. Further, the *range* of activities he may or may not be free from this or that to engage in, or the range of character states he may or may not be free to develop, should make a difference in our evaluations of his situation and of his society; but this too is not called for strongly enough when one asks simply, 'Is the man free?' Only when we determine what the men in question are free from, and what they are free to do or become, will we be in a position to estimate the value for human happiness and fulfilment of being free from *that* (whatever *it* is), to do *the other thing* (whatever *it* is). Only then will we be in a position to make rational evaluations of the relative merits of societies with regard to freedom.

---

[16] e.g., is it logically possible for a person to be free to do something immoral? Cf. Berlin, *Two Concepts*, p. 10 n. [pp. 37–8, this volume].

5

The above remarks can be tied again to the controversy concerning negative and positive freedom by considering the following argument by friends of 'negative' freedom. Freedom is always and necessarily *from* restraint; thus, in so far as the adherents of positive freedom speak of persons being made free *by means of* restraint, they cannot be talking about freedom.

The issues raised by this argument (which is seldom stated more fully than here) can be revealed by investigating what might be done to make good sense out of the claim that, for example, Smith is (or can be) made free by restraining (constraining, coercing) him.[17] Use of the format of specifications recommended above reveals two major possibilities:

1. Restraining Smith by means *a* from doing *b* produces a situation in which he is now able to do *c* because restraint *d* is lifted. He is thereby, by means of restraint *a*, made free from *d* to do *c*, although he can no longer do *b*. For example, suppose that Smith, who always walks to where he needs to go, lives in a tiny town where there have been no pedestrian crosswalks and where automobiles have had right of way over pedestrians. Suppose further that a series of pedestrian crosswalks is instituted along with the regulation that pedestrians must use only these walks when crossing, but that while in these walks pedestrians have right of way over automobiles. The regulation restrains Smith (he can no longer legally cross streets where he pleases) but it also frees him (while in crosswalks he no longer has a duty to defer to automobile traffic). Using the schema above, the regulation (*a*) restrains Smith from crossing streets wherever he likes (*b*), but at the same time is such as to (make it practicable to) give him restricted right of way (*c*) over automobile traffic. The regulation (*a*) thus gives him restricted right of way (*c*) because it lifts the rule (*d*) giving automobiles general right of way over pedestrians.

This interpretation of the assertion that Smith can be made free by restraining him is straightforward enough. It raises

---

[17] This presumes that the prospect of freeing Smith by restraining *someone else* would be unproblematic even for the friends of negative freedom.

problems only if one supposes that persons must be either free or not free *simpliciter*, and that the claim in question is that Smith is made free *simpliciter*. But there is no obvious justification for either of these suppositions.

If these suppositions *are* made, however, then the following interpretation may be appropriate:

2. Smith is being 'restrained' only in the ordinary acceptance of that term; actually, he is not being restrained at all. He is being helped to do what he really wants to do, or what he *would* want to do if he were reasonable (moral, prudent, or such like); compare Locke's words: 'that ill deserves the name of confinement which hedges us in only from bogs and precipices'.[18] Because of the 'constraint' put upon him, a *genuine* constraint that *was* upon him (for example, ignorance, passion, the intrusions of others) is lifted, and he is free from the latter to do what he really wishes (or would wish if . . .).

This interpretation is hardly straightforward, but the claim that it embodies is nevertheless arguable; Plato argues it in the *Republic* and implies such a claim in the *Gorgias*. Furthermore, insistence upon the format of specifications recommended above can lead one to see clearly the kind of arguments needed to support the claim. For example, if a person is to be made free, whether by means of restraint or otherwise, there must be something *from* which he is made free. This must be singled out. Its character may not always be clear; for example, in Locke's discussion the confinement from which one is liberated by law is perhaps the constraint produced by the arbitrary uncontrolled actions of one's neighbours, or perhaps it is the 'constraint' arising from one's own ignorance or passion, or perhaps it is both of these. If only the former, then the specification is unexceptionable enough; that kind of constraint is well within the range of what is ordinarily thought to be constraint. If the latter, however, then some further argument is needed; one's own ignorance and passion are at least not unquestionably within the range of what can restrain him and limit his freedom. The required argument may attempt to show that ignorance and passion prevent persons from doing

---

[18] *The Second Treatise of Government*, s. 57. As is remarked below, however, the proper interpretation of this passage is not at all clear.

what they want to do, or what they 'really' want to do, or what they *would* want to do if . . . The idea would be to promote seeing the removal of ignorance and passion, or at least the control of their effects, as the removal or control of something preventing a person from doing as he wishes, really wishes, or would wish, and so forth, and thus, plausibly, an increase of that person's freedom.

Arguments concerning the 'true' identity of the person in question and what *can* restrict such a person's freedom are of course important here and should be pushed further than the above discussion suggests. For the present, however, one need observe only that they are met again when one presses for specification of the full range of what, on interpretation (2), Smith is made free to *do*. Apparently, he is made free to do as he wishes, really wishes, or *would* wish if . . . But, quite obviously, there is also something that he is prima facie *not* free to do; otherwise, there would be no point in declaring that he was being made free *by means of* restraint. One may discover how this difficulty is met by looking again to the arguments by which the claimer seeks to establish that something which at first appears to be a restraint is not actually a restraint at all. Two main lines may be found here: (*a*) that the activities being 'restrained' are so unimportant or minor (relative, perhaps, to what is gained) that they are not worth counting, or (*b*) that the activities are such that no one could ever want (or really want, and so forth) to engage in them. If the activities in question are so unimportant as to be negligible, the restraints that prevent one from engaging in them may be also 'not worthy of consideration'; if, on the other hand, the activities are ones that no one would conceivably freely choose to engage in, then it might indeed be thought 'idle' to consider our inability to do them as a restriction upon our freedom.

Admittedly, the persons actually making the principal claim under consideration may have been confused, may not have seen all these alternatives of interpretation, and so forth. The intention here is not to say what such persons did mean when uttering the claims, but only more or less plausibly what they might have meant. The interpretations provide the main lines for the latter. They also provide a clear picture of what needs to be done in order to assess the worth of the claims in each case; for, of course, no pretence is being made here that such arguments are always or even very often ultimately convincing.

Interpretation (2) clearly provides the most difficult and interesting problems. One may analyse and discuss these problems by considering them to be raised by attempts to answer the following four questions:

(*a*) What is to count as an interference with the freedom of persons?
(*b*) What is to count as an action that persons might reasonably be said to be either free or not free to perform?
(*c*) What is to count as a legitimate interference with the freedom of persons?
(*d*) What actions are persons best left free to do?

As was mentioned above, there is a tendency to telescope (*c*) into (*a*), and to telescope (*d*) into (*b*). It was also noted that (*c*) and (*d*) are not distinct questions: they are logically related in so far as criteria of legitimacy are connected to beliefs about what is best or most desirable. (*a*) and (*b*) are also closely related in that an answer to one will affect what can reasonably be considered an answer to the other. The use of these questions as guides in the analysis and understanding of discussions of freedom should not, therefore, be expected to produce always a neat ordering of the discussion. But it *will* help further to delimit the alternatives of reasonable interpretation.

6

In the end, then, discussions of the freedom of agents can be fully intelligible and rationally assessed only after the specification of each term of this triadic relation has been made or at least understood. The principal claim made here has been that insistence upon this single 'concept' of freedom puts us in a position to see the interesting and important ranges of issues separating the philosophers who write about freedom in such different ways, and the ideologies that treat freedom so differently. These issues are obscured, if not hidden, when we suppose that the important thing is that the fascists, communists, and socialists on the one side, for example, have a different concept of freedom from that of the 'libertarians' on the other. These issues are also hidden, of course, by the facile assumption that the adherents on one side or the other are never sincere.

SIX

INDIVIDUAL LIBERTY

Hillel Steiner

An individual is unfree if, and only if, his doing of any action is rendered impossible by the action of another individual.[1] That is, the unfree individual is so because the particular action in question is *prevented* by another. In the following essay I shall, first, briefly defend this 'negative' conception of individual liberty, and then proceed to elicit several of its implications— particularly those which touch upon our understanding of the relation between liberty and threats. The nature of my argument will be such as to suggest that many of the kinds of circumstance in which an individual is said, by the proponents of the negative conception, to lack the liberty to do a certain action, cannot be held to be so without self-contradiction. Arguments about the nature of individual liberty—and they are legion—are usually disputes concerning either the relation between a prevented action and its subject, or that which is to count as prevention. Quite clearly, the two issues are connected. Hence what occasions this essay is my belief that many writers who have argued for what I take to be the correct position on the first issue, have nevertheless failed to draw the appropriate conclusions concerning what is to count as prevention. In so doing they have failed to appreciate an important aspect of the concept of individual liberty itself. My defence of the negative conception will thus be 'brief' inasmuch as I shall only cursorily rehearse the arguments establishing the correct position on the relation between prevented actions and their subjects, and shall refer the reader

H. Steiner, 'Individual Liberty', *Proceedings of the Aristotelian Society*, 75 (1974–5), 33–50. Reprinted by courtesy of the Editor of the Aristotelian Society: © 1975.

[1] I am particularly indebted to G. A. Cohen for his comments on an earlier draft of this paper.

to those writings in which these arguments are set out in greater detail.

I

Sir Isaiah Berlin, in the introduction to a revised version of his lecture 'Two Concepts of Liberty', undertakes to correct what he considers to be an error in the original version.[2] In that earlier version Berlin had argued that liberty, properly understood, consists in not being prevented by other persons from doing whatever one *desires* to do, and thus that one is free to the degree that one is not prevented by another from doing what one desires to do. Berlin rightly acknowledges that this formulation permits the unacceptably paradoxical (and positive libertarian) inference that one can increase the extent to which one is free simply by suppressing those of one's practical desires the satisfaction of which is prevented by others. It permits the inference that ultimately one is one's own gaoler, so to speak. As J. P. Day has pointed out, ridding oneself of the desire to do an action which is prevented by another, does not render one free to do that action.[3] Since the question of whether one is prevented from doing a particular action can always be said to arise in regard to actions of a kind which one is able to do, it is absurd to suggest that the extent of one's liberty can be increased by increasing the number of instances in which the question of *whether* one is free does not arise. The class of cases in which this question does not arise clearly includes those kinds of action which one is unable to do. The conception of liberty as the absence of prevention of only *actually desired* actions—permitting, as it does, the aforementioned inference about the expansion of liberty— logically requires that we extend this class to include those actions which one has no actual desire to do. On this suggestion, a necessary condition of our being either free or unfree to do an action is not merely that we are able to do that kind of action, but also that we in fact want to do it. But to assert this is to confuse the condition of 'being free' with that

---

[2] Published in his *Four Essays on Liberty* (Oxford, 1969), pp. xxxviii–xl.
[3] 'On Liberty and the Real Will', *Philosophy*, 45 (1970), 177–92; p. 191.

of 'feeling free'. For if there are persons who make it impossible for me to import cannabis into this country, I am free to do so irrespective of whether I want to do so, am indifferent to doing so, or want not to do so.[4] Being placed in a locked prison cell renders me unfree to go to the theatre regardless of whether I want to go to the theatre or not.

Obviously the extent to which such prevention engenders in me a feeling of frustration, the extent to which I experience it as an obstacle to my satisfaction or contrary to my interests, does depend on what I actually desire or want to do. Perhaps the only freedom that matters to me is the freedom to do what I desire to do or believe I ought to do. But it does not follow from this that I can only be free or unfree with regard to those actions which I want or believe I ought to do. For I can equally be free to do actions which I do not want to do. It is not unintelligible—on the contrary, it makes perfect sense—to assert that 'I am free to do *A*, i.e., am not prevented from doing *A*, though I have no desire to do so'. Again, it is perfectly intelligible to say that 'I am unfree to do *A*, and have no desire to do so.'

The same may be said of actions whose relation to their subject is defined in normative terms. To ask whether an individual is free to do *A*, is not to ask a moral question. It is, rather, to ask a factual question the answer to which is logically prior to any moral question about his doing *A*. Indeed, it is difficult to comprehend how one could perform an action which one ought not to perform—a wrong action— unless one is free to do it, not prevented from doing it. Thus it is mistaken to imagine that 'our conception of freedom is bounded by our notions of what might be worthwhile doing'.[5] For such an argument implies *inter alia* that 'incomprehension, not hostility, is the first obstacle to toleration' (ibid.). Whereas, apart from the tautologous character of the suggestion that comprehending the (possible) value of an action is a reason for finding it worthwhile, there is absolutely no reason to suppose that we are incapable of tolerating actions the worthwhileness of which we do not accept. It follows from

[4] The example is Day's; ibid. 179.
[5] S. I. Benn and W. L. Weinstein, 'Being Free to Act and Being a Free Man', *Mind*, 80 (1971), 194–211; p. 195.

these considerations that statements to the effect that '*X* is free to do *A*' do not imply or presuppose statements to the effect either that '*X* wants to do *A*' or that '*X* has no obligation to do not-*A*'. Nor, therefore, do they imply or presuppose statements about what *X* 'really' wants or about what it is in his 'real' interest to do or have done to him. Judgements about whether an individual is free to do a certain action do not presuppose any judgement concerning either his desires or his obligations.

2

Suppose that I am offered a teaching post at a university other than the one which at present employs me. Suppose, further, that the duties and privileges attached to the offered post are quite similar to those pertaining to my present post, except in this respect: that the offered salary is considerably greater than my present one. Suppose, finally, that I am not averse to receiving a higher salary and, indeed, would positively welcome it. Is there some significant sense in which this offer has rendered it *impossible* for me to remain in my present post and to reject the offered one? Alternatively, suppose that I have no offer of a teaching post at a university other than the one which at present employs me. Suppose, further, that the relevant university authorities have informed me that unless I substantially increase the amount of teaching I am to do in the next academic session and, moreover, undertake to teach several courses in subjects unrelated to my own, my contract of employment will not be renewed. And suppose, finally, that I entertain considerable doubt as to the conceptual soundness of these prospective courses, that I am therefore averse to teaching them, and that in any case I am loath to surrender still more of my time to teaching as I much prefer to spend it reading. Is there some significant sense in which this threat has rendered it *impossible* for me to remain in my present post and to renew my contract?

Offers and threats are interventions, by others, in individuals' practical deliberations. They are intended by their authors to influence how a recipient individual behaves, by altering the extent to which he actually desires to do a particular action of a kind which he is able to do. If the intervener is correct in his assessment of the desires of the recipient, and if he has designed his intervention accordingly, he necessarily succeeds in bringing about the intended alteration in the recipient's desire to do the particular action in behalf of which the intervention is made. However, despite this shared characteristic of interventions which are offers and interventions which are threats, few writers who subscribe to the negative conception of personal liberty contend that the making of an offer constitutes a diminution of the liberty of its recipient; while many of them would insist that a threat does so constitute. (Positive libertarians allow that both offers and threats, as heteronomous influences, may diminish personal liberty and they tend to suggest that the distinction between the two is therefore of little moment.)

Thus we are faced with four questions. What, if any, are the grounds for distinguishing those interventions which are offers from those which are threats? If such a distinction can be established, does it imply a difference between the ways in which offers and threats, respectively, affect the practical deliberations of their recipients? If such a difference exists, does it constitute a reason for asserting that threats, but not offers, diminish personal liberty? If such a difference does *not* exist, can we nevertheless claim—as do positive libertarians— that both offers and threats diminish personal liberty? In pursuing answers to these questions I shall put aside the further complications which could be introduced into the discussion by a consideration of the obvious truth that what counts as a threatening intervention to some individuals may often count as an offer to others. Attaching the intervening consequence, of accommodation in a gaol cell, to the action of sleeping on a park bench at night, may well constitute an offer to vagrants while at the same time constituting a threat to other members of the public. Similarly, what counts as a strong threat or offer to some individuals may constitute only a weak threat or offer to others. Interpersonal variations of these kinds—whether between different recipients or between a recipient and an intervener—though important for the purposes of some discussions, are not relevant to this one. Such considerations can therefore be excluded by adopting the assumption that everyone knows the nature and extent of the desires of everyone else, and intervenes accordingly.

Cinema-goers will doubtless recall a recent popular film concerning the Mafia in which the *padrone*, periodically confronted with an uncooperative business associate, declares his intention of making the recalcitrant 'an offer he can't refuse'. The amusing irony of this turn of phrase might understandably be taken as proof that we are all reasonably able to distinguish an offer from a threat, because we all know the difference between a benefit and a penalty. But if a distinction of this kind can be drawn, it cannot be done simply upon such grounds as these. For it is true of both offers and threats that compliance promises to make one better off than non-compliance, i.e., that for both offers and threats, there is a clear sense in which compliance is seen to involve beneficial consequences and non-compliance to involve penal consequences. So the differences which must exist if a distinction is to be drawn between offers and threats are those (1) between the benefits conferred by compliance with an offer and a threat, respectively, and correspondingly (2) between the penalties incurred by non-compliance with an offer and a threat, respectively.

It is not necessary to rehearse the accounts provided by the growing body of literature on this subject, to appreciate that an affirmation of the existence of such differences logically presupposes a conception of 'normalcy' into which the threatening or offering action is taken to be an extrinsic intrusion.[6] That such a presupposition is required is evident from the fact that the casual distinction commonly drawn between offering interventions and threatening interventions— that compliance with the former results in an augmentation of well-being while non-compliance with the latter results in a diminution of well-being—tends to obscure the point that non-compliance with offers results in a relative diminution of

---

[6] Cf. Robert Nozick, 'Coercion', in S. Morgenbesser, P. Suppes, and M. White (eds.), *Philosophy, Science and Method: Essays in Honor of Ernest Nagel* (New York, 1969); Harry G. Frankfurt, 'Coercion and Moral Responsibility', in T. Honderich (ed.), *Essays on Freedom of Action* (London, 1973); and the papers by M. D. Bayles, B. Gert, and V. Held in J. R. Pennock and J. W. Chapman (eds.), *Nomos XIV: Coercion* (Chicago, 1972).

well-being while compliance with threats results in a relative augmentation of well-being. To establish the distinction between offers and threats it is therefore necessary to establish that the compliance-consequences of the former and the non-compliance-consequences of the latter are not merely relative augmentations and diminutions (respectively) of well-being, but absolute ones. And this presupposes a standard or norm from which such consequences are judged to be departures. In the literature, the conception of the norm to be employed for this purpose is the description of the normal and predictable course of events, that is, the course of events which would confront the recipient of the intervention were the intervention not to occur. (Thus a shopkeeper is not threatening his customers when he raises his prices during a generally inflationary period.) Given this conception of the norm, we get the following configuration of alternative consequences: for an offer—'You may use my car whenever you like'—the compliance-consequence represents a situation which is preferred to the norm, while the non-compliance-consequence represents a situation on the norm, no more or less preferred than it because identical to it; for a threat—'Your money or your life'—the compliance-consequence represents a situation which is less preferred than the norm (no money), but the non-compliance-consequence represents a situation which is still less preferred (no life). We can, in addition, distinguish a third kind of intervention which I shall call a 'throffer', e.g. 'Kill this man and you'll receive £100—fail to kill him and I'll kill you.' Here the compliance-consequence represents a situation which is (let us suppose) preferred to the norm, while the non-compliance-consequence represents a situation which is less preferred than the norm. This configuration can be displayed diagrammatically:

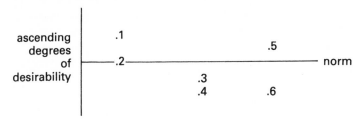

where the vertically ordered pairs of points represent the alternative consequences posed by offers, threats, and throffers, respectively; and where the odd-numbered points represent compliance-consequences, even-numbered points representing non-compliance-consequences. Hence it would appear that the answer to our first question is an affirmation that we can distinguish offers from threats, and that the grounds for doing so consist in the fact that the alternative consequences posed by the former occupy a different position relative to the norm than do those posed by the latter.

We may now consider our answer to the second question in the light of this distinction. Does this distinction, between those interventions which are offers and those which are threats, imply any difference between the ways in which each affects the practical deliberations of their recipients? The short answer to this question is 'No'. The way in which both offers and threats affect the practical deliberations of their recipients consists in the reversal of the relative desirability of doing a particular action with that of not doing it. Whereas in the normal course of events—in the absence of an intervention—X's desire to do A is greater than his desire to do not-A, in the presence of an intervention his desire to do A is less than his desire to do not-A. Now what is consequential for the deliberations of the recipient of an intervention is *not* whether the pair of alternatives confronting him is above (and on) or below the norm. Rather it is the fact—true of both offers and threats—that compliance leaves him in a more desired position than does non-compliance. The *modus operandi* of an intervention—its method of promoting a compliant response—consists in effecting a positive remainder when the degree of desirability attached to the non-compliance-consequence is subtracted from that of the compliance-consequence. This is true irrespective of whether that pair of consequences lies above (and on) or below the norm, that is, irrespective of whether that intervention is an offer or a threat. And while it is necessarily true that an action complying with an offer is more desired than an action complying with a threat, it is very far from being necessarily true that the difference in desirability between compliance and non-compliance with offers is of a lesser magnitude than the corresponding difference pertaining to threats. This means, as will be shown, that it is not necessarily true that offers are more resistible or exert less influence than threats. With respect to any intervention, it is the existence of this difference which affects the practical deliberations of the recipient, and not the kind of intervention involved.

If (and only if) this argument is correct, it should be true that the factor determining the strength of a recipient's desire to comply with an intervention is the magnitude of this difference, and not the position of either of its consequences relative to the norm. That this is indeed the case can be seen by comparing the following threatening interventions:

    (i) Give me £100 or I shall kill you;
    (ii) Give me £1,000 or I shall kill you;
    (iii) Give me £1,000 or I shall kill you and your brother;
    (iv) Give me £100 or I shall kill you and your brother.

Making all the usual (though by no means incontrovertible) assumptions about individuals' relative preferences concerning money, personal survival, and fraternal welfare, we can readily see that the desire of a recipient to comply would be greatest in the case of (iv) and least in the case of (ii). (Whether his desire to comply would be greater or less in the case of (i) than of (iii) is undecidable on these preference assumptions.) What this indicates is that the strength of a threat is not a function of the desirability of its compliance-consequence relative to that of the norm: (ii) is weaker than both (i) and (iv). Nor is the strength of a threat a function of the desirability of its non-compliance-consequence relative to that of the norm: (iii) is weaker than (iv), and (ii) is weaker than (i). Differences in degree of desirability between consequences and the norm are utterly irrelevant in assessing the strength of a threat. All that is relevant is the difference in degree of desirability between compliance- and non-compliance-consequences. In that respect, it is not strictly mistaken—as it is in the case of threats—to claim that the strength of an offer is a function of the desirability of its compliance-consequence relative to that of the norm. But this is not a reason to suppose that the strength of offers is determined by considerations different from those of threats, i.e. that their respective strengths are incommensurable. It is merely an analytic fact that the non-compliance-consequence of an offer lies on the norm. Its strength, like that of other interventions, is purely a function of the difference in desirability between the two alternative consequences. That this is indeed a rule covering all interventions is also to be seen in a comparison of the strength of the following throffers:

(i)   Do *A* and I shall give you £100—fail and I shall kill you;

(ii)   Do *A* and I shall give you £1,000—fail and I shall kill you;

(iii) Do *A* and I shall give you £100—fail and I shall kill you and your brother;

(iv) Do *A* and I shall give you £1,000—fail and I shall kill you and your brother.

Again, making all the usual assumptions about relative preferences, it is clear that the greatest desire to comply arises in (iv) and the least in (i), with (ii) and (iii) in the middle position (and not susceptible of mutual ranking on these assumptions). This ranking, in terms of capacity to affect the desire to comply, exactly corresponds to the ranking of these throffers in terms of the difference of desirability between their alternative consequences. It does *not* correspond to their ranking in terms either of the difference of desirability between their compliance-consequences and the norm, or of the difference of desirability between their non-compliance-consequences and the norm.

There is one further point which requires to be made. The preceding discussion of offers and threats has been in terms of how they affect their recipients' *desires* to do and not do a particular action. It is equally possible, however, to reformulate the discussion in terms of the effect of such interventions on their recipients' *obligations* to do and not do a particular action. Whereas in the normal course of events *X* may have a duty to do *A*, in the presence of a circumstance created by an intervention, he may have a duty to do not-*A*. The only difference between the descriptive account and the prescriptive one is that, in the latter case, the reversal in the desirability of the two alternatives is not a matter of degree: interventions, in the prescriptive account, do not make compliance more desirable and non-compliance less desirable. Rather, compliance becomes obligatory and non-compliance prohibited. The reversal in the prescriptive account is, as it were, one of quality rather than quantity. This, however, does not alter the point that whether interventions are spoken of as affecting desires or obligations, the ways in which these are affected are the same—namely, by the reversal of the desirability of a complying action with that of a non-complying action.

Briefly then, both the *modus operandi* of an intervention and its strength are specifiable without reference to the norm. Since it is in the concept of the norm that the distinction between offering and threatening interventions is grounded, we may conclude—in answer to the second question—that there is no difference between the ways in which offers and threats respectively affect the practical deliberations of their recipients.

And this provides us with the answer to the third question, as well: since no such difference exists, it cannot constitute a reason for asserting that threats, but not offers, diminish personal liberty. Furthermore, since there appears to be no other way that threats can be said to affect personal liberty—other than through their effect on the deliberations of their recipients—there is no reason to believe that, if they do affect it, these effects are different from those of offers.

We have now to consider the answer to the fourth question which asks whether, in the absence of such a difference, it is nevertheless possible to claim—as do positive libertarians—that both threats and offers diminish personal liberty. We have already seen that statements to the effect that 'X is free to do A' do not imply or presuppose statements to the effect either that 'X wants to do A' or that 'X has no obligation to do not-A'. Interventions of an offering or threatening kind effect changes either in individuals' relative desires to do certain actions or in the evaluative status assigned to their doing certain actions. Whereas in the normal course of events it might be the case that 'X wants to do A' or 'X has no obligation to do not-A', the occurrence of an intervention may cause it to be the case that 'X wants to do not-A' or 'X ought to do not-A'. But neither of these latter two statements, nor the fact that they are true as a consequence of another's intervention, entails that 'X is unfree to do A'. They do not imply that '*X* doing *A*' is rendered impossible. It is, of course, not disputed that the truth of the first of these two statements rules out the possibility of '*X* doing *A* eagerly' and that the truth of the second rules out the possibility of '*X* doing *A* justifiably'. But that is another matter. Hence it would appear that neither the making of threats nor that of offers constitutes a diminution of personal liberty. Intervention does not count as prevention.

The argument to the contrary—that *Y*'s intervening action *B*, in behalf of '*X* doing not-*A*', does render '*X* doing *A*' impossible—presupposes that rendering a compliant action (not-*A*) more desirable than its non-compliant alternative (*A*), entails rendering the latter impossible and the former, therefore, necessary. And this in turn presupposes that only that one which is the more desirable of two alternative courses of action, can be done. But if this were true, then *Y*'s intervening action *B* must have been more desirable than not-*B*. And this would imply that '*Y* doing not-*B*' was impossible and that '*Y* doing *B*' was necessary. But if this were so, then '*Y* doing *B*'—as a necessary occurrence—must itself be part of the normal and predictable course of events, since it is analytically true that all necessary events are inevitable events and all inevitable events are predictable events. In which case, however, '*Y* doing *B*' cannot be construed as an intervention. Thus the argument that intervention is prevention is self-contradictory, because its proponents are logically committed both to affirming and to denying that an intervening action is part of the normal and predictable course of events. This contradiction seems to me to be implicitly present in the political writings of many of those who defend the positive conception of individual liberty. It is therefore all the more surprising that it is also to be found in the opposed conception presented by some negative libertarians.

3

The preceding arguments have been brought in support of a single claim: that since an individual is unfree to do—is prevented from doing—a particular action if and only if the action of another renders it impossible for him to do it, an *intervening* action on the part of one individual in behalf of another's not doing an action does not render the latter unfree to do that action. The intervention does not count as the prevention of his doing that action. We have now to consider what *does* count as prevention.

Prevention is a relation between the respective actions of two (or more) individuals such that the occurrence of one of those actions rules out, or renders impossible, the occurrence of the other (or others). If there are two individuals' actions which can both occur, neither can be preventive of the other. Hence what we want to know is the kind of condition under which either of two individuals' actions can occur, but not both. Acknowledging the immense diversity of actions and of the circumstances of their prevention, can we nevertheless specify a universally valid description of the conditions of prevention? The grounds for an affirmative answer to this question should furnish us with the conceptual equipment to formulate more positively what it is to be free to do a particular action.

Consider the case of an individual incarcerated in a locked gaol cell which is ten feet high, wide and long, which is devoid of any furniture or fittings, and for the lock of which he lacks a key. There is, we might say, an indefinitely long list of actions which this individual is prevented from doing. It is also true that there is an indefinitely long list—though not as long as the previous one—of actions which this individual is not prevented from doing. He is not prevented from jumping up and down, nor from singing 'Waltzing Matilda', nor from twiddling his thumbs in a clockwise direction, nor from twiddling his thumbs in a counter-clockwise direction, and so forth. Now consider the change that would be wrought, in the extent to which he is subject to prevention, were his gaolers to place in his cell a (ventilated) mummy-case and to lock him inside it. We should say that his list of prevented actions, however indefinitely long it had been, would lengthen; and his list of unprevented actions would shorten. It is true, however, that there would now (in the mummy-case) be certain actions possible for him to do which were not so before. Before, he was prevented from, among other things, rubbing his foot against the inside of a mummy-case. Indeed, one could compile a considerable inventory of actions now open to him by virtue of his access to the mummy-case, which were previously rendered impossible by the denial of such access by his gaolers. Hence, in order to establish a clear-cut comparison between any two hypothetical situations in terms of the relative amount of prevention each would involve, we must eliminate as many differences between them as possible, without rendering them exactly alike. Let us say then, that in the first situation the incarcerated individual finds himself in the aforementioned locked cell, which also contains a mummy-case which is not locked though which he can lock from the inside. And in the second situation the individual is locked inside the mummy-case (not lockable/unlockable from inside) which is, in turn, located within the locked cell. It seems clear that however indefinitely long are the lists of prevented and unprevented actions respectively pertaining to the individual in each of these situations, the extent of prevention is greater in the second than in the first.

Next, compare the extent of prevention obtaining in the case of an individual confined in a cell like the one just mentioned and which is devoid of any furnishings, to that obtaining in the case of an individual similarly confined but who can secure writing materials for limited periods of time when he requests them from his gaolers. We should not hesitate to say that prevention is greater in the former case than in the latter. A similar judgement would be rendered in comparing the circumstance in which an individual is compelled to pay a fine of £1,000, with that in which he is fined only £100. For even if the money economy in which he lives and works were to cease to exist while he was still in the court-room, there would still be more actions open to him were he to be deprived of only £100 than there would be if he were deprived of £1,000. Again, an individual is more free if he is chained to a dungeon wall by a shackle on only one wrist, than if both wrists are shackled. And finally, the number of actions rendered impossible for one individual by another, is less if the preventer has crippled only one of his victim's legs than if he has crippled both of them.

In all of these cases we should, of course, be hard pressed to specify precisely the extent to which one individual's action prevents the other from acting. This is because the number of actions which the prevented individual is and is not thereby prevented from doing, is incalculably great. Nevertheless, the fact that this number cannot be specified does not constitute an insurmountable obstacle to any further analysis of the manner in which one action may stand in a preventive relation to others. For the fact that we are able to compare at least some hypothetical situations where prevention occurs, and to form judgements as to the *relative* amounts of prevention respectively obtaining in these compared situations, indicates that—despite the vast diversity of preventive conditions—there is some limitedly quantifiable common element present in them.

The reason why we judge an individual to be subject to less prevention in the cell with the unlocked mummy-case than in the cell with the locked one is, obviously enough, that he is unprevented from doing all those actions which would be open to him were he to be locked inside the case, as well as others which would not be open to him were he so confined. Yet upon what grounds is this comparative judgement made? What is the nature of the difference, between these two situations, which enables us to claim with complete confidence—and in the absence of an actual comparative inventory of prevented actions—that the one allows of greater freedom than the other? The difference is, simply and solely, that in the former situation the incarcerated individual can make use of a greater amount of physical space and material objects than his confinement in the locked case would permit. No other difference exists between these two situations. The same kind of claim can be made about the other hypothetical situations compared above. In other words, the greater the amount of physical space and/or material objects the use of which is blocked to one individual by another, the greater is the extent of the prevention to which that former individual is subject.

This is because to act is, among other things, to occupy particular portions of physical space and to dispose of particular material objects including, in the first instance, parts of one's own body. I shall call the particular portions of physical space occupied in a particular action, and the particular material objects disposed of in that action, the 'physical components' of that action. Thus, pursuing the universally valid description desiderated at the beginning of this section, the kind of condition under which the occurrence of one action renders impossible the occurrence of another is that at least one of the physical components of one action is (simultaneously) identical with one of the physical components of another. If two agents' respective actions (simultaneously) have no common physical components, there is no reason why they cannot both occur. It follows that to prevent an individual from doing a particular action is (simultaneously) to occupy and/or to dispose of at least one of the physical components of that individual's action. To be free to do A therefore entails that all of the physical components of doing A are (simultaneously) unoccupied and/or disposed of by another.

The relation between an agent and a portion of physical space which he occupies, and between an agent and a material object of which he disposes, is commonly called *possession*. An individual is said to possess an object when he enjoys exclusive physical control of it, that is, when what happens to that object—allowing for the operation of the laws of physics—is not subject to the determination of any other agent and is therefore subject only to his own determination. Possession is thus a *triadic* relation obtaining between an agent, an object, and all other agents. Statements about the freedom of an individual to do a particular action are therefore construable as claims about the agential location of possession of the particular physical components of that action. The statement that 'X is free to do A' entails that none of the physical components of doing A is possessed by an agent other than X. The statement that 'X is unfree to do A' entails that at least one of the physical components of doing A is possessed by an agent other than X. My theorem is, then, that *freedom is the personal possession of physical objects*.

At least one interesting inference may be drawn from this theorem. It has to do with what is implied by any statement about either the expansion or diminution of his personal liberty that may be experienced by an individual. If X's freedom consists in the physical objects X possesses, any expansion in his freedom must consist in an increase in the physical objects X possesses. But if a physical object P is in X's possession, it cannot be in the possession of any agent other than X. In this circumstance, another agent Y is prevented from doing any action of which P is a physical component. Y is unfree to do any action of which one or more of the physical components are possessed by X. If there were only two agents, X and Y, the extent of X's freedom and of Y's unfreedom would both be functions of the extent of X's possessions. Any expansion in the freedom of X would constitute a diminution in the freedom of Y: it would extend the list of actions which Y is prevented from doing. In a universe of more than two agents, any increase in the number of physical objects controlled by one agent must constitute an increase in the number of physical objects the control of which is denied to other agents. Conversely, any decrease in the number of physical objects controlled by one agent, must constitute a decrease in the number of physical objects the control of which is denied to other agents. This much at least is analytically true and, perhaps, reasonably obvious.

Hence it is often asserted, with some justification, that the paradigm instance of being unfree is that in which an individual is imprisoned. Certainly it is true that, for most people, imprisonment involves a very considerable decrease in the amount of physical objects they control. (Where it does not, imprisonment may fail to penalize.) And, in the case of any one individual, this decrease implies a corresponding increase in the amount of physical objects over which other individuals enjoy control. Nevertheless the paradigmatic character of imprisonment is doubtful since, as was noted previously, certain actions are possible even in prison and, to that extent, a prisoner does enjoy control over some physical objects. Therefore the true paradigm of prevention, the condition under which an individual is maximally unfree, is that in which another individual controls his voluntary nervous system and thereby renders it impossible for him to dispose of the various parts of his body in a manner appropriate to the doing of any action whatever. In such a case it is readily apparent that the diminution in the extent of control enjoyed by the one individual corresponds to the expansion in the extent of control enjoyed by the other. It does not stretch our conceptual capacities too far, even if it is somewhat unidiomatic, to say that the latter possesses the body of the former. Of course, most instances of prevention are rather less drastic and thus less thoroughgoing. But the paradigm does serve to exemplify the nature of the relation obtaining between the extent of one agent's freedom and that of others.

Berlin observes, in a figurative vein, that ' "Freedom for the pike is death for the minnows" ' and interprets this epigram literally to mean that 'the liberty of some must depend on the restraint of others'.[7] It is thus inconsistent as well as mistaken to suggest, as he does just slightly further on in his argument, that there can be circumstances in which 'an absolute loss of liberty occurs', i.e. that one individual can lose freedom without thereby increasing the individual liberty of others (*Four Essays*, p. 125 [p. 38 this volume]). Within the universe of agents, that is, within the class of beings who count as authors of actions and who are therefore the subjects of statements concerning freedom and prevention, there can be no such thing as an absolute loss of (or gain in) individual liberty.

[7] *Four Essays*, p. 124 [p. 36 this volume]; see also S. I. Benn and R. S. Peters, *Social Principles and the Democratic State* (London, 1966), 213.

SEVEN

WHAT'S WRONG WITH NEGATIVE LIBERTY

Charles Taylor

This is an attempt to resolve one of the issues that separate 'positive' and 'negative' theories of freedom, as these have been distinguished in Isaiah Berlin's seminal essay, 'Two Concepts of Liberty'.[1] Although one can discuss almost endlessly the detailed formulation of the distinction, I believe it is undeniable that there are two such families of conceptions of political freedom abroad in our civilization.

Thus there clearly are theories, widely canvassed in liberal society, which want to define freedom exclusively in terms of the independence of the individual from interference by others, be these governments, corporations, or private persons; and equally clearly these theories are challenged by those who believe that freedom resides at least in part in collective control over the common life. We unproblematically recognize theories descended from Rousseau and Marx as fitting in this category.

There is quite a gamut of views in each category. And this is worth bearing in mind, because it is too easy in the course of polemic to fix on the extreme, almost caricatural variants of each family. When people attack positive theories of freedom, they generally have some Left totalitarian theory in mind, according to which freedom resides exclusively in exercising collective control over one's destiny in a classless society, the kind of theory which underlies, for instance, official Communism. This view, in its caricaturally extreme form, refuses to recognize the freedoms guaranteed in other societies as

Charles M. Taylor, 'What's Wrong with Negative Liberty', in *The Idea of Freedom*, ed. A. Ryan (Oxford: Oxford University Press, 1979), 175–93. Reprinted by permission of the author.

[1] *Four Essays on Liberty* [Oxford, 1969], 118–72.

genuine. The destruction of 'bourgeois freedoms' is no real loss of freedom, and coercion can be justified in the name of freedom if it is needed to bring into existence the classless society in which alone men are properly free. Men can, in short, be forced to be free.

Even as applied to official Communism, this portrait is a little extreme, although it undoubtedly expresses the inner logic of this kind of theory. But it is an absurd caricature if applied to the whole family of positive conceptions. This includes all those views of modern political life which owe something to the ancient republican tradition, according to which men's ruling themselves is seen as an activity valuable in itself, and not only for instrumental reasons. It includes in its scope thinkers like Tocqueville, and even arguably the J. S. Mill of *On Representative Government*. It has no necessary connection with the view that freedom consists *purely and simply* in the collective control over the common life, or that there is no freedom worth the name outside a context of collective control. And it does not therefore generate necessarily a doctrine that men can be forced to be free.

On the other side, there is a corresponding caricatural version of negative freedom which tends to come to the fore. This is the tough-minded version, going back to Hobbes, or in another way to Bentham, which sees freedom simply as the absence of external physical or legal obstacles. This view will have no truck with other less immediately obvious obstacles to freedom, for instance, lack of awareness, or false consciousness, or repression, or other inner factors of this kind. It holds firmly to the view that to speak for instance of someone's being less free because of false consciousness, is to abuse words. The only clear meaning which can be given to freedom is that of the absence of external obstacles.

I call this view caricatural as a representative portrait of the negative view, because it rules out of court one of the most powerful motives behind the modern defence of freedom as individual independence, viz., the post-Romantic idea that each person's form of self-realization is original to him/her, and can therefore only be worked out independently. This is one of the reasons for the defence of individual liberty by among others J. S. Mill (this time in his *On Liberty*). But if we think of freedom as including something like the freedom of self-fulfilment, or self-realization according to our own pattern, then we plainly have something which can fail for inner reasons as well as because of external obstacles. We can fail to achieve our own self-realization through inner fears, or false consciousness, as well as because of external coercion. Thus the modern notion of negative freedom which gives weight to the securing of each person's right to realize him/herself in his/her own way cannot make do with the Hobbes/Bentham notion of freedom. The moral psychology of these authors is too simple, or perhaps we should say too crude, for its purposes.

Now there is a strange asymmetry here. The extreme caricatural views tend to come to the fore in the polemic, as I mentioned above. But whereas the extreme 'forced-to-be-free' view is one which the opponents of positive liberty try to pin on them, as one would expect in the heat of the argument, the proponents of negative liberty themselves often seem anxious to espouse their extreme, Hobbesian view. Thus even Isaiah Berlin, in his eloquent exposition of the two concepts of liberty, seems to quote Bentham[2] approvingly and Hobbes[3] as well. Why is this?

To see this we have to examine more closely what is at stake between the two views. The negative theories, as we saw, want to define freedom in terms of individual independence from others; the positive also want to identify freedom with collective self-government. But behind this lie some deeper differences of doctrines.

Isaiah Berlin points out that negative theories are concerned with the area in which the subject should be left without interference, whereas the positive doctrines are concerned with who or what controls. I should like to put the point behind this in a slightly different way. Doctrines of positive freedom are concerned with a view of freedom which involves essentially the exercising of control over one's life. On this view, one is free only to the extent that one has effectively determined oneself and the shape of one's life. The concept of freedom here is an exercise-concept.

[2] *Four Essays*, 148 n. 1 [n. 24 this volume].
[3] Ibid. 164.

By contrast, negative theories can rely simply on an opportunity-concept, where being free is a matter of what we can do, of what it is open to us to do, whether or not we do anything to exercise these options. This certainly is the case of the crude, original Hobbesian concept. Freedom consists just in there being no obstacle. It is a sufficient condition of one's being free that nothing stand in the way.

But we have to say that negative theories *can* rely on an opportunity-concept, rather than that they necessarily do so rely, for we have to allow for that part of the gamut of negative theories mentioned above which incorporates some notion of self-realization. Plainly this kind of view can't rely simply on an opportunity-concept. We can't say that someone is free, on a self-realization view, if he is totally unrealized, if for instance he is totally unaware of his potential, if fulfilling it has never even arisen as a question for him, or if he is paralysed by the fear of breaking with some norm which he has internalized but which does not authentically reflect him. Within this conceptual scheme, some degree of exercise is necessary for a man to be thought free. Or if we want to think of the internal bars to freedom as obstacles on all fours with the external ones, then being in a position to exercise freedom, having the opportunity, involves removing the internal barriers; and this is not possible without having to some extent realized myself. So that with the freedom of self-realization, having the opportunity to be free requires that I already be exercising freedom. A pure opportunity-concept is impossible here.

But if negative theories can be grounded on either an opportunity- or an exercise-concept, the same is not true of positive theories. The view that freedom involves at least partially collective self-rule is essentially grounded on an exercise-concept. For this view (at least partly) identifies freedom with self-direction, i.e. the actual exercise of directing control over one's life.

But this already gives us a hint towards illuminating the above paradox, that while the extreme variant of positive freedom is usually pinned on its protagonists by their opponents, negative theorists seem prone to embrace the crudest versions of their theory themselves. For if an opportunity-concept is incombinable with a positive theory, but either it or its alternative can suit a negative theory, then one way of ruling out positive theories in principle is by firmly espousing an opportunity-concept. One cuts off the positive theories by the root, as it were, even though one may also pay a price in the atrophy of a wide range of negative theories as well. At least by taking one's stand firmly on the crude side of the negative range, where only opportunity concepts are recognized, one leaves no place for a positive theory to grow.

Taking one's stand here has the advantage that one is holding the line around a very simple and basic issue of principle, and one where the negative view seems to have some backing in common sense. The basic intuition here is that freedom is a matter of being able to do something or other, of not having obstacles in one's way, rather than being a capacity that we have to realise. It naturally seems more prudent to fight the Totalitarian Menace at this last-ditch position, digging in behind the natural frontier of this simple issue, rather than engaging the enemy on the open terrain of exercise-concepts, where one will have to fight to discriminate the good from the bad among such concepts; fight, for instance, for a view of individual self-realization against various notions of collective self-realization, of a nation, or a class. It seems easier and safer to cut all the nonsense off at the start by declaring all self-realization views to be metaphysical hog-wash. Freedom should just be tough-mindedly defined as the absence of external obstacles.

Of course, there are independent reasons for wanting to define freedom tough-mindedly. In particular there is the immense influence of the anti-metaphysical, materialist, natural-science-oriented temper of thought in our civilization. Something of this spirit at its inception induced Hobbes to take the line that he did, and the same spirit goes marching on today. Indeed, it is because of the prevalence of this spirit that the line is so easy to defend, forensically speaking, in our society.

Nevertheless, I think that one of the strongest motives for defending the crude Hobbes–Bentham concept, that freedom is the absence of external obstacles, physical or legal, is the strategic one above. For most of those who take this line thereby abandon many of their own intuitions, sharing as

they do with the rest of us in a post-Romantic civilization
which puts great value on self-realization, and values freedom
largely because of this. It is fear of the Totalitarian Menace, I
would argue, which has led them to abandon this terrain to
the enemy.

I want to argue that this not only robs their eventual
forensic victory of much of its value, since they become
incapable of defending liberalism in the form we in fact value
it, but I want to make the stronger claim that this Maginot
Line mentality actually ensures defeat, as is often the case
with Maginot Line mentalities. The Hobbes–Bentham view, I
want to argue, is indefensible as a view of freedom.

To see this, let's examine the line more closely, and the
temptation to stand on it. The advantage of the view that
freedom is the absence of external obstacles is its simplicity.
It allows us to say that freedom is being able to do what you
want, where what you want is unproblematically understood
as what the agent can identify as his desires. By contrast an
exercise-concept of freedom requires that we discriminate
among motivations. If we are free in the exercise of certain
capacities, then we are not free, or less free, when these
capacities are in some way unfulfilled or blocked. But the
obstacles can be internal as well as external. And this must be
so, for the capacities relevant to freedom must involve some
self-awareness, self-understanding, moral discrimination, and
self-control, otherwise their exercise couldn't amount to
freedom in the sense of self-direction; and this being so, we can
fail to be free because these internal conditions are not
realized. But where this happens, where, for example, we are
quite self-deceived, or utterly fail to discriminate properly the
ends we seek, or have lost self-control, we can quite easily be
doing what we want in the sense of what we can identify as our
wants, without being free; indeed, we can be further en-
trenching our unfreedom.

Once one adopts a self-realization view, or indeed, any
exercise-concept of freedom, then being able to do what
one wants can no longer be accepted as a sufficient condition
of being free. For this view puts certain conditions on
one's motivation. You are not free if you are motivated,
through fear, inauthentically internalized standards, or false

consciousness, to thwart your self-realization. This is some-times put by saying that for a self-realization view, you have to be able to do what you really want, or to follow your real will, or to fulfil the desires of your own true self. But these formulas, particularly the last, may mislead, by making us think that exercise-concepts of freedom are tied to some particular metaphysic, in particular that of a higher and lower self. We shall see below that this is far from being the case, and that there is a much wider range of bases for discriminating authentic and inauthentic desires.

In any case, the point for our discussion here is that for an exercise-concept of freedom, being free can't just be a question of doing what you want in the unproblematic sense. It must also be that what you want doesn't run against the grain of your basic purposes, or your self-realization. Or to put the issue in another way, which converges on the same point, the subject himself can't be the final authority on the question whether he is free; for he cannot be the final authority on the question whether his desires are authentic, whether they do or do not frustrate his purposes.

To put the issue in this second way is to make more palpable the temptation for defenders of the negative view to hold their Maginot Line. For once we admit that the agent himself is not the final authority on his own freedom, do we not open the way to totalitarian manipulation? Do we not legitimate others, supposedly wiser about his purposes than himself, redirecting his feet on the right path, perhaps even by force, and all this in the name of freedom?

The answer is that of course we don't. Not by this concession alone. For there may be good reasons for holding that others are not likely to be in a better position to understand his real purposes. This indeed plausibly follows from the post-Romantic view above that each person has his/her own original form of realization. Some others, who know us intimately, and who surpass us in wisdom, are undoubtedly in a position to advise us, but no official body can possess a doctrine or a technique whereby they could know how to put us on the rails, because such a doctrine or technique cannot in principle exist if human beings really differ in their self-realization.

Or again, we may hold a self-realization view of freedom, and hence believe that there are certain conditions on my motivation necessary to my being free, but also believe that there are other necessary conditions which rule out my being forcibly led towards some definition of my self-realization by external authority. Indeed, in these last two paragraphs I have given a portrait of what I think is a very widely held view in liberal society, a view which values self-realization, and accepts that it can fail for internal reasons, but which believes that no valid guidance can be provided in principle by social authority, because of human diversity and originality, and holds that the attempt to impose such guidance will destroy other necessary conditions of freedom.

It is however true that totalitarian theories of positive freedom do build on a conception which involves discriminating between motivations. Indeed, one can represent the path from the negative to the positive conceptions of freedom as consisting of two steps: the first moves us from a notion of freedom as doing what one wants to a notion which discriminates motivations and equates freedom with doing what we really want, or obeying our real will, or truly directing our lives. The second step introduces some doctrine purporting to show that we cannot do what we really want, or follow our real will, outside of a society of a certain canonical form, incorporating true self-government. It follows that we can only be free in such a society, and that being free *is* governing ourselves collectively according to this canonical form.

We might see an example of this second step in Rousseau's view that only a social contract society in which all give themselves totally to the whole preserves us from other-dependence and ensures that we obey only ourselves; or in Marx's doctrine of man as a species-being who realizes his potential in a mode of social production, and who must thus take control of this mode collectively.

Faced with this two-step process, it seems safer and easier to stop it at the first step, to insist firmly that freedom is just a matter of the absence of external obstacles, that it therefore involves no discrimination of motivation and permits in principle no second-guessing of the subject by any one else.

This is the essence of the Maginot Line strategy. It is very tempting. But I want to claim that it is wrong. I want to argue that we cannot defend a view of freedom which doesn't involve at least some qualitative discrimination as to motive, i.e. which doesn't put some restrictions on motivations among the necessary conditions of freedom, and hence which could rule out second-guessing in principle.

There are some considerations one can put forward straight off to show that the pure Hobbesian concept won't work, that there are some discriminations among motivations which are essential to the concept of freedom as we use it. Even where we think of freedom as the absence of external obstacles, it is not the absence of such obstacles *simpliciter*. For we make discriminations between obstacles as representing more or less serious infringements of freedom. And we do this, because we deploy the concept against a background understanding that certain goals and activities are more significant than others.

Thus we could say that my freedom is restricted if the local authority puts up a new traffic light at an intersection close to my home; so that where previously I could cross as I liked, consistently with avoiding collision with other cars, now I have to wait until the light is green. In a philosophical argument, we might call this a restriction of freedom, but not in a serious political debate. The reason is that it is too trivial, the activity and purposes inhibited here are not really significant. It is not just a matter of our having made a trade-off, and considered that a small loss of liberty was worth fewer traffic accidents, or less danger for the children; we are reluctant to speak here of a loss of liberty at all; what we feel we are trading off is convenience against safety.

By contrast a law which forbids me from worshipping according to the form I believe in is a serious blow to liberty; even a law which tried to restrict this to certain times (as the traffic light restricts my crossing of the intersection to certain times) would be seen as a serious restriction. Why this difference between the two cases? Because we have a background understanding, too obvious to spell out, of some activities and goals as highly significant for human beings and others as less so. One's religious belief is recognized, even by atheists, as supremely important, because it is that by which the believer defines himself as a moral being. By contrast my rhythm of movement through the city traffic is trivial. We don't want to speak of these two in the same breath. We don't even readily admit that liberty is at stake in the traffic light case. For *de minimis non curat libertas*.

But this recourse to significance takes us beyond a Hobbesian scheme. Freedom is no longer just the absence of external obstacle *tout court*, but the absence of external obstacle to significant action, to what is important to man. There are discriminations to be made; some restrictions are more serious than others, some are utterly trivial. About many, there is of course controversy. But what the judgement turns on is some sense of what is significant for human life. Restricting the expression of people's religious and ethical convictions is more significant than restricting their movement around uninhabited parts of the country; and both are more significant than the trivia of traffic control.

But the Hobbesian scheme has no place for the notion of significance. It will allow only for purely quantitative judgements. On the toughest-minded version of his conception, where Hobbes seems to be about to define liberty in terms of the absence of physical obstacles, one is presented with the vertiginous prospect of human freedom being measurable in the same way as the degrees of freedom of some physical object, say a lever. Later we see that this won't do, because we have to take account of legal obstacles to my action. But in any case, such a quantitative conception of freedom is a non-starter.

Consider the following diabolical defence of Albania as a free country. We recognize that religion has been abolished in Albania, whereas it hasn't been in Britain. But on the other hand there are probably far fewer traffic lights per head in Tirana than in London. (I haven't checked for myself, but this is a very plausible assumption.) Suppose an apologist for Albanian Socialism were nevertheless to claim that this country was freer than Britain, because the number of acts restricted was far smaller. After all, only a minority of Londoners practise some religion in public places, but all have to negotiate their way through traffic. Those who do practise a religion generally do so on one day of the week, while they are held up at traffic lights every day. In sheer quantitative terms, the number of acts restricted by traffic lights must be greater than that restricted by a ban on public religious practice. So if Britain is considered a free society, why not Albania?

So the application even of our negative notion of freedom requires a background conception of what is significant, according to which some restrictions are seen to be without relevance for freedom altogether, and others are judged as being of greater and lesser importance. So some discrimination among motivations seems essential to our concept of freedom. A minute's reflection shows why this must be so. Freedom is important to us because we are purposive beings. But then there must be distinctions in the significance of different kinds of freedom based on the distinction in the significance of different purposes.

But of course, this still doesn't involve the kind of discrimination mentioned above, the kind which would allow us to say that someone who was doing what he wanted (in the unproblematic sense) wasn't really free, the kind of discrimination which allows us to put conditions on people's motivations necessary to their being free, and hence to second-guess them. All we have shown is that we make discriminations between more or less significant freedoms, based on discriminations among the purposes people have.

This creates some embarrassment for the crude negative theory, but it can cope with it by simply adding a recognition that we make judgements of significance. Its central claim that freedom just is the absence of external obstacles seems untouched, as also its view of freedom as an opportunity-concept. It is just that we now have to admit that not all opportunities are equal.

But there is more trouble in store for the crude view when we examine further what these qualitative discriminations are based on. What lies behind our judging certain purposes/feelings as more significant than others? One might think that there was room here again for another quantitative theory; that the more significant purposes are those we want more. But this account is either vacuous or false.

It is true but vacuous if we take wanting more just to mean being more significant. It is false as soon as we try to give wanting more an independent criterion, such as, for instance, the urgency or force of a desire, or the prevalence of one desire over another, because it is a matter of the most banal experience that the purposes we know to be more significant are not always those which we desire with the greatest urgency to encompass, nor the ones that actually always win out in cases of conflict of desires.

When we reflect on this kind of significance, we come up against what I have called elsewhere the fact of strong evaluation, the fact that we human subjects are not only subjects of first-order desires, but of second-order desires, desires about desires. We experience our desires and purposes as qualitatively discriminated, as higher or lower, noble or base, integrated or fragmented, significant or trivial, good and bad. This means that we experience some of our desires and goals as intrinsically more significant than others: some passing comfort is less important than the fulfilment of our lifetime vocation, our *amour propre* less important than a love relationship; while we experience some others as bad, not just comparatively, but absolutely: we desire not to be moved by spite, or some childish desire to impress at all costs. And these judgements of significance are quite independent of the strength of the respective desires: the craving for comfort may be overwhelming at this moment, we may be obsessed with our *amour propre*, but the judgement of significance stands.

But then the question arises whether this fact of strong evaluation doesn't have other consequences for our notion of freedom, than just that it permits us to rank freedoms in importance. Is freedom not at stake when we find ourselves carried away by a less significant goal to override a highly significant one? Or when we are led to act out of a motive we consider bad or despicable?

The answer is that we sometimes do speak in this way. Suppose I have some irrational fear, which is preventing me from doing something I very much want to do. Say the fear of public speaking is preventing me from taking up a career that I should find very fulfilling, and that I should be quite good at, if I could just get over this 'hang-up'. It is clear that we experience this fear as an obstacle, and that we feel we are less than we would be if we could overcome it.

Or again, consider the case where I am very attached to comfort. To go on short rations, and to miss my creature comforts for a time, makes me very depressed. I find myself making a big thing of this. Because of this reaction I can't do certain things that I should like very much to do, such as going on an expedition over the Andes, or a canoe trip in the Yukon. Once again, it is quite understandable if I experience this attachment as an obstacle, and feel that I should be freer without it.

Or I could find that my spiteful feelings and reactions which I almost can't inhibit are undermining a relationship which is terribly important to me. At times, I feel as though I am almost assisting as a helpless witness at my own destructive behaviour, as I lash out again with my unbridled tongue at her. I long to be able not to feel this spite. As long as I feel it, even control is not an option, because it just builds up inside until it either bursts out, or else the feeling somehow communicates itself, and queers things between us. I long to be free of this feeling.

These are quite understandable cases, where we can speak of freedom or its absence without strain. What I have called strong evaluation is essentially involved here. For these are not just cases of conflict, even cases of painful conflict. If the conflict is between two desires with which I have no trouble identifying, there can be no talk of lesser freedom, no matter how painful or fateful. Thus if what is breaking up my relationship is my finding fulfilment in a job which, say, takes me away from home a lot, I have indeed a terrible conflict, but I would have no temptation to speak of myself as less free.

Even seeing a great difference in the significance of the two terms doesn't seem to be a sufficient condition of my wanting to speak of freedom and its absence. Thus my marriage may be breaking up because I like going to the pub and playing cards on Saturday nights with the boys. I may feel quite unequivocally that my marriage is much more important than the release and comradeship of the Saturday night bash. But nevertheless I wouldn't want to talk of my being freer if I could slough off this desire.

The difference seems to be that in this case, unlike the ones above, I still identify with the less important desire, I still see it as expressive of myself, so that I couldn't lose it without altering who I am, losing something of my personality. Whereas my irrational fear, my being quite distressed by discomfort, my spite—these are all things which I can easily see myself losing without any loss whatsoever to what I am. This is why I can see them as obstacles to my purposes, and hence to my freedom, even though they are in a sense unquestionably desires and feelings of mine.

Before exploring further what's involved in this, let's go back and keep score. It would seem that these cases make a bigger breach in the crude negative theory. For they seem to be cases in which the obstacles to freedom are internal; and if this is so, then freedom can't simply be interpreted as the absence of *external* obstacles; and the fact that I'm doing what I want, in the sense of following my strongest desire, isn't sufficient to establish that I'm free. On the contrary, we have to make discriminations among motivations, and accept that acting out of some motivations, for example irrational fear or spite, or this too great need for comfort, is not freedom, is even a negation of freedom.

But although the crude negative theory can't be sustained in the face of these examples, perhaps something which springs from the same concerns can be reconstructed. For although we have to admit that there are internal, motivational, necessary conditions for freedom, we can perhaps still avoid any legitimation of what I called above the second-guessing of the subject. If our negative theory allows for strong evaluation, allows that some goals are really important to us, and that other desires are seen as not fully ours, then can it not retain the thesis that freedom is being able to do what I want, that is, what I can identify myself as wanting, where this means not just what I identify as my strongest desire, but what I identify as my true, authentic desire or purpose? The subject would still be the final arbiter of his being free/unfree, as indeed he is clearly capable of discerning this in the examples above, where I relied precisely on the subject's own experience of constraint, of motives with which he can't identify. We should have sloughed off the untenable Hobbesian reductive-materialist metaphysics, according to which only external obstacles count, as though action were just movement, and there could be no internal, motivational obstacles to our deeper purposes. But we would be retaining the basic concern of the negative theory, that the subject is still the final authority as to what his freedom consists in, and cannot be second-guessed by external authority. Freedom would be modified to read: the absence of internal or external obstacle to what I truly or authentically want. But we would still be holding the Maginot Line. Or would we?

I think not, in fact. I think that this hybrid or middle position is untenable, where we are willing to admit that we can speak of what we truly want, as against what we most strongly desire, and of some desires as obstacles to our freedom, while we still will not allow for second-guessing. For to rule this out in principle is to rule out in principle that the subject can ever be wrong about what he truly wants. And how can he never, in principle, be wrong, unless there is nothing to be wrong about in this matter?

That in fact is the thesis our negative theorist will have to defend. And it is a plausible one for the same intellectual (reductive-empiricist) tradition from which the crude negative theory springs. On this view, our feelings are brute facts about us; that is, it is a fact about us that we are affected in such and such a way, but our feelings can't themselves be understood as involving some perception or sense of what they relate to, and hence as potentially veridical or illusory, authentic or in-authentic. On this scheme, the fact that a certain desire represented one of our fundamental purposes, and another a mere force with which we cannot identify, would concern merely the brute quality of the affect in both cases. It would be a matter of the raw feel of these two desires that this was their respective status.

In such circumstances, the subject's own classification would be incorrigible. There is no such thing as an impercept-ible raw feel. If the subject failed to experience a certain desire as fundamental, and if what we meant by 'fundamental' applied to desire was that the felt experience of it has a certain quality, then the desire couldn't be fundamental. We can see this if we look at those feelings which we can agree are brute in this sense: for instance, the stab of pain I feel when the dentist jabs into my tooth, or the crawling unease when someone runs his fingernail along the blackboard. There can be no question of misperception here. If I fail to 'perceive' the pain, I am not in pain. Might it not be so with our fundamental desires, and those which we repudiate?

The answer is clearly no. For first of all, many of our feelings and desires, including the relevant ones for these kinds of conflicts, are not brute. By contrast with pain and the fingernail-on-blackboard sensation, shame and fear, for instance, are emotions which involve our experiencing the situation as bearing a certain import for us, as being dangerous or shameful. This is why shame and fear can be inappropriate, or even irrational, where pain and a *frisson* cannot. Thus we can be in error in feeling shame or fear. We can even be consciously aware of the unfounded nature of our feelings, and this is when we castigate them as irrational.

Thus the notion that we can understand all our feelings and desires as brute, in the above sense, is not on. But more, the idea that we could discriminate our fundamental desires, or those which we want to repudiate, by the quality of brute affect is grotesque. When I am convinced that some career, or an expedition in the Andes, or a love relationship, is of fundamental importance to me (to recur to the above examples), it cannot be just because of the throbs, *élans*, or tremors I feel; I must also have some sense that these are of great significance for me, meet important, long-lasting needs, represent a fulfilment of something central to me, will bring me closer to what I really am, or something of the sort. The whole notion of our identity, whereby we recognize that some goals, desires, allegiances are central to what we are, while others are not or are less so, can make sense only against a background of desires and feelings which are not brute, but what I shall call import-attributing, to invent a term of art for the occasion.

Thus we have to see our emotional life as made up largely of import-attributing desires and feelings, that is, desires and feelings which we can experience mistakenly. And not only can we be mistaken in this, we clearly must accept, in cases like the above where we want to repudiate certain desires, that we are mistaken.

For let us consider the distinction mentioned above between

conflicts where we feel fettered by one desire, and those where we do not, where, for instance, in the example mentioned above, a man is torn between his career and his marriage. What made the difference was that in the case of genuine conflict both desires are the agent's, whereas in the cases where he feels fettered by one, this desire is one he wants to repudiate.

But what is it to feel that a desire is not truly mine? Presumably, I feel that I should be better off without it, that I don't lose anything in getting rid of it, I remain quite complete without it. What could lie behind this sense?

Well, one could imagine feeling this about a brute desire. I may feel this about my addiction to smoking, for instance—wish I could get rid of it, experience it as a fetter, and believe that I should be well rid of it. But addictions are a special case; we understand them to be unnatural, externally induced desires. We couldn't say in general that we are ready to envisage losing our brute desires without a sense of diminution. On the contrary, to lose my desire for, and hence delectation in, oysters, mushroom pizza, or Peking duck would be a terrible deprivation. I should fight against such a change with all the strength at my disposal.

So being brute is not what makes desires repudiable. And besides, in the above examples the repudiated desires aren't brute. In the first case, I am chained by unreasoning fear, an import-attributing emotion, in which the fact of being mistaken is already recognized when I identify the fear as irrational or unreasoning. Spite, too, which moves me in the third case, is an import-attributing emotion. To feel spite is to see oneself and the target of one's resentment in a certain light; it is to feel in some way wounded, or damaged, by his success or good fortune, and the more hurt the more he is fortunate. To overcome feelings of spite, as against just holding them in, is to come to see self and other in a different light, in particular, to set aside self-pity, and the sense of being personally wounded by what the other does and is.

(I should also like to claim that the obstacle in the third example, the too great attachment to comfort, while not itself import-attributing, is also bound up with the way we see things. The problem is here not just that we dislike discomfort, but that we are too easily depressed by it; and this is something which we overcome only by sensing a different order of priorities, whereby small discomforts matter less. But if this is thought too dubious, we can concentrate on the other two examples.)

Now how can we feel that an import-attributing desire is not truly ours? We can do this only if we see it as mistaken, that is, the import or the good it supposedly gives us a sense of is not a genuine import or good. The irrational fear is a fetter, because it is irrational; spite is a fetter because it is rooted in a self-absorption which distorts our perspective on everything, and the pleasures of venting it preclude any genuine satisfaction. Losing these desires we lose nothing, because their loss deprives us of no genuine good or pleasure or satisfaction. In this they are quite different from my love of oysters, mushroom pizza, and Peking duck.

It would appear from this that to see our desires as brute gives us no clue as to why some of them are repudiable. On the contrary it is precisely their not being brute which can explain this. It is because they are import-attributing desires which are mistaken that we can feel that we would lose nothing in sloughing them off. Everything which is truly important to us would be safeguarded. If they were just brute desires, we couldn't feel this unequivocally, as we certainly do not when it comes to the pleasures of the palate. True, we also feel that our desire to smoke is repudiable, but there is a special explanation here, which is not available in the case of spite.

Thus we can experience some desires as fetters, because we can experience them as not ours. And we can experience them as not ours because we see them as incorporating a quite erroneous appreciation of our situation and of what matters to us. We can see this again if we contrast the case of spite with that of another emotion which partly overlaps, and which is highly considered in some societies, the desire for revenge. In certain traditional societies this is far from being considered a despicable emotion. On the contrary, it is a duty of honour on a male relative to avenge a man's death. We might imagine that this too might give rise to conflict. It might conflict with the attempts of a new regime to bring some order to the land.

The government would have to stop people taking vengeance, in the name of peace.

But. short of a conversion to a new ethical outlook, this would be seen as a trade-off, the sacrifice of one legitimate goal for the sake of another. And it would seem monstrous were one to propose reconditioning people so that they no longer felt the desire to avenge their kin. This would be to unman them.[4]

Why do we feel so different about spite (and for that matter also revenge)? Because the desire for revenge for an ancient Icelander was his sense of a real obligation incumbent on him, something it would be dishonourable to repudiate; while for us, spite is the child of a distorted perspective on things.

We cannot therefore understand our desires and emotions as all brute, and in particular we cannot make sense of our discrimination of some desires as more important and fundamental, or of our repudiation of others, unless we understand our feelings to be import-attributing. This is essential to there being what we have called strong evaluation. Consequently the half-way position which admits strong evaluation, admits therefore that there may be inner obstacles to freedom, and yet will not admit that the subject may be wrong or mistaken about these purposes—this position doesn't seem tenable. For the only way to make the subject's assessment incorrigible in principle would be to claim that there was nothing to be right or wrong about here; and that could only be so if experiencing a given feeling were a matter of the qualities of brute feeling. But this it cannot be if we are to make sense of the whole background of strong evaluation, more significant goals, and aims that we repudiate. This whole scheme requires that we understand the emotions concerned as import-attributing, as, indeed, it is clear that we must do on other grounds as well.

But once we admit that our feelings are import-attributing, then we admit the possibility of error, or false appreciation. And indeed, we have to admit a kind of false appreciation which the agent himself detects in order to make sense of the

---

[4] Compare the unease we feel at the reconditioning of the hero of Anthony Burgess's *A Clockwork Orange*.

cases where we experience our own desires as fetters. How can we exclude in principle that there may be other false appreciations which the agent does not detect? That he may be profoundly in error, that is, have a very distorted sense of his fundamental purposes? Who can say that such people can't exist? All cases are, of course, controversial; but I should nominate Charles Manson and Andreas Baader for this category, among others. I pick them out as people with a strong sense of some purposes and goals as incomparably more fundamental than others, or at least with a propensity to act the having such a sense so as to take in even themselves a good part of the time, but whose sense of fundamental purpose was shot through with confusion and error. And once we recognize such extreme cases, how avoid admitting that many of the rest of mankind can suffer to a lesser degree from the same disabilities?

What has this got to do with freedom? Well, to resume what we have seen: our attributions of freedom make sense against a background sense of more and less significant purposes, for the question of freedom/unfreedom is bound up with the frustration/fulfilment of our purposes. Further, our significant purposes can be frustrated by our own desires, and where these are sufficiently based on misappreciation, we consider them as not really ours, and experience them as fetters. A man's freedom can therefore be hemmed in by internal, motivational obstacles, as well as external ones. A man who is driven by spite to jeopardize his most important relationships, in spite of himself, as it were, or who is prevented by unreasoning fear from taking up the career he truly wants, is not really made more free if one lifts the external obstacles to his venting his spite or acting on his fear. Or at best he is liberated into a very impoverished freedom.

If through linguistic/ideological purism one wants to stick to the crude definition, and insist that men are equally freed from whom the same external obstacles are lifted, regardless of their motivational state, then one will just have to introduce some other term to mark the distinction, and say that one man is capable of taking proper advantage of his freedom, and the other (the one in the grip of spite, or fear) is not. This is because in the meaningful sense of 'free', that for which we value it, in the sense of being able to act on one's important purposes, the internally fettered man is not free. If we choose to give 'free' a special (Hobbesian) sense which avoids this issue, we'll just have to introduce another term to deal with it.

Moreover since we have already seen that we are always making judgements of degrees of freedom, based on the significance of the activities or purposes which are left unfettered, how can we deny that the man, externally free but still stymied by his repudiated desires, is less free than one who has no such inner obstacles?

But if this is so, then can we not say of the man with a highly distorted view of his fundamental purpose, the Manson or Baader of my discussion above, that he may not be significantly freer when we lift even the internal barriers to his doing what is in line with this purpose, or at best may be liberated into a very impoverished freedom? Should a Manson overcome his last remaining compunction against sending his minions to kill on caprice, so that he could act unchecked, would we consider him freer, as we should undoubtedly consider the man who had done away with spite or unreasoning fear? Hardly, and certainly not to the same degree. For what he sees as his purpose here partakes so much of the nature of spite and unreasoning fear in the other cases, that is, it is an aspiration largely shaped by confusion, illusion, and distorted perspective.

Once we see that we make distinctions of degree and significance in freedoms depending on the significance of the purpose fettered/enabled, how can we deny that it makes a difference to the degree of freedom not only whether one of my basic purposes is frustrated by my own desires but also whether I have grievously misidentified this purpose? The only way to avoid this would be to hold that there is no such thing as getting it wrong, that your basic purpose is just what you feel it to be. But there is such a thing as getting it wrong, as we have seen, and the very distinctions of significance depend on this fact.

But if this is so, then the crude negative view of freedom, the Hobbesian definition, is untenable. Freedom can't just be the absence of external obstacles, for there may also be internal ones. And nor may the internal obstacles be just confined to those that the subject identifies as such, so that he is the final arbiter; for he may be profoundly mistaken about his purposes and about what he wants to repudiate. And if so, he is less capable of freedom in the meaningful sense of the word. Hence we cannot maintain the incorrigibility of the subject's judgements about his freedom, or rule out second-guessing, as we put it above. And at the same time, we are forced to abandon the pure opportunity-concept of freedom.

For freedom now involves my being able to recognize adequately my more important purposes, and my being able to overcome or at least neutralize my motivational fetters, as well as my way being free of external obstacles. But clearly the first condition (and, I would argue, also the second) require me to have become something, to have achieved a certain condition of self-clairvoyance and self-understanding. I must be actually exercising self-understanding in order to be truly or fully free. I can no longer understand freedom just as an opportunity-concept.

In all these three formulations of the issue—opportunity-versus exercise-concept; whether freedom requires that we discriminate among motivations; whether it allows of second-guessing the subject—the extreme negative view shows up as wrong. The idea of holding the Maginot Line before this Hobbesian concept is misguided not only because it involves abandoning some of the most inspiring terrain of liberalism, which is concerned with individual self-realization, but also because the line turns out to be untenable. The first step from the Hobbesian definition to a positive notion, to a view of freedom as the ability to fulfil my purposes, is one we cannot help taking. Whether we must also take the second step, to a view of freedom which sees it as realizable or fully realizable only within a certain form of society; and whether in taking a step of this kind one is necessarily committed to justifying the excesses of totalitarian oppression in the name of liberty; these are questions which must now be addressed. What is certain is that they cannot simply be evaded by a philistine definition of freedom which relegates them by fiat to the limbo of metaphysical pseudo-questions. This is altogether too quick a way with them.

EIGHT

CAPITALISM, FREEDOM, AND THE PROLETARIAT

G. A. Cohen

1. In capitalist societies everyone owns something, be it only his own labour power, and each is free to sell what he owns, and to buy whatever the sale of what he owns enables him to buy. Many claims made on capitalism's behalf are questionable, but here is a freedom which it certainly provides.

It is easy to show that under capitalism everyone has some of this freedom, especially if being free to sell something is compatible with not being free not to sell it, two conditions whose consistency I would defend. Australians are free to vote, even though they are not free not to vote, since voting is mandatory in Australia. One could say that Australians are forced to vote, but that proves that they are free to vote, as follows: one cannot be forced to do what one cannot do, and one cannot do what one is not free to do. Hence one is free to do what one is forced to do. Resistance to this odd-sounding but demonstrable conclusion comes from failure to distinguish the idea of being free to do something from other ideas, such as the idea of doing something freely.

Look at it this way: before you are forced to do A, you are, except in unusual cases, free to do A and free not to do A.

G. A. Cohen, 'Capitalism, Freedom, and the Proletariat', from *The Idea of Freedom*, ed. A. Ryan (Oxford: Oxford University Press, 1979). The present extensively revised version draws heavily on two of Cohen's later papers: 'Illusions about Private Property and Freedom', in John Mepham and David Ruben (eds.), *Issues in Marxist Philosophy*, iv (Brighton, 1981), and 'The Structure of Proletarian Unfreedom', *Philosophy and Public Affairs*, 12. 1 (Winter, 1983), reprinted as ch. 13 of Cohen's *History, Labour, and Freedom* (Oxford, 1988).

The force removes the second freedom, not the first. It puts no obstacle in the path of your doing A, so you are still free to. Note, too, that you could frustrate someone who sought to force you to do A by making yourself not free to do it.

I labour this truth—that one is free to do what one is forced to do—because it, and failure to perceive it, help to explain the character and persistence of a certain ideological disagreement. Marxists say that working-class people are forced to sell their labour power, a thesis we shall look at later. Bourgeois thinkers celebrate the freedom of contract manifest not only in the capitalist's purchase of labour power but in the worker's sale of it. If Marxists are right, then workers, being forced to sell their labour power, are, in an important way, unfree. But it must remain true that (unlike chattel slaves) they are free to sell their labour power. Accordingly, the unfreedom asserted by Marxists is compatible with the freedom asserted by bourgeois thinkers. Indeed: if the Marxists are right, the bourgeois thinkers are right, unless they also think, as characteristically they do, that the truth they emphasize refutes the Marxist claim. The bourgeois thinkers go wrong not when they say that the worker is free to sell his labour power, but when they infer that the Marxist cannot therefore be right in his claim that the worker is forced to. And Marxists[1] share the bourgeois thinkers' error when they think it necessary to deny what the bourgeois thinkers say. If the worker is not free to sell his labour power, of what freedom is a foreigner whose work permit is removed deprived? Would not the Marxists who wrongly deny that workers are free to sell their labour power nevertheless protest, inconsistently, that

---

[1] Such as Ziyad Husami, if he is a Marxist, who says of the wage-worker: 'Deprived of the ownership of means of production and means of livelihood he is forced (not free) to sell his labour power to the capitalist' ('Marx on Distributive Justice', *Philosophy and Public Affairs*, 8. 1 (Autumn, 1978), 51–2). I contend that the phrase in parentheses introduces a falsehood into Husami's sentence, a falsehood which Karl Marx avoided when he said of the worker that 'the period of time for which he is free to sell his labour power is the period of time for which he is forced to sell it' (*Capital*, i, (Harmondsworth, 1976), 415; cf. p. 932: 'the wage-labourer . . . is compelled to sell himself of his own free will').

such disfranchised foreigners have been deprived of a freedom?[2]

2. Freedom to buy and sell is one freedom of which in capitalism there is a great deal. It belongs to capitalism's essential nature. But many think that capitalism is, quite as essentially, a more comprehensively free society. They believe that, *if* what you value is freedom, as opposed, for example, to equality, then you should be in favour of an unmixed capitalist economy without a welfare sector. In the opinion I am describing, one may or may not favour such a purely capitalist society, but, if one disfavours it, then one's reason for doing so must be an attachment to values other than freedom, since, from the point of view of freedom, there is little to be said against pure capitalism. It is in virtue of the prevalence of this opinion that so many English-speaking philosophers and economists now call the doctrine which recommends a purely capitalist society 'libertarianism'.

It is not only those who call themselves 'libertarians' who believe that that is the right name for their party. Many who reject their aim endorse their name: they do not support unmodified capitalism, but they agree that it maximizes freedom. This applies to *some* of those who call themselves 'liberals', and Thomas Nagel is one of them. Nagel says that 'libertarianism exalts the claim of individual freedom of action', and he believes that it does so too much. He believes that it goes too far towards the liberty end of a spectrum on which he believes leftists go too far towards the equality end.[3]

Nagel-like liberals—and henceforth, by 'liberals', I shall mean ones of the Nagel kind—assert, plausibly, that liberty is

---

[2] For a more developed account of the relations between force and freedom, see *History, Labour, and Freedom*, pp. 239–47.

[3] 'Libertarianism . . . fastens on one of the two elements [that is, freedom and equality—G. A. Cohen] of the liberal ideal and asks why its realization should be inhibited by the demands of the other. Instead of embracing the ideal of equality and the general welfare, libertarianism exalts the claim of individual freedom of action and asks why state power should be permitted even the interference represented by progressive taxation and public provision of health care, education and a minimum standard of living' ('Libertarianism without Foundations', in J. Paul (ed.), *Reading Nozick* (Totowa, NJ, 1981), 192).

a good thing, but they say that it is not the only good thing. So far, libertarians will agree. But liberals also believe that libertarians wrongly sacrifice other good things in too total defence of the one good of liberty. They agree with libertarians that pure capitalism is liberty pure and simple, or anyway *economic* liberty pure and simple, but they think the various good things lost when liberty pure and simple is the rule justify restraints on liberty. They want a capitalism modified by welfare legislation and state intervention in the market. They advocate, they say, not unrestrained liberty, but liberty restrained by the demands of social and economic equality. They think that what they call a free economy is too damaging to those who, by nature or circumstance, are ill placed to achieve a minimally proper standard of life within it, so they favour, within limits, taxing the better off for the sake of the worse off, although they believe that such taxation interferes with liberty. They also think that what they call a free economy is subject to fluctuations in productive activity and misallocations of resources which are potentially damaging to everyone, so they favour measures of interference in the market, although, again, they believe that such interventions diminish liberty. They do not question the libertarian description of capitalism as the (economically) free society, the society whose economic agents are not, or only minimally, interfered with by the state. But they believe that economic freedom may rightly and reasonably be abridged. They believe in a compromise between liberty and other values, and that what is known as the welfare state mixed economy approaches the right sort of compromise.

3. I shall argue that libertarians, and liberals of the kind described, misuse the concept of freedom. That is not, as it stands, a comment on the attractiveness of the institutions they severally favour, but on the rhetoric they use to describe those institutions. If, however, and as I contend, they misdescribe those institutions, then a correct description of them might make them appear less attractive, and then my critique of the defensive rhetoric would indirectly be a critique of the institutions the rhetoric defends.

My principal contention is that, while liberals and libertarians see the freedom which is intrinsic to capitalism, they overlook the unfreedom which necessarily accompanies capitalist freedom.

To expose this failure of perception, I shall begin by criticizing a description of the libertarian position provided by the libertarian philosopher Antony Flew in his *Dictionary of Philosophy*. Flew defines 'libertarianism' as 'whole-hearted political and economic liberalism, opposed to any social or legal constraints on individual freedom'. Liberals of the Nagel kind would avow themselves *un*whole-hearted in the terms of Flew's definition. For they would say that they support certain (at any rate) legal constraints on individual freedom. Indeed, after laying down his definition of 'libertarianism', Flew adds that 'the term was introduced in this sense by people who believe that, especially but not only in the United States, those who pass as liberals are often much more sympathetic to socialism than to classical liberalism'.[4]

Now a society in which there are *no* 'social and legal constraints on individual freedom' is perhaps imaginable, at any rate by people who have highly anarchic imaginations. But, be that as it may, the Flew definition misdescribes libertarians, since it does not apply to defenders of capitalism, which is what libertarians profess to be, and are. For consider: If the state prevents me from doing something I want to do, it evidently places a constraint on my freedom. Suppose, then, that I want to perform an action which involves a legally prohibited use of your property. I want, let us say, to pitch a tent in your large back garden, perhaps just in order to annoy you, or perhaps for the more substantial reason that I have nowhere to live and no land of my own, but I have got hold of a tent, legitimately or otherwise. If I now try to do this thing I want to do, the chances are that the state will intervene on your behalf. If it does, I shall suffer a constraint on my freedom. The same goes for all unpermitted uses of a piece of private property by those who do not own it, and there are always those who do not own it, since 'private ownership by one person presupposes non-ownership on the part of other persons'.[5] But the free enterprise economy advocated by

[4] *A Dictionary of Philosophy* (London, 1979), 188.
[5] Karl Marx, *Capital*, iii (Harmondsworth, 1978), 812.

libertarians and described as the 'free' economy by liberals rests upon private property: you can sell and buy only what you respectively own and come to own. It follows that the Flew definition is untrue to its *definiendum*, and that the term 'libertarianism' is a gross misnomer for the position it now standardly denotes among philosophers and economists.

4. How could Flew have brought himself to publish the definition I have criticized? I do not think that he was being dishonest. I would not accuse him of appreciating the truth of this particular matter and deliberately falsifying it. Why then is it that Flew, and libertarians like him, *and* liberals of the kind I described, see the unfreedom in state interference with a person's use of his property, but fail to note the unfreedom in the standing intervention against anyone else's use of it entailed by the fact that it is that person's private property? What explains their monocular vision? (By that question, I do not mean: what motive do they have for seeing things that way? I mean: how is it possible for them to see things that way? What intellectual mechanism or mechanisms operate to sustain their view of the matter?)

Notice that we can ask similar questions about how anti-libertarian liberals are able to entertain the description which they favour of *modified* capitalism. According to Nagel, 'progressive taxation' entails 'interference' with individual freedom.[6] He regards the absence of such interference as a value, but one which needs to be compromised for the sake of greater economic and social equality, as what he calls the 'formidable challenge to liberalism . . . from the left' maintains.[7] Yet it is quite unclear that social democratic restriction on the sway of private property, through devices like progressive taxation and the welfare minimum, represents *any* enhancement of governmental interference with freedom. The government certainly interferes with a land-owner's freedom when it establishes public rights of way and the right of others to pitch tents on his land. But it also interferes with the freedom of a would-be walker or tent-pitcher when it prevents

---

[6] See n. 3 above.
[7] 'Libertarianism without Foundations', p. 191.

them from indulging *their* individual inclinations. The general point is that incursions against private property which *reduce* owners' freedom and transfer rights over resources to non-owners thereby *increase* the latter's freedom. The net effect on freedom of the resource transfer is, therefore, in advance of further information and argument, a moot point.

Libertarians are against what they describe as an 'interventionist' policy in which the state engages in 'interference'. Nagel is not, but he agrees that such a policy 'intervenes' and 'interferes'. In my view, the use of words like 'interventionist' to designate the stated policy is an ideological distortion detrimental to clear thinking and friendly to the libertarian point of view. It is, though friendly to that point of view, consistent with rejecting it, and Nagel does reject it, vigorously. But, by acquiescing in the libertarian use of 'intervention', he casts libertarianism in a better light than it deserves. The standard use of 'intervention' esteems the private property component in the liberal or social democratic settlement too highly, by associating that component too closely with freedom.

5. I now offer a two-part explanation of the tendency of libertarians and liberals to overlook the interference in people's lives induced by private property. The two parts of the explanation are independent of each other. The first part emerges when we remind ourselves that 'social and legal constraints on freedom' (see p. 167 above) are not the only source of restriction on human action. It restricts my possibilities of action that I lack wings, and therefore cannot fly without major mechanical assistance, but that is not a social or legal constraint on my freedom. Now I suggest that one explanation of our theorists' failure to note that private property constrains freedom is a tendency to take as part of the structure of human existence in general, and therefore as no social or legal constraint on freedom, any structure around which, *merely as things are*, much of our activity is organized. A structure which is not a permanent part of the human condition can be misperceived as being just that, and the institution of private property is a case in point. It is treated as so given that the obstacles it puts on freedom are not

perceived, while any impingement on private property itself is immediately noticed. Yet private property, like any system of rights, pretty well *is* a particular way of distributing freedom *and unfreedom*. It is necessarily associated with the liberty of private owners to do as they wish with what they own, but it no less necessarily withdraws liberty from those who do not own it. To think of capitalism as a realm of freedom is to overlook half of its nature.

I am aware that the tendency to the failure of perception which I have described and tried to explain is stronger, other things being equal, the more private property a person has. I do not think really poor people need to have their eyes opened to the simple conceptual truth I emphasize. I also do not claim that anyone of sound mind will for long deny that private property places restrictions on freedom, once the point has been made. What is striking is that the point so often needs to be made, against what should be *obvious* absurdities, such as Flew's definition of 'libertarianism'.

6. But there is a further and independent and conceptually more subtle explanation of how people[8] are able to believe that there is no restriction, or only minimal restriction, of freedom under capitalism, which I now want to expound.

You will notice that I have supposed that to prevent someone from doing something he wants to do is to make him, in that respect, unfree; I am *pro tanto* unfree *whenever* someone interferes with my actions, whether *or not I have a right to perform them, and whether or not my obstructor has a right to interfere with me.* But there is a definition of freedom which informs much libertarian writing and which entails that interference is not a sufficient condition of unfreedom. On that definition, which may be called the rights definition of freedom, I am unfree only when someone prevents me from doing what I have a right to do, so that he, consequently, has no right to prevent me from doing it. Thus Robert Nozick says: 'Other people's actions place limits on one's available opportunities. Whether

---

[8] This part of the explanation applies more readily to libertarian than to liberal ideological perception. It does also apply to the latter, but by a route too complex to set out here.

this makes one's resulting action non-voluntary depends upon whether these others had the right to act as they did.'[9]

Now, if one combines this rights definition of freedom with a moral endorsement of private property, with a claim that, in standard cases, people have a moral right to the property they legally own, then one reaches the result that the protection of legitimate private property cannot restrict anyone's freedom. It will follow from the moral endorsement of private property that you and the police are justified in preventing me from pitching my tent on your land, and, because of the rights definition of freedom, it will then further follow that you and the police do not thereby restrict my freedom. So here we have a further explanation of how intelligent philosophers are able to say what they do about capitalism, private property, and freedom. But the characterization of freedom which figures in the explanation is unacceptable. For it entails that a properly convicted murderer is not rendered unfree when he is justifiably imprisoned.

Even justified interference reduces freedom. But suppose for a moment that, as libertarians say or imply, it does not. On that supposition one cannot argue, without further ado, that interference with private property is wrong *because* it reduces freedom. For one can no longer take it for granted, what is evident on a normatively neutral account of freedom, that interference with private property *does* reduce freedom. On a rights account of what freedom is one must abstain from that assertion until one has shown that people have moral rights to their private property. Yet libertarians tend *both* to use a rights definition of freedom *and* to take it for granted that interference with his private property diminishes the owner's freedom. But they can take that for granted only on the normatively neutral account of freedom, on which, however, it is equally obvious that the protection of private property diminishes the freedom of *non*-owners, to avoid which consequence they adopt a rights definition of the concept. And so they go, back and forth, between inconsistent definitions of freedom, not because they cannot make up their minds which one they like better, but under the propulsion of their desire to

[9] *Anarchy, State and Utopia* (New York, 1974), 262.

occupy what is in fact an untenable position. Libertarians want to say that interferences with people's use of their private property are unacceptable because they are, quite obviously, abridgements of freedom, and that the reason why protection of private property does not similarly abridge the freedom of non-owners is that owners have a right to exclude others from their property and non-owners consequently have no right to use it. But they can say all that only if they define freedom in two inconsistent ways.

7. Now, I have wanted to show that private property, and therefore capitalist society, limit liberty, but I have not said that they do so more than communal property and socialist society. Each form of society is by its nature congenial and hostile to various sorts of liberty, for variously placed people. And concrete societies exemplifying either form will offer and withhold additional liberties whose presence or absence may not be inferred from the nature of the form itself. Which form is better for liberty, all things considered, is a question which may have no answer in the abstract. Which form is better for liberty may depend on the historical circumstances.[10]

I say that capitalism and socialism offer different sets of freedoms, but I emphatically do not say that they provide freedom in two different senses of that term. To the claim that capitalism gives people freedom some socialists respond that what they get is *merely bourgeois* freedom. Good things can be meant by that response: that there are important particular liberties which capitalism does not confer; and/or that I do not have freedom, but only a necessary condition of it, when a course of action (for example, skiing) is, though not *itself* against the law, unavailable to me anyway, because other laws (for example, those of private property, which prevent a poor man from using a rich man's unused skis) forbid me the means to perform it. But when socialists suggest that there is no 'real' freedom under capitalism, at any rate for the workers, or that socialism promises freedom of a higher and as yet unrealized kind, then, so I think, their line is theoretically incorrect and politically disastrous. For there is freedom

[10] For further discussion of that question, see 'Illusions about Private Property and Freedom', pp. 232–5.

under capitalism, in a plain, good sense, and if socialism will not give us more of it, we shall rightly be disappointed. If the socialist says he is offering a new variety of freedom, the advocate of capitalism will carry the day with his reply that he prefers freedom of the known variety to an unexplained and unexemplified rival. But if, as I would recommend, the socialist argues that capitalism is, all things considered, inimical to freedom *in the very sense* of 'freedom' in which, as he should concede, a person's freedom is diminished when his private property is tampered with, then he presents a challenge which the advocate of capitalism, by virtue of his own commitment, cannot ignore.

For it is a contention of socialist thought that capitalism does not live up to its own professions. A fundamental socialist challenge to the libertarian is that pure capitalism does not protect liberty in general, but rather those liberties which are built into private property, an institution which also limits liberty. And a fundamental socialist challenge to the liberal is that the modifications of modified capitalism modify not liberty, but private property, often in the interest of liberty itself. Consequently, transformations far more revolutionary than a liberal would contemplate might be justified on grounds similar to those which support liberal reform.

A homespun example shows how communal property offers a differently shaped liberty, in no different sense of that term, and, in certain circumstances, more liberty than the private property alternative. Neighbours *A* and *B* own sets of household tools. Each has some tools which the other lacks. If *A* needs a tool of a kind which only *B* has, then, private property being what it is, he is not free to take *B*'s one for a while, even if *B* does not need it during that while. Now imagine that the following rule is imposed, bringing the tools into partly common ownership: each may take and use a tool belonging to the other without permission provided that the other is not using it and that he returns it when he no longer needs it, or when the other needs it, whichever comes first. *Things being what they are* (a substantive qualification: we are talking, as often we should, about the real world, not about remote possibilities) the communizing rule would, I contend, increase tool-using freedom, on any reasonable view. To be sure, some freedoms are removed by the new rule. Neither neighbour is as assured of the same easy access as before to the tools that were wholly his. Sometimes he has to go next door to retrieve one of them. Nor can either now charge the other for use of a tool he himself does not then require. But these restrictions probably count for less than the increase in the range of tools available. No one is as sovereign as before over any tool, so the privateness of the property is reduced. But freedom is probably expanded.

It is true that each would have more freedom still if he were the sovereign owner of *all* the tools. But that is not the relevant comparison. I do not deny that full ownership of a thing gives greater freedom than shared ownership of that thing. But no one did own all the tools before the modest measure of communism was introduced. The kind of comparison we need to make is between, for example, sharing ownership with ninety-nine others in a hundred things and fully owning just one of them. I submit that which arrangement nets more freedom is a matter of cases. There is little sense in one hundred people sharing control over one hundred tooth-brushes. There is an overwhelming case, from the point of view of freedom, in favour of our actual practice of public ownership of street pavements. Denationalizing the pavements in favour of private ownership of each piece by the residents adjacent to it would be bad for freedom of movement.

8. Sensible neighbours who make no self-defeating fetish of private property might contract into a communism of household tools. But that way of achieving communism cannot be generalized. We could not by contract bring into fully mutual ownership those non-household tools and resources which Marxists call means of production. They will never be won for socialism by contract, since they belong to a small minority, to whom the rest can offer no quid pro quo.[11]

---

[11] Unless the last act of this scenario qualifies as a contract: in the course of a general strike a united working class demands that private property in major means of production be socialized, as a condition of their return to work, and a demoralized capitalist class meets the demand. (How, by the way, could libertarians object to such a revolution? For hints, see Robert

Most of the rest must hire out their labour power to members of that minority, in exchange for the right to some of the proceeds of their labour on facilities in whose ownership they do not share.

So we reach, at length, the third item in the title of this paper, and an important charge, with respect to liberty, which Marxists lay against capitalism. It is that in capitalist society the great majority of people are forced to sell their labour power, because they do not own any means of production. The rest of this paper addresses a powerful objection to that Marxist charge.

To lay the ground for the objection, I must explain how the predicate 'is forced to sell his labour power' is used in the Marxist charge. Marxism characterizes classes by reference to social relations of production, and the claim that workers are forced to sell their labour power is intended to satisfy that condition: it purports to say something about the proletarian's position in capitalist relations of production. But relations of production are, for Marxism, *objective*: what relations of production a person is in does not turn on his consciousness. It follows that if the proletarian is forced to sell his labour power in the relevant Marxist sense, then this must be because of his objective situation, and not merely because of his attitude to himself, his level of self-confidence, his cultural attainment, and so on. It is in any case doubtful that limitations in those subjective endowments can be sources of what interests us: unfreedom, as opposed to something similar to it but also rather different: incapacity. But even if diffidence and the like could be said to force a person to sell his labour power, that would be an irrelevant case here.[12]

9. Under the stated interpretation of 'is forced to sell his labour power', a serious problem arises for the thesis under examination. For if there are persons whose objective position is

Nozick, 'Coercion', in P. Laslett, W. G. Runciman, and Q. Skinner, *Philosophy, Politics and Society*, 4th ser. (Oxford, 1972).

[12] Except, perhaps, where personal subjective limitations are explained by capitalist relations of production: see *History, Labour, and Freedom*, pp. 278–9.

standardly proletarian but who are not forced to sell their labour power, then the thesis is false. And there do seem to be such persons.

I have in mind those proletarians who, initially possessed of no greater resources than most, secure positions in the petty bourgeoisie and elsewhere, thereby rising above the proletariat. Striking cases in Britain are members of certain immigrant groups, who arrive penniless, and without good connections, but who propel themselves up the class hierarchy with effort, skill, and luck. One thinks—it is a contemporary example—of those who are willing to work very long hours in shops bought from native British petty bourgeois, shops which used to close early. Their initial capital is typically an amalgam of savings, which they accumulated, perhaps painfully, while still in the proletarian condition, and some form of external finance. *Objectively speaking*, most[13] British proletarians are in a position to obtain these. Therefore most British proletarians are not forced to sell their labour power.

10. I now refute two predictable objections to the above argument.

The first says that the recently mentioned persons were, *while they were proletarians*, forced to sell their labour power. Their cases do not show that proletarians are not forced to sell their labour power. They show something different: that proletarians are not forced to remain proletarians.

This objection illegitimately contracts the scope of the Marxist claim that workers are forced to sell their labour power. But before I say what Marxists intend by that statement, I must defend this general claim about freedom and constraint: *fully explicit attributions of freedom and constraint contain two temporal indexes*. To illustrate: I may now be in a position truly to say that I am free to attend a concert tomorrow night, since nothing has occurred, up to now, to prevent my doing so. If so, I am *now* free to attend a concert *tomorrow night*. In similar fashion, the time when I am

---

[13] At least most: it could be argued that *all* British proletarians are in such a position, but I stay with 'most' lest some ingenious person discover objective proletarian circumstances worse than the worst one suffered by now prospering immigrants. But see also n. 14 below.

constrained to perform an action need not be identical with the time of the action: I might *already* be forced to attend a concert *tomorrow night* (since you might already have ensured that if I do not, I shall suffer some great loss).

Now when Marxists say that proletarians are forced to sell their labour power, they mean more than '*X* is a proletarian at time *t* only if *X* is at *t* forced to sell his labour power at *t*'; for that would be compatible with his not being forced to at time *t* + *n*, no matter how small *n* is. *X* might be forced on Tuesday to sell his labour power on Tuesday, but if he is not forced on Tuesday to sell his labour power on Wednesday (if, for example, actions open to him on Tuesday would bring it about that on Wednesday he need not do so), then, though still a proletarian on Tuesday, he is not then someone who is forced to sell his labour power in the relevant Marxist sense. The manifest intent of the Marxist claim is that the proletarian is forced at *t* to *continue* to sell his labour power, throughout a period from *t* to *t* + *n*, for some considerable *n*. It follows that because there is a route out of the proletariat, which our counter-examples travelled, reaching their destination in, as I would argue, an amount of time less than *n*,[14] they were, though proletarians, not forced to sell their labour power in the required Marxist sense.

Proletarians who have the option of class ascent are not forced to continue to sell their labour power, just because they do have that option. Most proletarians have it as much as our counter-examples did. Therefore most proletarians are not forced to sell their labour power.

11. But now I face a second objection. It is that necessarily not more than a few proletarians can exercise the option of

---

[14] This might well be challenged, since the size of *n* is a matter of judgement. I would defend mine by reference to the naturalness of saying to a worker that he is not forced to (continue to) sell his labour power, since he can take steps to set himself up as a shopkeeper. Those who judge otherwise might be able, at a pinch, to deny that most proletarians are not forced to sell their labour power, but they cannot dispose of the counter-examples to the generalization that all are forced to. For our prospective petty bourgeois is a proletarian on the eve of his ascent when, unless, absurdly, we take *n* as 0, he is not forced to sell his labour power.

upward movement. For capitalism requires a substantial hired labour force, which would not exist if more than just a few workers rose.[15] Put differently, there are necessarily only enough petty bourgeois and other non-proletarian positions for a small number of the proletariat to leave their estate.

I agree with the premiss, but does it defeat the argument against which it is directed? Does it refute the claim that most proletarians are not forced to sell their labour power? I think not.

An analogy will indicate why I do not think so. Ten people are placed in a room, the only exit from which is a huge and heavy locked door. At various distances from each lies a single heavy key. Whoever picks up this key—and each is physically able, with varying degrees of effort, to do so—and takes it to the door will find, after considerable self-application, a way to open the door and leave the room. But if he does so he alone will be able to leave it. Photoelectric devices installed by a gaoler ensure that it will open only just enough to permit one exit. Then it will close, and no one inside the room will be able to open it again.

It follows that, whatever happens, at least nine people will remain in the room.

Now suppose that not one of the people is inclined to try to obtain the key and leave the room. Perhaps the room is no bad place, and they do not want to leave it. Or perhaps it is pretty bad, but they are too lazy to undertake the effort needed to escape. Or perhaps no one believes he would be able to secure the key in face of the capacity of the others to intervene (though no one would in fact intervene, since, being so diffident, each also believes that he would be unable to remove the key from anyone else). Suppose that, whatever may be their reasons, they are all so indisposed to leave the room that if, counterfactually, one of them were to try to leave, the rest

---

[15] 'The truth is this, that in this bourgeois society every workman, if he is an exceedingly clever and shrewd fellow, and gifted with bourgeois instincts and favoured by an exceptional fortune, can possibly convert himself into an *exploiteur du travail d'autrui*. But if there were no *travail* to be *exploité*, there would be no capitalist nor capitalist production' (Karl Marx, 'Results of the Immediate Process of Production', in *Capital*, i. 1079). For commentary on similar texts, see my *Karl Marx's Theory of History* (Oxford, 1978), 243.

would not interfere. The universal inaction is relevant to my argument, but the explanation of it is not.

Then whomever we select, it is true of the other nine that not one of them is going to try to get the key. Therefore it is true of the selected person that he is free to obtain the key, and to use it.[16] He is therefore not forced to remain in the room. But all that is true of whomever we select. Therefore it is true of each person that he is not forced to remain in the room, even though necessarily at least nine will remain in the room, and in fact all will.

Consider now a slightly different example, a modified version of the situation just described. In the new case there are two doors and two keys. Again, there are ten people, but this time one of them does try to get out, and succeeds, while the rest behave as before. Now necessarily eight will remain in the room, but it is true of each of the nine who do stay that he or she is free to leave it. The pertinent general feature, present in both cases, is that there is at least one means of egress which none will attempt to use, and which each is free to use, since, *ex hypothesi*, no one would block his way.

By now the application of the analogy may be obvious. The number of exits from the proletariat is, as a matter of objective circumstance, small. But most proletarians are not trying to escape, and, as a result, *it is false that each exit is being actively attempted by some proletarian*. Therefore for most[17] proletarians there exists a means of escape. So even though necessarily most proletarians will remain proletarians, and will sell their labour power, perhaps none, and at most a minority, are forced to do so.

In reaching this conclusion, which is about the proletariat's *objective* position, I used some facts of consciousness, regarding workers' aspirations and intentions. That is legitimate. For if

[16] For whatever may be the correct analysis of '*X* is free to do *A*', it is clear that *X* is free to do *A* if *X* would do *A* if he tried to do *A*, and that sufficient condition of freedom is all that we need here. (Some have objected that the stated condition is not sufficient: a person, they say, may do something he is not free to do, since he may do something he is not legally, or morally, free to do. Those who agree with that unhelpful remark can take it that I am interested in the non-normative use of 'free', which is distinguished by the sufficient condition just stated.)

[17] See nn. 13, 14 above.

workers are objectively forced to sell their labour power, then they are forced to do so whatever their subjective situation may be. But their actual subjective situation brings it about that they are not forced to sell their labour power. Hence they are not objectively forced to sell their labour power.

12. One could say, speaking rather broadly, that we have found more freedom in the proletariat's situation than classical Marxism asserts. But if we return to the basis on which we affirmed that most proletarians are not forced to sell their labour power, we shall arrive at a more refined description of the objective position with respect to force and freedom. What was said will not be withdrawn, but we shall add significantly to it.

That basis was the reasoning originally applied to the case of the people in the locked room. Each is free to seize the key and leave. But note the conditional nature of his freedom. He is free not only *because* none of the others tries to get the key, but *on condition* that they do not (a condition which, in the story, is fulfilled). Then *each is free only on condition that the others do not exercise their similarly conditional freedom.* Not more than one can exercise the liberty they all have. If, moreover, any one were to exercise it, then, because of the structure of the situation, all the others would lose it.

Since the freedom of each is contingent on the others not exercising their similarly contingent freedom, we can say that there is a great deal of unfreedom in their situation. Though each is individually free to leave, he suffers with the rest from what I shall call *collective unfreedom.*

In defence of that description, let us reconsider the question why the people do not try to leave. None of the reasons suggested earlier—lack of desire, laziness, diffidence—go beyond what a person wants and fears for himself alone. But sometimes people care about the fate of others, and they sometimes have that concern when they share a common oppression. Suppose, then, not so wildly, that there is a sentiment of solidarity in that room. A fourth possible explanation of the absence of attempt to leave now suggests itself. It is that no one will be satisfied with a personal escape which is not part of a general liberation.

The new supposition does not upset the claim that each is free to leave, for we may assume that it remains true of each person that he would suffer no interference if, counterfactually, he sought to use the key (assume that the others would have contempt for him, but not try to stop him). So each remains free to leave. Yet we can envisage members of the group communicating to their gaoler a demand for freedom, to which he could hardly reply that they are free already (even though, individually, they are). The hypothesis of solidarity makes the collective unfreedom evident. But unless we say, absurdly, that the solidarity creates the unfreedom to which it is a response, we must say that there is collective unfreedom whether or not solidarity obtains.

Returning to the proletariat, we can conclude, by parity of reasoning, that although most proletarians are free to escape the proletariat, and, indeed, even if every one is, the proletariat is collectively unfree, an imprisoned class.

Marx often maintained that the worker is forced to sell his labour power not to any particular capitalist, but just to some capitalist or other, and he emphasized the ideological value of that distinction.[18] The present point is that although, in a collective sense, workers are forced to sell their labour power, scarcely any particular proletarian is forced to sell himself even to some capitalist or other. And this too has ideological value. It is part of the genius of capitalist exploitation that, by contrast with exploitation which proceeds by 'extra-economic compulsion',[19] it does not require the unfreedom of specified individuals. There is an ideologically valuable anonymity on *both* sides of the relationship of exploitation.

13. It was part of the argument for affirming the freedom to escape of proletarians, taken individually, that not every exit from the proletariat is crowded with would-be escapees. Why should this be so? Here are some of the reasons.

1. It is possible to escape, but it is not easy, and often people do not attempt what is possible but hard.

2. There is also the fact that long occupancy, for example from birth, of a subordinate class position nurtures the

---

[18] See *Karl Marx's Theory of History*, p. 223, for exposition and references.

[19] Karl Marx, *Capital*, iii. 926.

illusion, which is as important for the stability of the system as the myth of easy escape, that one's class position is natural and inescapable.

3. Finally, there is the fact that not all workers would like to be petty or trans-petty bourgeois. Eugene Debs said 'I do not want to rise above the working class, I want to rise with them',[20] thereby evincing an attitude like the one lately attributed to the people in the locked room. It is sometimes true of the worker that, in Brecht's words,

> He wants no servants under him
> And no boss over his head.[21]

Those lines envisage a better liberation: not just from the working class, but from class society.[22]

---

[20] And R. H. Tawney remarked that it is not 'the noblest use of exceptional powers . . . to scramble to shore, undeterred by the thought of drowning companions' (*Equality* (London, 1964), 106.

[21] From his 'Song of the United Front'.

[22] See *History, Labour, and Freedom*, ch. 13, for a fuller and more nuanced presentation of ss. 8–13 of the foregoing article. See, too, J. Gray, 'Against Cohen on Proletarian Unfreedom', in Ellen F. Paul *et al.* (eds.), *Capitalism* (Oxford, 1989), which criticizes the material presented above. What Gray says against the claims developed in ss. 1–7 strikes me as feeble, but his critique of the idea of collective proletarian unfreedom demands a response, which I hope in due course to provide.

NINE

CONSTRAINTS ON FREEDOM

David Miller

Among the most intractable questions facing political theorists are those concerning the overall amounts of freedom provided by particular social systems.[1] Consider, as an example, the radical disagreement between libertarians and socialists over how much freedom the average person enjoys in a capitalist society. For those in the first camp, freedom under capitalism is restricted only by rules of law backed by sanctions and by such occurrences of force and fraud as the law fails to prevent.[2] Thus whatever the extent of inequality generated by the workings of the economy, any person taken at random enjoys a very great deal of freedom indeed, even if he lacks the ability or opportunity to perform a number of the actions that he is free to perform, such as becoming an employer of labor or dining at the Ritz. Capitalism, in this view, deserves its self-applied title 'the free society', since it imposes only such restrictions on freedom as are necessary to secure an equal amount of freedom for all. Those in the socialist camp take a very different view. Freedom under capitalism is unequally distributed, since freedom depends not only on the absence of legal restrictions, force, and fraud, but also on having the effective opportunity to pursue courses of action. Moreover, since conditions of work under capitalism are such as to deny

A revised and abridged version of David Miller, 'Constraints on Freedom', *Ethics* 94 (1983–84): 66–86.

[1] An earlier version of this essay was presented to the Workshop on Liberty at the European Consortium for Political Research Joint Sessions of Workshops, Florence, 1980. I should like to thank the other members of the workshop for their valuable comments. Bob Goodin commented extensively on a second draft, and I have adopted a number of his suggestions.

[2] A more extreme view still, attributable to Hayek, is that legal rules do not restrict freedom, since freedom consists in the absence of *arbitrary* coercion. This is gilding the capitalist lily. As John Gray has pointed out, Hayek's venture along this path leads him directly to a positive conception of liberty. See J. N. Gray, 'Hayek on Liberty, Rights, and Justice', *Ethics* 92 (1981–82): 73–84.

most employees the effective opportunity to perform many actions important to them, the average degree of freedom is small—indeed possibly smaller than under systems that impose many more legal restrictions on human action.

This disagreement has a number of possible sources, including disputes over the core notion of liberty itself and disputes over how different specific freedoms are to be aggregated to give an overall total for the society, but I shall focus here on one specific question, namely, what should count as a constraint on freedom. Part of what libertarians and socialists disagree about is whether certain salient features of a capitalist society, notably economic inequalities, reduce freedom, or merely make some people less able to get what they want. I shall argue that this disagreement cannot be conclusively resolved, because it involves ascribing moral responsibility for barriers to action, and this in turn depends on which theory of moral obligation one holds. Debates about social freedom cannot be kept separate from wider debates about social obligation, an issue over which libertarians and socialists are unlikely to agree.

I

Discussions of freedom and constraint usually and properly start from the distinction between being free to do something, being able to do it, and desiring to do it. A commonplace example illustrates the distinction in question. Suppose that I enjoy taking walks along the bank of a certain river, and consider the following three possibilities:

1. The local authority that administers the riverbank erects fences around it and employs a warden to keep people off. When this happens, I shall say that I am no longer free to take my walk.
2. Brambles grow and block the path so that I can't walk on the bank without tearing my clothes. In this event, I shall say that although I am still free to walk there, I am no longer able to do so.
3. The river becomes littered with offensive debris. Under these circumstances I shall say that, although I am both free and able to walk, I no longer wish to do so.

We have here three changes in my environment, each of which has the same behavioral consequence (namely, that I cease walking on the riverbank) but which we describe in different terms. In order to clarify the distinction we need to understand the point of making it. If we were only interested in behavior and its explanation, it might seem prodigal to have three alternative descriptions for the same behavioral change. But in fact we are equally interested in questions of justification. From that point of view, the source of an obstacle to potential action may be as important as its very existence. The concepts of ability and desirability make no reference to the genesis of the set of possible actions open to an agent, and the distinction between them is merely one of degree; that is, we say that an agent is unable to perform an action when it is literally impossible for him to perform it, or the performance would be so costly that it is effectively excluded from the scope of his consideration, while we say that an action is simply undesirable when the costs outweigh the benefits but not so overwhelmingly.[3] We use the notion of freedom, however, in the subclass of cases where the presence of an obstacle can be attributed to the action of another human being or beings, and we do so in order to draw attention to that fact. There are, in other words, numerous instances that can equally properly be described as cases of unfreedom or of inability, and our choice of terms will depend on whether we want to emphasize the human source of the obstacle. If, in example 1 above, I wish merely to lament the fact that a pleasurable activity is no longer open to me, I may well say that I am unable to walk on the riverbank; but if, in addition, I want to draw attention to the human agency responsible for the deprivation, I shall use the language of freedom.

This question about the origins of an obstacle is closely linked to a question about justification. Our language embodies a presumption that humans should not obstruct one another's activity. When we say of an obstacle that it renders a person unfree to act, we make a charge that stands in need of rebuttal.[4] Reasons have to be given for the continued presence of the obstacle. Of course such reasons may not be far to seek. Many restrictions of freedom are justified, whether to protect the freedom of other agents, to pro-

---

[3] We make a distinction here between 'being able to' do something and 'having the ability to' do it. The latter notion is narrower and refers to the agent's physical or psychological capacity. The former also covers cases where an agent has the capacity to act but is deterred by the costliness of an option. We should say of a badly paid worker, e.g., that he is unable to take a holiday abroad, but not that he hasn't the ability to do so.

[4] Cf. S. I. Benn and W. L. Weinstein, 'Being Free to Act, and Being a Free Man', *Mind* 80 (1971): 194–211. The present discussion is greatly indebted to this paper.

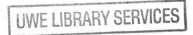

mote competing values such as welfare and equality, or to protect the agent himself. It is a mistake to think that to describe a state of affairs as involving unfreedom is to settle a political argument; it is, however, to make a *move* in a political argument.[5] There is no such presumption in cases of inability that cannot also be described as cases of unfreedom. Someone's inability to act in a certain way is morally or politically relevant only where the inability serves to bring other values into play. The fact that a speleologist is unable to escape from a cave moves us to act because we are independently concerned for his welfare; but the fact that millions of people are unable to fly to the moon doesn't move us at all.

In embodying this presumption, our language of freedom reflects the view that 'the nature of things does not madden us, only ill will does'.[6] From certain perspectives this view may appear irrational. A full-blooded determinist will see no relevant difference between obstacles brought about by human agency and obstacles arising from natural causes. If we were examining a society of robots and wanted to describe the options open to one particular robot, there would be no point in distinguishing actions that it was unfree to perform from actions that it was free but unable to perform. The behavior of the other robots would not appear to be a circumstance that was relevantly different from the rest of the environment. The language of social freedom presupposes a view of human agents as (in another sense) free and responsible for their actions.[7] We are thereby licensed to complain about restrictions of freedom in a way that would be inappropriate in the case of natural obstacles.

This view of the human agent need not be a matter of controversy between libertarians and socialists. Some socialists have indeed wanted to define freedom as the opportunity to satisfy all of one's needs, a definition that appears to obliterate the distinction between humanly caused and naturally occurring obstacles. But this might arise from

---

[5] This error may underlie Hayek's attempt to show that rules of law do not diminish freedom—so that freedom under capitalism is almost complete. See n. 2 above.

[6] Rousseau, cited in I. Berlin, 'Two Concepts of Liberty' in *Liberty,* ed. Henry Hardy (Oxford, UK: Oxford University Press, 2002) p.170 [p. 35 this volume].

[7] The freedom at issue here is freedom of the will. I have not wanted to be drawn into the debate about the compatibility of determinism and free will. The relevant line of division for our purposes lies not between determinists and indeterminists, but between strong, or 'incompatibilist,' determinists, who maintain that the truth of determinism makes ordinary notions of human choice and responsibility redundant, and everyone else.

the belief that all obstacles to the satisfaction of needs are as a matter of fact humanly caused, together with the belief that ordinary definitions of freedom invite too narrow an interpretation of the notion of constraint. (I hope that arguments in this essay will allay the latter fear.) It is hard to believe that anyone would, on political grounds alone, wish to obliterate the distinction between unfreedom and inability altogether. Since human capacities are limited and unequal, and resources are finite, under any social system we can imagine there will be actions that cannot be performed and ends that cannot be achieved. No change in social arrangements would enable me to run 100 meters in ten seconds, and no *reasonable* change would enable me, and everyone else who wanted to, to travel in space. In describing these cases, we need to be able to say that people are free, but unable, to do certain things, which distinguishes them from other cases where agents' freedom is restricted. The relevant issue is then to determine where that line should be drawn—precisely when an obstacle should be considered a constraint on freedom. This is the real issue over which libertarians and socialists disagree. The metaphysical challenge posed by a strong version of determinism can be kept to one side.

2

Having examined the context in which the problem about constraints arises we can now begin to investigate the problem itself. It has two main dimensions. First, what causal history must an obstacle to action have in order for it to count as a constraint on freedom? Up to now I have loosely contrasted 'natural' obstacles with obstacles 'attributable to human agency'. How is this contrast to be made more precise? Second, what features must the obstacle itself have for it to qualify as a constraint? Must it, at one extreme, be an obstruction that renders the proposed action impossible? Or, at the other extreme, should anything that has been done to make the action less attractive count as a reduction in one's freedom to perform it? These two dimensions are obviously separate, but it will turn out that resolving the first issue helps to resolve the second. For the sake of clarity, I shall begin by considering cases where an action has been rendered impossible in order to tackle the causal history problem and then go on to ask when, if ever, agents should be considered unfree to perform actions that they are not physically prevented from performing.

Take a simple, if mildly improbable, example. Suppose that I am the unfortunate possessor of a room whose door can only be opened from the outside, and consider the following ways in which I might become trapped in the room.

1. I am working in my room. Y, knowing that I am inside and wishing to confine me, pushes the door shut.
2. Y walks along the corridor and, without checking to see whether anybody is inside, closes my door.
3. The wind blows the door shut. It is Y's job to check rooms at 7 P.M. each evening, but he is engaged on a private errand, and this evening he fails to do so.
4. The wind blows the door shut. At 6.30 P.M. I call to a passerby to unlock the door, but the passerby, who knows about Y's duties, is busy and pays no attention.
5. Y, whose job it is to check rooms, comes to my room and looks round it. I have concealed myself in a cupboard, and he closes the door without having seen me.
6. The wind blows the door shut. There is no one assigned to check rooms and no passerby within earshot.

We are likely to be most confident in our judgments about cases 1 and 6. In case 1, I am rendered unable to leave my room by the deliberate action of another human being, and this is clearly a case where I have been made unfree to leave by Y. On the other hand, in case 6, the cause of my imprisonment is entirely natural, and we should say that I am free but unable to leave.[8] The intermediate cases are more complex. In cases 2 and 5 Y's action is the main cause of my confinement, but in another respect the cases are significantly different. In case 2 Y, although not intending to imprison me, behaves in a negligent fashion. Shutting doors without checking to see whether anyone is behind them is, under the circumstances, likely to lead to

---

[8] An alternative view here is that when I am unable to do A, the question of my freedom to do A does not arise; I can properly be described neither as free nor as unfree to do A. This view gains its strength from the observation that it is often pointless and sometimes cynical to say that people are free to do things that they are clearly unable to do. It may nonetheless be conceptually proper to say such a thing. In defense of the view taken in the essay, consider the case where the government decides to fence off Scafell Pike. We may well want to say that this action makes everyone unfree to climb Scafell Pike, without waiting to make an elaborate calculation of the number of people able to climb it in the first place.

people being trapped. Y ought to know this. In case 5, by contrast, Y does everything that could reasonably be expected of someone whose job it is to check rooms. My imprisonment results from a quite unforeseeable combination of circumstances, notwithstanding the fact that Y's action is its direct cause. We should normally mark this difference by saying that Y was responsible for my imprisonment in case 2 but not in case 5. 'Responsible' here cannot simply mean 'causally responsible', since Y's causal role is approximately the same in both cases; the responsibility in question is a morally relevant form of responsibility.[9] My proposal is that it is the presence of such responsibility in one case but not the other that justifies us in saying that Y has rendered me unfree to leave in case 2 but not in case 5.

Before considering more fully why this should be so, let me deal with cases 3 and 4. In case 3 the main cause of my imprisonment is a natural event, but a contributory cause is Y's omission, his failure to check the room at the appropriate time. Y has an obligation to check rooms and so is morally responsible for my subsequent confinement. In case 4, on the other hand, the passerby is so placed that he could if he wished release me, but in the circumstances he has no obligation to do so.[10] From a causal point of view his omission is partly responsible for my confinement, but from a moral point of view he is not responsible at all. This difference permits us to say that in case 3 I am unfree to leave my room from 7 P.M. on (when Y is supposed to check), whereas in case 4, I am merely unable to leave from 6.30 P.M. to 7 P.M. (between the passerby's passing and Y's arriving).

I have identified three circumstances in which some Y may be held morally responsible for the existence of an obstacle to some X's action: Y may have imposed the obstacle intentionally, he may have imposed it negligently, or he may have failed to remove it despite having an obligation to do so. Why should moral responsibility so

---

[9] I shall refer to this as 'moral responsibility', but with the caveat that this concept is to be interpreted broadly. As I note later, to be morally responsible for an outcome is to be potentially blamable for it, but in many cases it is possible to preempt blame by showing that the action in question was justified. In a narrower use, being morally responsible may entail being blameworthy—this is not how I understand the concept here. Note also that moral responsibility may be a matter of degree, and this is relevant when we are judging the agent, but not when we are deciding whether the recipient's freedom has been restricted.

[10] I assume as part of the story that when I call to the passerby I manifest no signs of distress. If I were to, then, with a few other conditions added, the passerby would have an obligation to come to my aid.

understood be the appropriate criterion for distinguishing between constraints on freedom and other hindrances to action? Notice that to say someone is morally responsible for a state of affairs is *not* to say that he is blamable for it, though it is to say that he is liable to blame if he fails to provide a justification for his conduct. Thus in case 3 Y might admit that he was responsible for my imprisonment but defend himself by stressing the importance of his private mission. This feature of the concept of moral responsibility precisely mirrors a feature of the concept of freedom that has already been noted. When we describe a person as unfree to do something, we imply that an obstacle exists that stands in need of justification, and we are in effect calling upon the human race collectively to vindicate its behavior in permitting the obstacle to exist. At the same time we allow that such justification may be forthcoming: we distinguish unfreedom from un-justified unfreedom.[11] This supports my proposal that the appropriate condition for regarding an obstacle as a constraint on freedom is that some other person or persons can be held morally responsible for its existence. When that condition obtains, we have achieved our two desiderata, namely, that the obstacle stands in need of justification and that justification may nonetheless be possible.

If this criterion were to be rejected, how else might we explain the distinction between constraints on freedom and other hindrances to action? First, we might say that obstacles were constraints on freedom only when they were deliberately imposed by other human agents. Second, we might argue that the relevant dividing line lay between obstacles that human beings had imposed (deliberately or not) and those they had merely failed to remove. Third, we might propose that a constraint on freedom was any obstacle for whose existence other humans were causally responsible, in whole or in part. Each of these proposals is unsatisfactory, as I shall try to show.

The first suggestion has some defenders—for instance it serves as the starting point for Berlin's classic account of negative liberty, though Berlin does not hold the position consistently[12]—and it seems

---

[11] This should make it clear that the definition of freedom I am offering is not a moralized definition of the sort that G. A. Cohen has found objectionable ('Capitalism, Freedom and the Proletariat', in *The Idea of Freedom*, ed. A. Ryan [Oxford: Oxford University Press, 1979], pp. 12–13) [pp. 170–2 this volume] though it is not a morally neutral definition either.

[12] Compare Berlin, 'Two Concepts of Liberty', p. 169 [p. 34 this volume] ('Coercion implies the deliberate interference of other human beings within the area in which I could otherwise act') with p. 170 [p. 35 this volume] ('The criterion of oppression is the part that I believe to be played by other human beings, directly or indirectly, with or without the intention of doing so, in frustrating my wishes').

to capture the idea that 'ill will' is what maddens us. But reflecting a little further along these lines, it is difficult to see why we should always resent deliberate obstruction more than, say, obstruction that is a by-product of action in pursuit of other ends. If a law is passed that is aimed at preventing me from leaving the country, I should regard it as an infringement of my freedom. But equally if a law is passed that requires me to repay the costs of my professional training (which I cannot as it happens do without remaining in the country), I shall to the same degree regard myself as unfree to leave. Indeed I may rail more strongly against incompetent legislators who fail to foresee the consequences of their actions than against misguided legislators who act in the light of sincere (though in my view mistaken) convictions.

The second proposal relies on a distinction between acts and omissions, between what people do and what they fail to do. It therefore faces two critical difficulties connected with that distinction. The first is simply one of drawing the dividing line in a clear way. If I allow trees to grow on my land that prevent you from driving your car into your garage, have I blocked your drive or merely failed to keep it clear? Either description of my behavior—as an act or as an omission—seems about as plausible as the other. The distinction might perhaps be firmed up in some ingenious way.[13] But then the second problem is that by itself it seems to have no moral significance.[14] For although the distinction might be *correlated* to some extent with features of behavior that are morally significant, the bare contrast between an act and an omission is not. It may, for instance, turn out that agents are morally responsible for the results of a larger proportion of those pieces of behavior we should call acts than of those pieces of behavior we should call omissions; but it does not of course follow from this that to describe a piece of behavior as an act (or an omission) is to say anything morally relevant about it. Now since I have assumed that the distinction between unfreedom and mere inability is morally loaded, it seems unlikely that it should rest on a distinction that is not.

[13] See, for instance, J. Bennett, '"Whatever the Consequences",' *Analysis* 26 (1965–66): 83–102, esp. pp. 93–97. Bennett has since developed his position more fully in 'Morality and Consequences', in *The Tanner Lectures on Human Values,* II, ed. S. M. McMurrin (Salt Lake City: University of Utah Press, 1981).

[14] See, for instance, J. Glover, *Causing Death and Saving Lives* (Harmondsworth, UK: Penguin Books, 1977), chapter 7; J. Harris, *Violence and Responsibility* (London: Routledge & Kegan Paul, 1980), chapters 3–4.

What the supporter of the second proposal has to show is that there are no cases in which agents are rendered unfree by others' omissions. But consider the case in which I am caving with a companion who is trapped by a fall of rock. If I fail to make reasonable attempts to extricate him, how can I avoid conceding that I have made him unfree to escape? To load the moral dice still further, suppose that I deliberately leave him trapped because I have designs upon his wife. My omission is then intentional but it is still on any reasonable account an omission. Why should this state of affairs be described differently in terms of freedom from one in which I precipitate the rockfall myself?

The final suggestion is that any obstacle for which human agents are in some way or other causally responsible should be regarded as a constraint on freedom. This might on the face of it seem a reasonable way of explaining the distinction between naturally occurring and humanly caused obstacles. But unless the suggestion relies on some version of the acts-and-omissions doctrine, it must involve a very broad interpretation of causal responsibility. A constraint will then be defined as any obstacle that it is possible for human beings to remove or fail to impose. This means in effect that the scope of mere inability will shrink almost to vanishing point, for who can say what impediments to individual action might not be removed by the concerted efforts of humanity? For instance, all those who wished to fly to the moon might be able to do so, if human resources were devoted entirely to this end, at the expense of all the other projects on which we are now engaged. So we should have to say that people are now unfree to fly to the moon, since among the causal conditions of their inability is the fact that the rest of the human race has not devoted itself single-mindedly to that aim.[15] It seems clear to me that this is not a helpful extension of the concept of freedom; it fails entirely to capture the intentions of those who want to retain a distinction between inability and unfreedom. One should, in other

---

[15] William Connolly has argued that an obstacle to action should count as a constraint when its removal is feasible and when such removal is regarded as sufficiently important by the person obstructed. This sounds much like the view I am attacking here. But Connolly also implies that judgments of feasibility must take into account the costs of removing the obstacle. 'The notion of a constraint, then, involves the idea of a normal range of conduct people can be expected to undertake or forgo when doing so restricts the options of others'. See W. E. Connolly, *The Terms of Political Discourse* (Lexington, MA: D. C. Heath, 1974), pp. 160–170.

words, either abandon the distinction altogether or reject the third proposal as extending the limits of unfreedom absurdly far.

Having eliminated several alternatives, we may return to my original proposal that constraints should be identified as those obstacles for whose existence other agents are morally responsible. The practical implications of this proposal will depend on how we understand moral responsibility: For how much of our conduct can we be made to answer morally? The crucial question here is how widely our moral obligations extend. In the series of examples involving the self-locking door, I tacitly invoked an everyday understanding of obligations, for instance those of janitors and casual passersby. A utilitarian view of obligation would on the other hand produce what has been called the 'strong doctrine of responsibility', namely, that we are morally responsible for outcomes to the extent to which we are causally responsible for them.[16] Acceptance of this view would bring us by a different route to the unacceptable conclusions of the third proposal outlined previously. I assume, therefore, that our theory of freedom will rest on a view of obligation that does not entail our being obliged to do everything in our power to promote human welfare; in other words, on a view of limited obligation and therefore of limited responsibility. This still leaves open, as we shall see later, a wide field for controversy.

3

We may now turn to the second dimension of the problem about constraints, namely, what features an obstacle must have for it to count as one. In my first set of examples the obstacle in question—the locked door—made the proposed action impossible; I was physically unable to leave the room. Everyone would, I assume, regard this as a paradigm case of unfreedom (when the causal history is of the appropriate sort). At the other extreme no one would wish to say that my freedom is impaired by just any decrease in the attractiveness of a contemplated action due to human agency—say the fact that on leaving my room I may run into an obnoxious colleague. Can we find a coherent position intermediate between these two extremes?

[16] I owe the phrase and the idea to Nancy Davis, 'Utilitarianism and Responsibility', *Ratio* 22 (1980–81): 15–35.

A powerful argument can be mounted for the first extreme view that one is unfree to perform an action only when someone else has rendered that action impossible. Hillel Steiner has defended this position by pointing out that any other mode of intervention merely alters the desirability of the action in question, and he claims that once any such intervention is allowed to count as a constraint on freedom, all such interventions must be.[17] By broadening the class of constraints, we undermine the essential distinction between X being free to do A and X wanting to do A.

We must concede to Steiner that any account of freedom that extends constraint beyond impossibility makes some assumptions about human desires. For if a constraint fails to make an action impossible, it must reduce freedom by making that action less eligible for the agent in question, and 'eligibility' depends on the desires and aversions of the agent himself. If these desires and aversions were to change radically enough, what was formerly a constraint might no longer be so. Against this theoretical disadvantage we must set the extreme narrowness of Steiner's view. Compare the following cases: in the first, a man is imprisoned in a ten-foot-square cage; in the second, a square of the same size is marked out on the ground, the man is placed inside, and told that moments after he steps out of the square he will be shot (there is ample evidence that the threat is not idle). On Steiner's view, the man is free to leave the square in the second case, but not the cage in the first. We may well doubt, however, whether the two cases are different in a way that bears upon our judgments of freedom. If we examine the relationship between the man and his jailers in both cases, we can say that in each case the man is effectively confined in a ten-foot square by his captors. It is true that in the second case the mechanism of confinement depends on the captive's aversion to being shot; yet this is not some idiosyncratic taste of his, but rather a well-entrenched feature of any normal person's psychology. When applying the notion of freedom, we are looking for morally relevant similarities and dissimilarities in relationships between persons, and it is perfectly appropriate if in doing so we rely on psychological facts for which there is such overwhelming evidence. We are after all using the concept to make judgments about *humans*.

---

[17] H. Steiner, 'Individual Liberty', *Proceedings of the Aristotelian Society* 65 (1974–75): 33–50 [pp. 123–40 this volume].

We might try to bring the second sort of case—where freedom is restricted by a threat of sanctions if action A is performed—under the rubric of the first by arguing that impossibility is indeed implied, but the impossibility here applies to a complex action A + B.[18] Thus when the jailer says, 'Step out of the square and you will be shot', he does not make it impossible for the man to step out of the square (he can imprudently choose to do that) but he does make it impossible for the man to step out of the square and remain alive. In other words, there was a conjunction of actions that it was possible for him to perform (stepping out of the square and staying alive) before the jailer intervened, which the latter has succeeded in rendering physically impossible.

But this solution is too permissive: for any disadvantageous change in the environment can be described as making some conjunction of actions impossible. Thus suppose I have been giving my neighbor some homegrown tomatoes free (out of the kindness of my heart). Finding myself short of cash one week, I offer to sell him some at a reasonable price. No one, I imagine, would argue that this limits his freedom, yet there is now a conjunctive action (having a pound of tomatoes *and* not parting with twenty pence) that it is impossible for him to perform, assuming that he cannot steal the tomatoes or obtain them free elsewhere. So on the proposal being considered, his freedom would have been reduced.

It follows that we cannot say everything that we want to say about freedom entirely in terms of impossibility. Simple impossibility is too restrictive (covers too few cases) and conjunctive impossibility is too permissive (covers too many). We need to include some instances where an action is made less eligible than it otherwise would be, while not including all such instances: we want a criterion that allows us to say that a threat of execution makes one unfree to step out of a square, while a demand for payment does not make one unfree (or even less free) to acquire tomatoes. A person's freedom to perform action A is infringed either when A is made impossible to perform, or when A is made less eligible, in certain ways. But which ways of making A less eligible should count?

One way of making prospective actions less eligible is by making them *punishable*. Oppenheim, for example, argues that Y makes X unfree to do A when Y either makes A impossible for X to do, or makes A punishable.[19] To make an action punishable, he states, is to be disposed to penalize the person in question when he performs it. This fits our commonly held belief that laws backed by sanctions restrict our freedom to perform the actions that are made illegal. However, it does not cover cases such as the man held in the ten-foot square unless 'penalization' is stretched beyond legal punishment to include other types of sanction. But if we widen the idea of punishability in this way, how are we to distinguish it from other cases in which the costs attaching to an action are increased, but not in such a way as to restrict freedom—such as charging my neighbor for tomatoes that he had previously been given for free? Penalizing an action must mean deliberately imposing a sanction in order to deter A (or others like him) from performing it, or exacting retribution if he does perform—in other words, it must depend on the intention and motive of the person or the agency imposing the costs.

A definition of unfreedom that refers to punishability must therefore exclude all cases where the obstacle to X's action results from Y's negligence or from an omission, since in these cases both intention and motive are lacking. I have already argued that there is no good reason for counting only intentionally imposed obstacles as constraints, and this applies with the same force when actions are rendered ineligible rather than impossible to perform. If Y carelessly leaves exposed electric cable lying across a piece of land so that I will receive severe (but nonfatal) shocks if I try to cross, I am unfree to walk there. Notice also that Oppenheim's definition would exclude all cases where a cost-imposing action is intentional but nonpunitive. Suppose that I have a neurotic neighbor who lets fly with a shotgun at anyone who approaches his front door. His aim is not to exact retribution or to deter people from walking up the drive, but purely to protect himself from (as he sees it) the threat posed by the intruder. The act of shooting is intentional, but the motive does not qualify it as one of penalization. I am nevertheless surely not free to walk up to this man's door.

If Oppenheim's definition of unfreedom is unacceptably narrow, it nonetheless points us forward by indicating that there is a relevant difference between a cost imposed on action by way of punishment and the same cost imposed by way of an economic charge, for example.

[19] F. E. Oppenheim, *Dimensions of Freedom* (New York: St. Martin's Press/London: Macmillan, 1961), chapter 4.

A notice that anyone who parks their car in a certain place will be fined restricts their freedom, whereas a parking fee does not, even if the monetary values are the same in both cases. So we cannot make judgments about freedom simply by looking at the tariff attached to actions. The parking fee does not reduce freedom because there is no intention to deter motorists from parking in that place. So far Oppenheim is right. His error is to think that intentional penalization is necessary as well as sufficient for unfreedom. He neglects the important class of situations where there is no intention to penalize and yet freedom is infringed.

To isolate this class, consider a shopkeeper who charges his customers standard market prices for their purchases. Suppose that the wholesale price of some commodity rises and the shopkeeper raises his price accordingly. Although the option of buying that commodity has become less eligible, we would not wish to say that the freedom of customers has been infringed in any way. This is not because we think that the price was fixed 'naturally' or that the shopkeeper 'had no choice' but to raise his price. The reason we would give is rather that the shopkeeper acted 'within his rights' in putting up his price in line with the increase in wholesale prices. He did not intend to deter customers; nor, on the other hand, did he act negligently or in breach of some obligation. He was not, in other words, morally responsible for the price rise.

Contrast this with two other cases. Suppose that there is a dramatic rise in the wholesale price of heating fuel, and the shopkeeper passes this on to his customers. As a result, some cannot afford to buy sufficient fuel to keep warm in winter. The price rise may in this case be considered a constraint on their freedom. We will make this judgment if we believe that there is a moral obligation to ensure that basic needs are met. The shopkeeper is, let us suppose, the person best placed to see what effect the price rise will have on the poor and to act in mitigation.[20] He then carries some portion of the moral responsibility for the increase. Because the price level falls

---

[20] This supposition may be thought unlikely; we are more likely to cast the government in the role described, and to hold *it* responsible for the obstacle faced by the poor. As a matter of fact, nineteenth-century shopkeepers in working-class districts quite regularly provided credit for their customers during the winter months (though mainly in response to reduced incomes due to seasonal work). But nothing hangs on the point, and I make the assumption simply to preserve the continuity of the argument.

within the bounds of moral responsibility, it can properly be seen as a constraint on freedom.

For the second case, suppose that the shopkeeper becomes a local monopolist. Let us say that some customers (the old and infirm, for example) find traveling to his nearest competitor prohibitively costly. If he takes advantage of this fact to raise his prices well above the competitive level, we may again feel that he is interfering with his customers' freedom. The underlying reason is once more that he is being held morally responsible for the increase. In this case he is seen to act in violation of an obligation of fairness, an obligation not to take advantage of his customers by virtue of their dependence on him.

This shows, I believe, that the notion of moral responsibility holds the key to both dimensions of our original problem; or rather, it shows that the dimensions are not really separate. By showing that some agency (person or persons) is morally responsible for an obstacle to X's action, we show both that the obstacle has origins of the right kind and that its nature is such as to count as a constraint on freedom. The sheer size of the obstacle turns out to have no intrinsic importance; at most there will be a contingent connection between the size of an obstacle and its constituting a constraint, turning on the fact that we are more likely to have an obligation to remove (or not to impose) large obstacles than small ones. (Perhaps obstacles that are so small that they barely act as deterrents at all would not count as constraints, even if deliberately imposed, but I shall not pursue this here.)

4

Let me return briefly now to the debate between libertarians and socialists that I outlined at the beginning of this essay. The key question that divides them, I suggested, is whether the distribution of wealth and the structure of opportunities facing the members of a capitalist society is relevant to an assessment of the degree of freedom each enjoys. One conclusion that follows directly from our analysis is that nothing in the nature of a wealth-and-opportunity distribution disqualifies it from featuring in a discussion of freedom. If it is impossible for me to obtain education of a certain kind because none is available, or if large price tags are attached to goods that I need, these obstacles potentially constrain my freedom as much as legal prohibitions. From the point of view of social freedom, legal obstacles have no special status. Equally, it is not a decisive argument against regarding a wealth-and-opportunity distribution as constraining that no one has intended the distribution to take the form that it has. Intention is not a necessary condition of moral responsibility.

So far my analysis lends support to the socialist view of freedom under capitalism. But to make a decisive case, it would be necessary to show that our moral obligations are such that we can be held morally responsible for obstacles such as the financial costs that others face in obtaining goods. In the previous discussion of the circumstances under which a shopkeeper might be judged to infringe on the freedom of his customers through the prices he attached to his goods, I invoked two such obligations: the obligation to ensure that the needs of others are met, and the obligation to deal fairly with people placed in a dependent position. Libertarians, as a general matter, deny that such obligations exist. They assume that all we owe each other is noninterference: I may not kill or imprison you, but I have no obligation to keep you alive or release you from natural entombment (these things may be morally desirable, but are not obligatory). Charging a price for some good cannot be seen as interference.

I have tried to show elsewhere that even libertarians do not consistently define interpersonal obligations in such a narrow way. When dealing with the position of a monopolist who controls access to some vital resource—the owner of the only water hole in the desert, for example—they recognize that charging an inflated price for the water may infringe rights or constitute coercion.[21] So a socialist may try to use that wider understanding of moral obligation to show that capitalism as a whole limits the freedom of most of those who live under it. This is a large task, but the main lesson I want to draw is that a responsibility-based view of freedom, such as I have set out here, makes judgments about when obstacles should count as constraints on freedom ultimately dependent on our preferred theory of moral obligation. Since this is likely to remain contestable, so too will be our verdicts on large questions, such as the question whether capitalism is indeed 'the free society' as it often claims to be.

[21] See the longer version of this essay, 'Constraints on Freedom', *Ethics* 94 (1983–84): 66–86, sect. V.

TEN

Toward a Feminist Theory of Freedom

Nancy J. Hirschmann

The March 15, 1992, issue of the *New York Times* ran an article about a twenty-three-year-old unemployed single mother in West Virginia who became pregnant as a result of date rape.[1] Due to federal policy, she had trouble locating an abortion clinic, but finally found one four hours away in Charleston. They told her she was seventeen weeks pregnant and they performed abortions only until sixteen weeks, and so they referred her to a clinic in Cincinnati, Ohio, that would perform an abortion up to nineteen and a half weeks for a cost of $850. When she went there a week and a half later, however, she was told that she was actually twenty-one weeks pregnant, and so the second clinic referred her to a clinic in Dayton, Ohio, that would perform the abortion for $1,675. She refinanced her car, sold her VCR, borrowed money, and went to Dayton. That clinic said that she was a high-risk patient because of an earlier Caesarean delivery, that she would have to go to Wichita, Kansas, and that it would cost $2,500. At this point, she decided that she no longer could manage the cost and logistics. Being opposed to adoption, she decided to have the baby and to try to love it in the same way that she loves her other child.[2] Can we say that this woman has freely chosen her role as mother?

A revised and abridged version of Nancy J. Hirschmann, 'Toward a Feminist Theory of Freedom', *Political Theory* 24 (1996), pp. 46–60, 62–67. Reprinted by permission of Sage Publications.

[1] This article was originally presented in a different form at the Young Scholars Seminar for the Program on Ethics and Public Life at Cornell University, May 1, 1993. Thanks to seminar participants, particularly Kathy Abrams, Lourdes Beneria, Zillah Eisenstein, Mary Katzenstein, Sally Ruddick, and Henry Shue. Thanks also to Tracy Strong for his critical insights and suggestions.

[2] Tamar Lewin, 'Hurdles Increase for Many Women Seeking Abortions', *New York Times,* March 15, 1992, 1, 18.

A woman in Philadelphia is beaten by her husband and goes to a battered women's shelter. This is the second time in a year that this woman has come to the shelter. However, she refuses to press charges with the police. After spending some time at the shelter, during which time her husband has initiated contact with her, she declares her intention to return to him. She says that he has apologized and that she forgives him, that he is basically a good person and has promised to change, that he loves her and is a good father, that she loves him, and that it was partly her fault anyway. Is she free if she returns to her husband?

In the movie *Mr. and Mrs. Bridge,* Joanne Woodward plays a woman who seems to submit completely to her husband. She rarely ventures a political opinion; she defers to her husband, is extremely self-deprecating, and has so effectively effaced herself that, at the end of the movie, she risks freezing to death while trapped in her car because she will not yell for help. (The implication is that she does not want to disturb anyone and so simply waits passively until her husband gets home to rescue her.) She does not appear to hold these views out of fear or coercion; her husband is somewhat overbearing but not violent, he does not overtly seek to control her, and he clearly loves his wife and demonstrates his consideration and respect in various ways. Is Mrs. Bridge free or not?

Charlene, a lesbian, is an attorney with an extremely conservative Wall Street firm that has never had a woman partner. Charlene wants very badly to become a partner. Accordingly, she is not open about her sexuality. Her lover, Sally, believes this is a mistake, not only tactically but from the perspective of personal cost as well. Although Charlene declares that the relationship is more important to her than anything else, she has become so fearful about colleagues finding out about the relationship that she and Sally have virtually stopped going out of the house together, and the stress is affecting not only Charlene's health but the relationship as well. Sally is beginning to contemplate 'outing' Charlene. She feels that this would liberate Charlene from her fears, anxiety, and extra stress and save the relationship. Is she right?

These dilemmas are not particularly special or unusual. Because of their familiarity, many people probably have immediate—perhaps even gut-level—reactions to these examples; for instance, most readers of this essay would probably say, at least initially, that the pregnant woman is unfree and that Sally is wrong. But I want to suggest that there is really no simple answer to the question of freedom in any of them. This is due partly to the amazing ambiguity displayed in popular (Western) usage of the term 'freedom'. But it is also due partly to the fact that the dominant discourse of freedom in philosophy and political theory, which founds as well as reflects popular everyday conceptions, is inadequate to encompass fully these complexities. And feminism, which many assume would maintain that the women in all four stories are unfree, highlights both this complexity and this inadequacy.

As theorists such as John Gray as well as S. I. Benn and W. L. Weinstein suggest,[3] determining the meaning of freedom is in part a matter of determining the context in which claims of unfreedom are made, such that my evaluation of freedom will depend on my evaluations of other things. For instance, a strong valuation of privacy might result in a context in which claims for husbands' 'freedom' to discipline their wives makes sense, whereas valuation of women's bodily security might result in a different context in which a counterclaim for governmental interference in the family is justified to protect women's 'freedom' from bodily harm.[4] Each of these alternatives involves some considerable cost—injury to women versus patriarchal and often racist state intervention in personal relationships—but that is precisely the point; by making a political evaluation of what is important, we determine the parameters of a meaningful freedom.

In this light, the task for feminist theorists is to stake out an overtly political territory of values—such as choice, bodily integrity, professional development, and/or nurturing relationships—that would allow theorists to point out the ways in which patriarchal practices and customs deny women access to the resources they need to satisfy these values. In this, women's experiences provide a powerful basis for highlighting the frequent sexism of liberty theory, precisely because these experiences often lie at the

---

[3] John Gray, 'On Negative and Positive Liberty', *Political Studies* 28, no. 4 (1980): 507–526; S. I. Benn and W. L. Weinstein, 'Being Free to Act and Being a Free Man', *Mind* 80 (1971): 194–211.

[4] I am aware that these might be considered the *same* context; for instance, the contemporary United States allows both sorts of claims to be made. By 'context', however, I am invoking a deeper notion of ideology, values, and perspective. In this light, at least two different contexts exist within contemporary U.S. family discourse.

crossroads of Enlightenment ideology of agency and choice with modern practices of sexism.

However, the notion that the context for women's desires and preferences is, for the most part, a patriarchal one does not mean that women are simply 'unfree'. Rather, feminism is one theoretical approach that permits a richer and more complex view. Feminists have been able to describe critically the ways in which desire, preferences, agency, and choice are as socially constructed as are the external conditions that enable or restrain them. This duality of social construction permits—even requires—a more complicated engagement of the question of freedom.

A MASCULINIST THEORY OF FREEDOM?

Although the political theory literature on freedom is extremely varied, ranging from a neo-Hobbesian descriptivist account of behavior to the most value-laden prescriptive account of actions,[5] most formulations of freedom still divide along the lines offered by Berlin in 1958 of 'negative' and 'positive' liberty.[6] The major difference between these two models involves the notion of what counts as a barrier to liberty, specifically whether one must consider strictly external barriers to action or whether one must be concerned with internal barriers. This division proves heuristically useful to understanding different notions of freedom and provides feminism with its critical purchase.

According to Berlin, negative liberty consists in an absence of external constraints. Berlin's general notion that restraints come from outside the self—that they are 'other'—is an important tenet of negative liberty; other people's direct (or, in some cases, indirect) participation 'in frustrating my wishes' is the relevant criterion in determining restraint. For this reason, negative liberty sometimes is called an 'opportunity concept',[7] and freedom as

---

[5] See Richard Flathman, *The Philosophy and Politics of Freedom* (Chicago, IL: University of Chicago Press, 1987), for an excellent survey of the range of definitions of freedom.

[6] Isaiah Berlin, 'Two Concepts of Liberty', *Four Essays on Liberty,* ed. Isaiah Berlin (New York: Oxford University Press, 1971), 118–172.

[7] Charles Taylor, 'What's Wrong with Negative Liberty', *The Idea of Freedom: Essays in Honor of Isaiah Berlin,* ed. Alan Ryan (New York: Oxford University Press), 177 [p. 144 this volume].

the 'nonrestriction of options' is the most popular formulation of negative liberty; the more opportunities and choices available to me, the freer I am.[8]

Furthermore, these desires, which I must be able to pursue unimpeded if I am to be free, are seen as coming from me and from me alone. Desires may be reactions to external stimuli (smelling newly baked cookies makes me want one), but the important fact is that I can identify a desire as *mine* regardless of *why* I have it (whether I am a sugar addict or simply hungry is immaterial). Negative liberty draws clear-cut lines between inner and outer, self and other, subject and object: desires come from within, restraints, from without; desires are formed by subjects, by selves, they are thwarted by objects, by others.

Positive liberty challenges this dichotomy by focusing on what might be called 'internal barriers': fears, addictions, and compulsions that are at odds with my 'true' self can all inhibit my freedom. This involves qualitative evaluation about our desires, which can be higher or lower, significant or trivial, genuine or false. Because of this, it is not enough to experience an absence of external restraints, for the immediate desires I have may frustrate my true will. For instance, while I am trying to quit smoking, a fight with my department chair makes me crave a cigarette: positive liberty says that if I were to sneak one in the bathroom, I would be not just weak willed but *unfree,* because I am violating my true desire, on which I have reflected at some length. Thus positive liberty sometimes is called an 'exercise concept';[9] people must exercise their full capacities if they are to be free.

Logically, then, as Taylor notes, positive liberty also involves the strong possibility that this evaluation can be performed by others who may know my true will as well as I do—indeed, sometimes better than I do, particularly when I am in the grip of these self-destructive short-term desires.[10] Indeed, if negative liberty exaggerates an opposition between self and other, it could be argued that positive liberty merges them altogether because

[8] Benn and Weinstein, 'Being Free to Act'; Gray, 'On Negative and Positive Liberty'; Isaiah Berlin, 'From Hope and Fear Set Free', *Concepts and Categories,* ed. Henry Hardy (New York: Viking, 1979), 191–192.

[9] Taylor, 'What's Wrong with Negative Liberty', 177 [p. 143 this volume].

[10] Ibid., 185–188 [pp. 152–6 this volume].

you can know my desires better than I know them myself. These others can 'interfere with' or 'guide' my actions to help me realize my true will and hence to realize my freedom; as you snatch the cigarette from my lips, you are preserving my true self from false desires and enhancing my liberty.[11]

Berlin's typology has been challenged by many, and some would suggest that couching a discussion of liberty in its terms is misdirected.[12] There are three reasons for retaining this framework, however. The first is that, debates and challenges notwithstanding, the typology of positive and negative liberty has in fact dominated theoretical discussions of freedom. Many theorists acknowledge the centrality of the typology to liberty theory.[13] Although individual theorists may *disagree* with Berlin's typology,

[11] Some critics will complain that I have collapsed two different conceptions of positive liberty here. Berlin, for instance, insists that positive liberty absolutely requires external determination of the will, and specifically determination by the state, as in Rousseau's infamous *forcer d'être libre*. A central element for many positive libertarians such as Rousseau, however, is that freedom consists in following your true will, and that in turn involves a 'freedom from' internal desires and passions that do not represent the true or higher self. Taylor emphasizes this same 'divided self' in his account of positive liberty, focusing on internal barriers to realizing the better or higher desire rather than on the external mechanism that directs you to it, but does so in an individualist fashion; in his examples, the subject always seems to know that he or she has a higher and lower desire and is struggling to achieve the former. However, Taylor points out that even this individualist account of positive liberty implicitly incorporates aspects of Berlin's view by maintaining that a focus on inner barriers inevitably leads to 'second guessing', and I follow him here; but he stops short of acknowledging the ways in which this second guessing in turn can lead inevitably to state intervention. On the other hand, Berlin's focus on state determination leads to his forgetting about the importance of the divided self and the internal barriers to realizing the preferred or 'true' will. See Berlin, 'Two Concepts of Liberty', esp. 133–134 [pp. 45–46 this volume]; Taylor, 'What's Wrong with Negative Liberty,' passim.

[12] Gerald MacCallum, 'Negative and Positive Freedom', *Philosophical Review* 76 (1967): 312–334 [pp. 100–122 this volume]; Orlando Patterson, *Freedom in the Making of Western Culture* (New York: Basic Books, 1991), 3.

[13] Stanley Benn, *A Theory of Freedom* (Cambridge, UK: Cambridge University Press, 1988); Ian Carter, 'The Measurement of Pure Negative Freedom', *Political Studies* 40 (1992): 38–50; Diana Coole, 'Constructing and Deconstructing Liberty: A Feminist and Poststructuralist Analysis', *Political Studies* 41 (1993): 83–95; Flathman, *The Philosophy and Politics of Freedom;* Gray, 'On Negative and Positive Liberty'; Kristjan Kristjansson, 'What's Wrong with Positive Liberty?' *Social Theory and Practice*

they seem unable to escape it, and it has retained a powerful grip on philosophical thinking about liberty.

Second, this grip is significantly due to the decidedly, if often overlooked, *political* character of the typology. Granted that Berlin's formulation is overdrawn and simplistic and that he clearly had cold war political motivations for his categories, wanting to ally positive liberty with 'bad-guy' Communist dictatorships and negative liberty with 'good-guy' Western democracies. But because Berlin manipulates philosophy to the end of politics should not lead us into the trap of separating the two and of missing the impact of the concepts as political and not 'just' philosophical. The two concepts of liberty reflect two different—although perhaps equally problematic—conceptions of a person: one as innately separate, individualistic, unconnected, rights oriented, even antagonistic; the other as innately connected, communitarian, even selfless, concerned with responsibility and care. Depending on which view of the subject one takes, a variety of conclusions follow about the relation between state and society, between society and individual—in short, political values. In this, the typology suggests that freedom is not *just* about 'who we are' but also about 'what kind of world we want to live in'.

Finally, and perhaps most importantly, both positive and negative conceptions inform *popular* understandings of liberty; after all, most of us can understand, in an everyday sense, how the cheating smoker is both free and not free. This is because the typology does in fact say something very important about freedom. Both variants of freedom are centrally about making choices. Choice is a complex process of negotiation and relationship between what we commonly call 'inside' and 'outside' factors: between will, desire, and preferences, on the one hand, and forces that not only inhibit or enable the realization of such desires but also contribute to or influence the *formation* of these desires, on the other. It is precisely in this notion of internal and external barriers to liberty that I think the positive-negative typology is the most powerful and at the same time, most problematic. Negative liberty emphasizes the role of external barriers, whereas posi-

(note 13 continued) 18 (1992): 63–70; Leslie Paul Thiele, 'Heidegger on Freedom: Political Not Metaphysical,' *American Political Science Review* 88 (1994): 278–291; David West, 'Spinoza on Positive Freedom': *Political Studies* 41 (1993): 284–296.

tive liberty highlights the internal; this is the key dividing line between the two models.[14]

These latter two reasons are particularly relevant to the argument I develop. In focusing on the internal/external theme, and in considering positive and negative liberty as political, not just philosophical, a feminist approach to liberty can suggest a way to hold on to the political usefulness of the differing models of self, subject, and politics and yet, in the process, develop a somewhat different conceptualization of freedom that transcends the duality even as it borrows from it.

Holding on to the models is also important because both positive and negative liberty models clearly inform feminist concerns. For instance, feminists such as Carol Gilligan assert that negative liberty ideals of individualism and rights display a masculinist bias, whereas positive liberty values of care and community are of greater historical importance to women.[15] At the same time, feminist discussions of reproductive and employment issues focus primarily on negative liberty issues of consent, opportunity, and choice. The freedom of women to control their bodies without external interference and to compete fairly in the marketplace without having to overcome obstacles not placed before men has been a central concern of the feminist movement since the late 1960s.

However, both models are also gender biased. Indeed, although the dualistic typology of positive and negative liberty is useful to understanding freedom, it is also theoretically inadequate to deal with many questions raised by women's historical and material experience. Indeed, although these two orientations toward liberty are generally seen by political theory as opposed, even mutually exclusive, from a feminist perspective, they can be seen to embody similar approaches and assumptions and demonstrate similar problems.

---

[14] Those who focus on Berlin's differentiation between 'freedom from' and 'freedom to' to illustrate its incoherence—every freedom from is a freedom to—miss the deeper point of this external/internal divide. See, for instance, Patterson, *Freedom;* MacCallum, 'Negative and Positive Freedom'.

[15] Carol Gilligan, *In a Different Voice: Psychological Theory and Women's Development* (Cambridge, MA: Harvard University Press, 1982).

FEMINIST FREEDOM AND SOCIAL CONSTRUCTION

Such criticisms invoke a rather superficial level of feminist analysis, however, pinning the gender bias of the concepts to individual theorists' treatment of women. A deeper level starts by challenging the naturalist basis to freedom altogether. In claiming that freedom discourse falsely universalizes a highly particularistic notion of humanity—white economically privileged men—I invoke the notion of 'social construction', the idea that human beings and their world are in no sense given or natural but the product of historical configurations of relationships. The desires and preferences we have, our beliefs and values, our way of defining the world are all shaped by the particular constellation of personal and institutional social relationships that constitute our individual and collective histories. Even the most intimate and supposedly 'internal' aspects of our being, such as our sexuality, must be understood in terms of the historical relations and actions that have imported meaning to our bodies. Context is what makes meaning possible, and meaning makes 'reality'.[16] Thus the value that we place on freedom, as well as the meaning we give to the word, are in no way essential or natural, but are the products of particular historical relationships that have developed through time.[17]

---

[16] See, for instance, Judith Butler, *Gender Trouble* (New York: Routledge, 1990), and *Bodies That Matter* (New York: Routledge, 1994); Jacques Derrida, *Margins of Philosophy,* trans. Alan Bass (Chicago: University of Chicago Press, 1982); Michel Foucault, *The History of Sexuality,* vol. I: *An Introduction* (New York: Vintage, 1980), and vol. 2: *The Use of Pleasure* (New York: Vintage, 1990); Jean François Lyotard, *The Postmodern Condition:* A *Report on Knowledge* (Minneapolis: University of Minnesota Press, 1979); Joan Scott, 'Experience', *Feminists Theorize the Political,* ed. J. Butler and J. Scott (New York: Routledge, 1992), 22–40; Jacquelyn Zita, 'The Male Lesbian', *Lesbian Ethics,* ed. Claudia Card (New York: Pantheon Books, 1994), 112–132.

[17] In this, it is important to note that social constructivism does not require that theorists reject individualism or negative freedom out of hand. Developed in part as a response to absolutist political authority and emerging political movements for parliamentarian and representative government, and motivated in turn by largely economic considerations (see Richard Ashcraft, *Revolutionary Politics and Locke's Two Treatises* [Princeton, NJ: Princeton University Press, 1986]; Isaac Kramnick, *Revolutionary Politics and Bourgeois Radicalism* [Ithaca, NY: Cornell University Press, 1990]; C. B. Macpherson, *The Political Theory of Possessive Individualism: Hobbes to Locke* [New York: Oxford University Press, 1964]), the emphasis on the individual as the unit of analysis and freedom

The idea of social construction is particularly important to feminist efforts to reject patriarchal arguments about men's and women's 'natures'. Not only can it challenge the hegemony of (dominant notions of) freedom, suggesting that other values allegedly more important to feminists (e.g., connection, responsibility, equality) have at least as great importance in social life, it can also offer important insights into who the 'subject' of liberty really is, namely, bourgeois white males at the dawn of capitalism and liberal representative democracy rather than 'natural man'. It also can help expose the battle between positive liberty's emphasis on inner barriers to my 'true' will and negative liberty's focus on outer barriers that are foreign to my radically autonomous will, as a false dichotomy, by suggesting that inner and outer are not opposed but in relationship.

The idea of social construction, however, contains a somewhat paradoxical character that feminist use of it can bring out. Feminists point out that if humans are socially constructed, male domination is and has been an important part of that construction. This has resulted in laws, customs, and social rules that come from men and are imposed on women to restrict their opportunities, choices, actions, and behaviours. Furthermore, and more problematic, these rules become constitutive not only of what women are allowed to do but of what they are allowed to *be* as well: how women are able to think and conceive of themselves, what they can and should desire, what their preferences are. Because our conceptual and material world has been formulated and developed by these masculinist perspectives, such rules are not simply external restrictions on women's otherwise natural desires; rather, they create an entire cultural context that makes women seem to choose what they are in fact restricted to.

Some, like Adriana Cavarero, a feminist philosopher, believe that this construction of reality takes root in our very language: 'Woman is not the subject of her language. Her language is not hers. She therefore speaks and represents herself in a language

(note 17 continued) as noninterference by governments is an understandable, although not the only possible, reaction to contemporary historical and political conditions. However, calling these conceptions natural and timeless obfuscates their origin and meaning, decontextualizes and dehistoricalizes, and thereby hides their biases. In such hidden biases lie the dangers of totalizing representation and the erasure of men and women of color, white women, workers, and the poor.

not her own, that is, through the categories of the language of the other. She thinks herself as thought by the other'.[18] This is a view shared by many French feminists as well.[19] If the language women speak is not 'ours', if it is a language and conceptual vocabulary of identity and being that is specifically masculinist, then categories of meaning become barriers to women's self-definition; epistemology itself is a restraint because dominant ways of knowing and categories of knowledge encode and derive from patriarchal constructions of women.

This notion is at once useful and troubling. By suggesting that the desires and preferences women have, and the choices they make, are determined to a large degree by a context that has women's subjugation at its core, this view suggests that we may be able to adapt a negative liberty model to feminist purposes by expanding the notion of what counts as a 'barrier' to freedom. From such a perspective, the existing patriarchal context—not only its generically inegalitarian customs and practices but also its language, conceptual framework, and epistemology—could be seen as a socially constructed external barrier to women's freedom. This would suggest that even the concept of 'freedom' itself must be premised on women's subservience to men, on the denial and obliteration of their humanity—in short, on their 'unfreedom'. Feminists using social constructivism can deconstruct the 'self-evident' and 'natural' claims of modernist ideologies into political claims specific to a particular time, history, class, race, and gender. And this recognition allows comparisons within the negative liberty framework: a woman who is not abused is freer (all other things being equal) than one who is; a woman who is able to obtain an abortion when she wants it is freer than one who cannot; a woman who can be open about her sexuality without fearing professional repercussions is freer than one who must hide. The essence of negative liberty as the absence

[18] Adriana Cavarero, 'Il pensiero della differenza sessuale' ('Toward a Theory of Sexual Difference'), *Diotima* (Milan, Italy: La Tartaruge, 1987), quoted and translated by Teresa de Lauretis, 'The Essence of the Triangle, or Taking the Risk of Essentialism Seriously: Feminist Theory in Italy, the U.S., and Britain', *Differences* 1, no. 2 (1989): 16.

[19] Luce Ingaray, *This Sex Which Is Not One* (Ithaca, NY: Cornell University Press, 1985); Julia Kristeva, *The Kristeva Reader,* ed. Toril Moi (Oxford, UK: Blackwell, 1986).

of external impediments is thus preserved, but the meaning of 'external impediment' is expanded considerably beyond what most negative libertarians conceive.

Indeed, this expanded notion of negative liberty would highlight the ways in which things that are considered 'internal' barriers within positive liberty terms are externally generated, culturally mediated and created, thus suggesting that positive liberty's focus on 'inner' barriers may be seen as a ploy to individualize and pathologize failures to break out of social conditioning. For instance, it is argued that battered women may stay with batterers because of 'internal' barriers such as shame, self-blame, guilt, low self-esteem, or love and its attendant belief that change is possible, as well as 'external' barriers such as fear of injury and economic dependence. But in a society where resources for battered women are a low funding priority, where courts and police openly disbelieve women, and where relatives and friends fail to help and protect, shame, guilt, and feelings of unworthiness and deservedness are predictable responses but are not just internal.[20] If we are who we are through social relations, and if those social relations construct women in negative terms, it is 'only human' for women to internalize them, to give them some credence, to accept them as 'truth', and to be who they say we are. On this view, Mrs. Bridge's self-effacement may be the product of an oppressive upbringing in a sexist society, and Charlene's fear of being fired may be a reasonable reaction to heterosexism and homophobia. Such examples suggest that the internal/external dichotomy is itself a construction.

On this reading, then, it would seem that for women to be free, the external forces of patriarchy must be eliminated. All 'inner' forces of will, desire, and preference as well as fear, compulsion, and revulsion would be seen as the products of patriarchal social forces over which women have little or no control.

Can this reading be sustained, however? Some would point out that it contradicts the fundamental underpinnings of negative

[20] See, for instance, Angela Brown, *When Battered Women Kill* (New York: Macmillan, 1987); R. Emerson and Russell P. Dobash, *Women, Violence and Social Change* (New York: Routledge, 1992); Mildred Pagelow, *Woman-Battering* (Beverly Hills, CA: Sage, 1981); Lenore Walker, *The Battered Woman Syndrome* (New York: Springer, 1984).

[21] Flathman, *Philosophy and Politics of Freedom,* 17.

liberty. For instance, Flathman says that negative liberty requires that barriers be the result of 'intentional and purposive actions by identifiable agents', thus ruling out generalized conditions of non-specific nature or origin (such as patriarchy); rather, these are part of our 'form of life'.[21] Ian Carter, who suggests that intentionality is not relevant, maintains that identifiable agency is.[22] This might allow us to identify a batterer who claims he 'didn't mean to hurt her' or a sexual harasser who thought he was simply paying his secretary a compliment as interfering with women's freedom even if neither of these men intended to do so. But both would prevent us from counting a more generalized 'patriarchy' that underlies abusive men's failure to understand or take responsibility for their actions as itself a barrier to women's freedom. Catharine MacKinnon's view that the existence of pornography inhibits all women's freedom by determining their sexuality, for instance, would not be considered a legitimate argument.[23]

Other theorists, however, have sympathy for expanding the negative liberty model. Gray, for instance, argues that to count as a barrier to liberty, restrictive conditions such as poverty do not have to be caused intentionally or by identifiable agents as long as they are avoidable (e.g., if 'mass unemployment resulted from misguided monetary policies whose application was in no way inevitable')[24] or at least remediable by human action. He argues that even Berlin is ambivalent about intentionality; although it is key to his conception of coercion, coercion is only one limitation on freedom, and other limitations may be only 'caused' unintentionally.[25] The extension of this view to sexism has considerable potential, because a key tenet of feminism is that sexism is literally 'man-made' and can—indeed must—be changed by human action.

But, as Gray notes, there are grave difficulties in determining whether social conditions *are* avoidable or remediable. This is a serious stumbling block for an expanded model of negative liberty

[22] Carter, 'The Measurement of Pure Negative Liberty'.

[23] Catherine MacKinnon, 'Not a Moral Issue', *Feminism Unmodified* (Cambridge, MA: Harvard University Press, 1984).

[24] Gray, 'On Negative and Positive Liberty', 522.

[25] Ibid., 522. See also Berlin, 'Two Concepts of Liberty', 122 [p. 35 this volume].

and is particularly problematic for feminists because many people would insist that patriarchy is natural and hence not avoidable at all, let alone remediable.[26] And yet, this entrenchment of patriarchy in many people's view of 'reality' is precisely what justifies the feminist claim that freedom requires changing the patriarchal context itself and not just particular practices *within* the context. The logic of a feminist expansion of negative freedom commits it to such a thoroughgoing and radical critique in spite of the practical difficulties involved in changing people's attitudes and understandings of what is 'real'.

But there is a deeper, more theoretical difficulty as well. Even if we put aside objections such as Flathman's and accept the expanded notion of 'external barrier', the unfreedom of women under patriarchy *cannot* be explained entirely in terms of external barriers. Even under a worse patriarchy than, say, the contemporary United States, it is difficult to count 'the world as we know it' as a barrier to liberty because this world is what makes our agency possible; it provides the language and conceptual vocabulary that make desire and intention possible.

That is, while some of the core beliefs of negative liberty must be preserved in a feminist reconceptualization (after all, the goal of enlarging the concept of external barriers in an expanded negative liberty model is not to meet positive liberty goals of a 'true will' but to meet *negative* liberty goals of choice and agency), these beliefs, ironically, are lost in the proposed expansion. By saying that everything in the patriarchal order is a barrier to women's freedom, possibilities for free action within those parameters disappear. For instance, not all men batter, harass, or rape women; not all battered women stay with their abusers; and not all victims of harassment and rape fail to press charges. Attributing such differences solely to external factors would require us to identify a set of conditions common to all the cases in which women display similar responses, an extremely unlikely (and perhaps intellectually futile) possibility. It also rests on an unacknowledged premise that women are all the same, belying the enormous diversity of

---

[26] Similar arguments are made about poverty, of course, but the central role of the body and reproduction in discussions of gender dominance seem to give the naturalist response even more of a historical hold.

coping and survival strategies that women in such situations have devised.[27]

Similarly, women who subscribe to traditional roles, who stay with mates who have exhibited some violence, or who fail to report rape to the police would have to be considered unfree by definition because they are externally restrained whether they realize it or not. To insist that women such as Mrs. Bridge and Charlene are victims of 'false consciousness', that their beliefs and values are only external barriers to the realization of their 'true' will, is to turn women into victims by denying their participation in structures of power and oppression that, while inhibiting some choices and activities (such as open sexuality), make other choices and activities possible (e.g., they both are financially well off).

Ironically, the attempt to develop an expanded model of *negative* liberty by externalizing the barriers to women's freedom thus returns us to the problems of *positive* liberty by second-guessing 'true' desires and motivations. A feminist theory of freedom must thus retain certain elements of positive liberty from the start, particularly by recognizing that some barriers *are* best described as 'internal', that individuals *can* have divided wills and complicated desires that may implicate them in supporting the very structures that apparently restrict them. It is only by recognizing this that feminists can achieve the recognition of women's choices within the context of attempts to reduce, if not eliminate, structural barriers to such choice. While removing external barriers is crucial, it may not be enough, because what these barriers have already constructed as internal identity may remain. That identity may be 'genuine'; it is not automatically 'false' just because it exists within—or even perhaps coheres with—the terms of patriarchy. But its 'genuineness' does not foreclose questions of liberty.

Social constructivism not only reveals that what is often called an 'inner barrier' is culturally mediated and externally generated but also highlights the *interaction* of 'inner' and 'outer' and reconceptualizes the meaning and relationship of those terms. Inner and outer are not mutually exclusive but interdependent in meaning and in practice; accordingly, any focus on external barriers will be weakened without attention to the internal. A

---

[27] See Brown, *When Battered Women Kill*; Lenore Walker, *Terrifying Love: Why Battered Women Kill and How Society Responds* (New York: Harper & Row, 1989).

feminist understanding of freedom acknowledges how external factors influence and generate inner feelings and motives as well as how those inner feelings act on and influence the external world. Indeed, without seeing the ways in which the relationship between the 'inner' self and the 'outer' environment must be re-defined and reconceptualized, an exclusive focus on external barriers reduces the complexities of patriarchy and women's choice to the very same individualist, rationalist assumptions that are blamed for Western liberalism's inability to respond adequately to women's needs.

The claim that the patriarchal context itself is a barrier to women's freedom must be viewed with self-critical ambivalence because it implicitly uses a concept of the subject that exists beyond, or outside of, not only this particular (patriarchal) context but any context whatsoever. The abstract 'woman' whose 'freedom' is allegedly restricted by her context is who she is *because* of that context. Feminists cannot operate from some abstract ideal of what a woman is 'really' like, what her desires and preferences 'truly' consist in, without then challenging the entire framework of social construction, which is necessary to the critique of patriarchy in the first place. Furthermore, it denies the reality that women, by living and acting within and on existing contexts, have always helped shape them. As Vaclav Havel points out, people who adapt to oppressive conditions 'help create those conditions. They are objects in a system of control, but at the same time they are its subjects as well'.[28] If such people—for example, women—are its subjects, then they have the power to change it. If humans are who they are through the social relations that make them, then even as those relations limit their options, they also create their options. The view that women are alienated from language itself ignores this duality of social construction or, at the least, fails to recognize the positive constructive elements. Self-definition *always* takes place in and through language; women have participated in that language and responded to it throughout history with their practices. Accordingly, although contexts such as patriarchy may restrict women's freedom, they also make such freedom possible.

Thus feminist freedom requires a double vision: while understanding that everyone 'always, already' participates in the

---

[28] Vaclav Havel, *Living In Truth* (London: Faber & Faber, 1987), 52.

Foucaultian 'field' of social construction,[29] feminists concerned with freedom also want to acknowledge that some groups of people systematically and structurally have more power to do the constructing than do others. That it may be more *difficult* for women to define themselves within a masculinist epistemology and language—as it is for people of color in a white language, lesbians and gays in a heterosexual language—is crucial to recognize. This greater difficulty means that women and other 'excluded others' *are* less free within these contexts and within the terms of masculinist discourse itself. But 'less free' does not mean 'unfree', and 'more difficult' does not mean 'impossible'; 'excluded others' participate in social construction to varying degrees. Furthermore, the meaning that has been created by these contexts enables people to understand who they are as much as who they are *not;* it conceptualizes powers as well as restrictions. Because of this duality, it is not the case that all men are free and all women are unfree; indeed, perhaps under patriarchy, no one is really free in the full senses meant by positive and negative liberty. Similarly, some women are better placed to support patriarchy—and accordingly freer—than are some men by virtue of race, class, or other privileging factors; although patriarchy is about gender domination, it cannot be completely separated from other kinds of domination, such as race, class, and physical ability. White women benefit from the race privilege that being white accords, just as black men benefit from the privileges of gender. Both thus share responsibility within the system of white patriarchy.[30] However, feminists also wish to recognize that patriarchy is defined by the general dominance of men over women, across race and class; it is premised on women's powerlessness

---

[29] Foucault, 'The Deployment of Sexuality', *History of Sexuality,* vol. I, esp. 92–95, and *Power/Knowledge: Selected Interviews and Other Writings, 1972–77,* ed. Colin Gordon (New York: Pantheon Books, 1980), 95–99.

[20] Furthermore, as Iris Young argues *(Justice and the Politics of Difference* [Princeton, NJ: Princeton University Press, 1990]), the distinction between responsibility and blame is important; while feminists may not be able to blame individual men for patriarchy because they are victimized by it—perhaps even (some? many?) white, economically privileged men—we nevertheless can hold men collectively responsible for it because they benefit from the power it gives them over women and they either tacitly or overtly refuse to resist those benefits just as many whites (women as well as men) tacitly accept the benefits of race privilege. As some benefit more than others, some are more responsible than others.

and men's power. And the power it confers includes the power to guide, direct, and shape social construction to a far greater degree than that available to the 'resisting' classes. Freedom for these groups thus requires increasing their ability to participate in the processes of construction.[31] Social construction commits us to this double-edged sword.

THE NEED FOR NEW CONTEXTS: RELATIONSHIPS AS POLITICAL PRACTICE

At the same time, however, such doubleness poses an even more troubling paradox, for if patriarchy constructs even language and epistemology, how are feminists to conceptualize challenges to the existing reality? How can comparisons be made between 'free' and 'unfree' (or 'less free') contexts? For instance, if patriarchy says that women realize their true freedom in bearing and raising children, how can women ever express—indeed, even formulate—the idea that this is not 'true'? In my opening abortion example, for instance, how is it possible to conclude that the woman is unfree? Should we not all be happy that she is being 'forced' to follow her nature and take as evidence of this that she is growing to love her baby?

In other words, if social constructivism is correct, then it would seem impossible to talk about 'women's freedom' outside of the conceptual vocabulary patriarchy provides; yet, that vocabulary has women's subjection at its core. And anyhow, what about men—are they not just as socially constructed as women? And if men themselves are socially constructed, how can 'patriarchy' even be conceptualized? Feminists need the idea of social construction to deconstruct the idea of freedom, to identify the ways in which patriarchy has limited not only women's options and choices but also their self-conceptions; yet, it paradoxically allows women no other way to see themselves. So what's a feminist to do?

---

[31] I use the wording 'participate in its processes' because I wish to avoid the impression that I think social construction is really as conscious and active as the term 'construction' implies. I believe that many men actively engage in perpetuating sexism, for instance, but its existence is much more complex than conscious conspiracy; perhaps it is its pervasiveness at the subconscious level that accounts for its tenacity.

The logical solution would seem to be to find another context, one in which language and epistemology generate a set of countermeanings that provide a critical perspective on the dominant language. Poststructuralist theory, for instance, sets forth the notion that every discourse (such as patriarchy) has aporia within which exist alternative discourses and counterdiscourses. So, for instance, patriarchy contains both the discursive ideal that it is men's right to discipline their wives and simultaneously that women should be worshipped and placed on a pedestal; the dissonance between these allows feminists to develop a 'counterdiscourse' identifying both of these ideals as false and objectifying.

The 'aporia' that is particularly relevant to a feminist theory of freedom involves relationships among women.[32] If women in patriarchal contexts internalize its image of their inferiority, then conversely the realization that this inferiority is a constructed image, that it is (at least at some level) false,[33] and that women's activities *have* value needs the support of other women's similar and simultaneous realization or consciousness.

Relationships among women provide this different context for the sharing of these realizations and hence the creation of a political 'feminist standpoint'.[34] Although patriarchy has dehumanized, decentered, dismissed, and disrupted women's relationships with one another throughout history, it has nevertheless permitted those relationships to exist, generally by default. In dismissing the private sphere and women's work as inessential and in directing their attention to the public sphere, men historically have been unable to completely repress or stop women's relations and communities

[32] Equality is another example of such an aporia; although the liberal discourse of equality has been critiqued for including only white propertied men, the logic of equality discourse has provided access for feminists from Mary Wollstonecraft onward, as well as people of color, to claim new powers and statuses within liberal society. See Patricia Williams, *The Alchemy of Race and Rights: Diary of a Law Professor* (Cambridge, MA: Harvard University Press, 1990).

[33] By this, I mean that social construction suggests that by saying women are inferior, women *are* inferior; that is, culture, ethics, and law encode the belief and it becomes materialized. But this materialization is never total, hence the ability to challenge the claim even as one lives it. See Butler, *Bodies that Matter;* Rosemary Hennessey, *Materialist Feminism and the Politics of Discourse* (New York: Routledge, 1993).

[34] Nancy Hartsock, *Money, Sex, and Power: Toward a Feminist Historical Materialism* (Boston: Northeastern University Press, 1984), 231–251.

from developing. These have often evolved as means of survival for women, ways that women have been able to help one another cope with their oppression, but they have simultaneously provided the basis for transcending it as well. And even though male domination often sets the parameters for these relationships—whether it is the oppressive conditions of a slave barracks, the Triangle Shirtwaist factory floor, a brothel, a tea for middle-class housewives, or the waiting room of a male gynecologist—such relationships have the potential to allow women to define themselves in ways that resist the patriarchal contexts that surround them. The most obvious contemporary example of this phenomenon is, of course, conscious-ness-raising groups in which the articulation of experience through patriarchal language gave way to a 'new', specifically feminist vo-cabulary of 'sexual politics'. However, such groups have existed in subtler, less recognized forms throughout history.[35]

Such relationship is central to the notion of liberty found in the Milan Women's Bookstore Collective's *Sexual Difference: A Theory of Social-Symbolic Practice,* which is one of the few contemporary works that attempts to theorize freedom in specifically feminist terms.[36] The book suggests that a feminist theory of freedom is based not on rights but on responsibility, not on separation but on connection, not on autonomy as rejection of or reaction to oth-ers but on relationship and interaction with others. Relationship is conceived not as a mere state of existence or as peripheral to what is important but rather as a vital political practice. Although context is all important, the fact that the patriarchal context in which women live so profoundly restricts women's ability to define themselves suggests the need for some sort of radical break, a po-litical and intellectual separatism that can yield a new relational context that is not—or at least has the potential not to be—totally constituted by patriarchy.

---

[35] See Kate Millet, *Sexual Politics* (New York: Doubleday, 1970), and Betty Friedan, *The Feminine Mystique* (New York: Norton, 1963), on consciousness-raising groups; see Patricia Hill Collins, *Black Feminist Thought* (Boston: Unwin Hyman, 1990), chapter 6, on black 'community othermothering'; and see Emily Martin, *The Woman in the Body* (Boston: Beacon, 1987), on menstruation huts.

[36] Milan Women's Bookstore Collective, *Sexual Difference: A Theory of Social-Sym-bolic Practice,* trans. Patricia Cicogna and Teresa de Lauretis (Bloomington: Indiana University Press, 1990).

In Italian feminism, the focus of such separatism was *autocoscienza* groups. Like consciousness-raising in the United States,
autocoscienza is a practice in which women gather together in
small groups to help themselves and each other to gain a deeper
understanding of themselves in the patriarchal world order. A
'separatism' of emotion and intellect, such groups provide, and
engage in the construction of, a new context of woman-to-woman
support, a 'safe space' for women to explore the dissonances between their experiences and the dominant discourse, to attempt
to describe those dissonances, and from there to rearticulate and
reformulate their 'original' experiences and create new experiences and descriptions. Such groups thus move from a negative
exploration—how their experience is *not* what patriarchy says it is,
how it cannot even find adequate expression there—to a positive
one, a new vocabulary of meaning that emerges from the new
feminist context's reinterpretation of women's historical and
current experiences.

If freedom requires self-definition but this self-definition is not
possible within patriarchal language and contexts, then women
need to create new ones; such new contexts provide women with
a critical perspective from which to evaluate their choices more
fully and to facilitate the creation of new choices. Engaging in
such community allows women to see how they have created, and
can create, the world; hence it enables women to identify their
agency, their ability to act on and shape their contexts, to make
choices and act on them.

This idea particularly resonates with the examples with which
this essay opened. For instance, a battered women's shelter provides a temporary 'separatist' community where women share
their experiences of abuse, validate one another, and gain a
clearer perspective on the abusive situations in which they live.
Studies show that even one visit to a battered women's shelter
often provides women with the resources they need to leave their
partners or otherwise alter their situations.[37] Abortion, rape,
and sexual harassment also particularly lend themselves to the
importance of community in the individual's attempt to attain
and protect control over her life and actions. For instance, in my

[37] Judy Woods Cox and Cal. D. Stoltenberg, 'Evaluation of a Treatment Program
for Battered Wives', *Journal of Family Violence* 6 (1991): 395–413.

opening abortion example, an important source of the woman's unfreedom lies in the fact that she is left to solve her dilemma on her own; we cannot blame Dayton for Cincinnati's mistake, but an organized community for reproductive choice could have aided in coordination, financial resources, and ultimately reducing bureaucratic and legal restrictions.

What about Mrs. Bridge? In her case, it would seem that relationship—namely, with her husband—undermines rather than enhances her freedom to define herself. But this is precisely why the Milan group argues for relationships among women specifically; relationship as political practice, rather than as a state of being, means that not just any relationship will do. Their apparent feminist separatism causes the greatest intellectual uneasiness among many feminists, but their central point is precisely that community among oppressed peoples who share certain histories is the kind of community that is needed for freedom to occur.

Community among lesbian women might logically fit such a description; could that be used to justify 'outing' Charlene in the name of freedom? In arguing that relationship is the necessary means to the end of self-definition, the Milan group rejects the positive libertarian's fusion of self and other; Sally cannot make such a decision *for* Charlene. Relationship provides a context that makes such choices possible (without the gay and lesbian movement, 'homophobia' and 'heterosexism' would not even be part of mainstream academic vocabulary), but Charlene ultimately must decide for herself, as must Mrs Bridge.

So the key to feminist freedom, and to the self-realization that lies at its core, is a notion of individual and group empowerment developing synchronically. Precisely because we are created and shaped by our contexts, a feminist practice of liberty must empower individuals to create and influence their contexts in more self-critical, self-reflexive ways. This requires negative liberty's absence of restraint as well as positive liberty's community assistance, but it simultaneously requires an expansion of external restraint beyond negative liberty's conventional formulation and a notion of community that pulls back from, or transforms, positive liberty's hierarchical social determination of desire. Equality is a vital component of relationships in this community, but the equality among individuals is one founded on difference, one that acknowledges and indeed depends on individuals' unique and particular ways of manifesting and living out the commonly shared and similarly encoded aspects of experience.

A notion of agency similarly lies at the heart of a feminist theory of freedom, but this agency is not the abstract and individualist agency of negative liberty's state of nature any more than it is the selfless collective agency of the general will. It involves a notion of self deeply situated in relationship; it involves recognition of the ways our powers and abilities have come from and been made possible by particular relationships and contexts. We are 'autonomous' in the sense that we have powers and abilities as well as desires, wants, and needs, but these are 'relational'; they come from, exist in the context of, and have meaning only in relation to others.[38] Other and self are thus not opposed but related. But to say they are 'related' is not to say that they are 'one', as positive liberty suggests, any more than they are two separate entities that must somehow be fitted together, as negative liberty asserts.

The focus on context requires an understanding of the ways in which the language, concepts, and epistemology of the patriarchal world constrain women's choices in ways in which men's choices are not constrained. But it also must be understood as a context of relationships that help create individuals—women as well as men—capable of making choices for themselves and of understanding themselves in and through those relationships that give us our 'desires' and 'will' in the first place. Through social constructivism, a feminist understanding of freedom requires the recognition that things *simultaneously* create and destroy, prevent and promote, prohibit and require. By emphasizing the centrality of agency and choice, but by deeply locating agents and their choices in relationships and contexts that can empower as well as inhibit them, such a conceptualization requires the collective creation of new contexts that will help people, particularly those on the margins (such as women), define themselves and become aware of their capacities and abilities. They must be able to exercise choice to affect the contexts themselves, for only then can the choices that occur within these contexts be conceived of as genuinely free.

---

[38] David Bakan, *The Duality of Human Existence: Isolation and Communion in Western Man* (Boston: Beacon, 1966); Nancy J. Hirschmann, *Rethinking Obligation* (Ithaca, NY: Cornell University Press, 1992), 139–140.

ELEVEN

THE REPUBLICAN IDEAL OF FREEDOM

Philip Pettit

THE CONSTANT CONNECTION

Early in the nineteenth century Benjamin Constant (1988) delivered a famous lecture entitled 'The Liberty of the Ancients and the Liberty of the Moderns'.[1] He depicted the liberty of the moderns, in the familiar negative or liberal fashion, as the absence of interference. I am free in this sense 'to the degree to which no human being interferes with my activity' (Berlin 1958: 7). Constant depicted the liberty of the ancients, on the other hand, as the liberty associated, ideally, with being a direct participant in a self-governing democracy. I am free in this sense, not through being uncontrolled by others, but through sharing with others the power to control all. The liberty of the ancients is the most prominent form of what Isaiah Berlin (1958) later called positive freedom.

The most important observation in introducing the republican conception of freedom is to recognize Constant's image of the liberty of the ancients as a caricature that served to hide the true republican way of thinking, only recently so prominent, from his contemporaries' eyes. Constant may not have been consciously propagandizing, but what he achieved was to mesmerize later generations into thinking that the only feasible, perhaps the only sensible, notion of freedom was the liberal idea of freedom as

Abridged from Philip Pettit, 'Republican Political Theory', in Andrew Vincent (ed.), *Political Theory: Tradition and Diversity* (Cambridge, UK: Cambridge University Press, 1997). Reprinted by permission of Cambridge University Press.

[1] I am most grateful to Geoffrey Brennan and Michael Smith for helpful discussions of the material. I was enormously helped by comments received when the paper was presented to a meeting in New Orleans organised by the Murphy Institute of Political Economy, Tulane University, and the International Society for Economics and Philosophy.

noninterference. The liberty of the ancients is no match for freedom as noninterference—even if it is thought desirable, it must be judged to be unattainable. The effect of setting up the two as the only relevant alternatives was to give victory, inevitably, to the liberal ideal.

The republican way of thinking about freedom, effectively suppressed by Constant, represents it as nondomination, not as direct democratic standing. And the difference between freedom as noninterference and freedom as nondomination is easily explained. Assume that one person dominates another to the extent that they have the capacity to interfere arbitrarily—to interfere on an arbitrary basis—in some or all of the other's choices (Pettit 1996; 1997). Freedom as noninterference makes the absence of interference sufficient for freedom; in contrast, freedom as nondomination requires the absence of a capacity on the part of anyone else—any individual or corporate agent—to interfere arbitrarily in another person's life or affairs. The difference between the two ways of conceiving of liberty may seem slight, but a little reflection will reveal hidden dimensions to the contrast.

INTERFERENCE AND ARBITRARY INTERFERENCE

The two conceptions of freedom both invoke the notion of interference, and we may begin our exploration of the contrast between the two ways of conceiving liberty with a comment on this. The first thing to note is that, on almost all accounts, the intrusions that count as interference have to be intentional acts, or at least acts for which the agent can be held responsible (Miller 1990: 35): they have to be intentional or quasi-intentional. The reason for this stipulation is that freedom under most accounts is a condition defined in relation to other intentional agents, not a condition defined by reference to favours bestowed by nature: not a condition defined by how far a person escapes various brute, nonintentionally imposed limitations (see Spitz 1995: 382–383).

The intrusions that constitute interference may be restricted to acts that make certain options impossible for the agent; or they may be extended to include acts that coerce or manipulate the agent in choosing between options. I shall assume that, for both conceptions of freedom, interference is to be understood in the broader fashion. Under this way of taking them, acts of interference include any acts that worsen the agent's situation—or at least worsen it significantly—either by reducing the alternatives available in choice, or by raising the actual or expected costs associated with some of the alternatives. Thus the agent may be stopped from doing something; the agent may be threatened with some extra cost, say some penalty, in the event of doing it; or the agent may simply be penalized for having done the act in question.

Freedom as noninterference invokes the notion of interference; freedom as nondomination goes further and invokes arbitrary interference: interference on an arbitrary basis. What makes an act of interference arbitrary, then, in the sense of being perpetrated on an arbitrary basis? An act is perpetrated on an arbitrary basis, we can say, if it is subject only to the *arbitrium,* the decision or judgment, of the agent; the agent was in a position to choose it or not choose it, at their pleasure. When we say that an act of interference is perpetrated on an arbitrary basis, then, we imply that like any arbitrary act it is chosen or not chosen at the agent's pleasure. And in particular, since interference with others is involved, we imply that it is chosen or rejected without reference to the interests, or the opinions, of those affected. The choice is not forced to track what the interests of those others require according to their own judgments.[2]

Under this conception of arbitrariness, then, an act of interference is nonarbitrary to the extent that it is forced to track the interests and ideas of the person suffering the interference. Since the interests and ideas of the person involved may make inconsistent demands, nonarbitrariness consists in recognition of the relevant ones. I may have an interest in the state imposing certain taxes or in punishing certain offenders, for example, and the state may pursue these ends according to procedures that conform to my ideas about appropriate means. But I may still

---

[2] Notice that an act of interference can be arbitrary in the procedural sense intended here—it may occur on an arbitrary basis—without being arbitrary in the substantial sense of actually going against the interests or judgments of the persons affected. An act is arbitrary, in this usage, by virtue of the controls—specifically, the lack of controls—under which it materializes, not by virtue of the particular consequences to which it gives rise. The usage I follow means that there is no equivocation involved in speaking, as I do, either of a power of arbitrary interference or of an arbitrary power of interference. What is in question in each case is a power of interfering on an arbitrary, unchecked basis.

not want the state to impose taxes on me—I may want to be an exception—or I may think that I ought not to be punished in the appropriate manner, even though I have been convicted of an offence. In such a case, my relevant interests and ideas are those that are shared in common with others, not those that treat me as exceptional, since the state is meant to serve others as well as me. And so, in these cases, the interference of the state in taxing or punishing me is not conducted on an arbitrary basis and does not represent domination.

The republican tradition of thinking took a distinctive view of what is required for an act of interference—in particular, an act of legal or government interference—to be nonarbitrary, and I follow that tradition in giving this account. Consider the complaint of Tom Paine (1989: 168) against monarchy: 'It means arbitrary power in an individual person; in the exercise of which, *himself,* and not the *res-publica,* is the object' (cf. Sydney 1996: 199–200). What is required for nonarbitrary state power, as this comment makes clear, is that the power be exercised in a way that tracks, not the power-holder's personal welfare or worldview, but rather the welfare and worldview of the public. The acts of interference perpetrated by the state must be triggered by the shared interests of those affected; and the interpretation of what those interests require must be shared, at least at the procedural level, by those affected.

Thus there are two antonyms for freedom: one opposes freedom directly to interference, but the second varies this opposition in two ways. The second antonym of freedom involves not interference as such, only interference on an arbitrary basis. Moreover, this second antonym of freedom does not require actual arbitrary interference, only vulnerability to someone with the capacity for such interference.

The second antonym has the effect of making it harder for someone to lose their freedom or to have their freedom reduced. For if an agent interferes nonarbitrarily in their choices, that does not offend as such against their freedom; whatever damage is done by the interference, the nonarbitrariness is enough to ensure that their freedom is not compromised. But the second antonym also has the contrary effect of making it easier, not harder, for someone to suffer a loss of freedom. For if an agent has the capacity to interfere arbitrarily in any of their choices, then that in itself compromises their freedom; they suffer a loss of freedom even if the other person does not actually exercise the capacity for interference.

THE HARDER-TO-LOSE-FREEDOM EFFECT

The harder-to-lose-freedom effect makes for a difference in the law's impact on liberty under the two conceptions. Under freedom as noninterference, a regime of law, being necessarily coercive, systematically compromises people's freedom, even if the consequence of putting the regime into operation is that less interference takes place overall. Subjection to the law, in and of itself, represents a loss of liberty. Under the second conception, however, subjection to the law need not represent a loss of liberty for anyone who lives under it, provided—and of course it is a big proviso—that the making, interpretation, and implementation of the law are not arbitrary: provided that the legal coercion involved is constrained to track the interests and ideas of those affected. The proviso, intuitively expressed, is that the legal regime represents a fair rule of law.

A regime of legal coercion and restraint, while not itself constituting a compromise of liberty, may have the same effect as a natural obstacle in limiting the choices available to people or in making them more costly: in defining the range over which people enjoy undominated choice. Proponents of freedom as noninterference do not count natural obstacles as factors that compromise liberty—because they are in no way intentional—but they do admit that such obstacles affect the range of choice over which freedom as noninterference may be exercised; the obstacles condition freedom, as we might put the distinction, but they do not compromise it.[3] Proponents of freedom as nondomination move the locus of this boundary between compromising and conditioning factors. For them, the interference associated with a fair rule of law, like the natural obstacle, conditions people's liberty but does not in

[3] When proponents of this ideal speak of making freedom as noninterference effective, not just leaving it as a formal freedom, I assume that they often have in mind removing or reducing the obstacles that condition the exercise of freedom as nondomination: extending the range of choice available to people. See Van Parijs 1995.

itself compromise it: the law does not in itself count as infringing or violating or reducing or offending against people's liberty.[4]

Hobbes and Bentham are the great advocates of the idea that law in itself represents a compromise of liberty. 'As against the coercion applicable by individual to individual, no liberty can be given to one man but in proportion as it is taken away from another. All coercive laws, therefore, and in particular all laws creative of liberty, are as far as they go abrogative of liberty' (Bentham 1843). Or as Hobbes had put it: 'The Liberty of a Subject, lyeth therefore only in those things, which in regulating their actions, the Soveraign hath praetermitted' (Hobbes 1968: 264).

But Hobbes and Bentham were consciously breaking with a longer tradition of thought—the republican or commonwealthman tradition—in taking this line (Skinner 1983). That tradition was defended in the first instance by James Harrington (1992: 20), who argued that Hobbes was confusing freedom from the law with freedom proper: freedom by the law. John Locke took Harrington's side, embracing 'freedom from Absolute, Arbitrary Power' as the essential thing and presenting law as essentially on liberty's side: 'that ill deserves the Name of Confinement which serves to hedge us in only from Bogs and Precipices ... the end of Law is not to abolish or restrain, but to preserve and enlarge Freedom' (1965: 325, 348). William Blackstone (1978: 126) represents the eighteenth-century orthodoxy when he follows the same line: 'laws, when prudently framed, are by no means subversive but rather introductive of liberty; for (as Mr Locke has well observed) where there is no law there is no freedom'.

The difference between the two conceptions of liberty in their attitude to the law was of great significance from the point of view of Hobbes and Bentham. The view that all law compromises people's liberty enabled Hobbes to withstand the criticism that he anticipated from republicans, that his Leviathan was utterly

---

[4] The extreme case of legal interference is punishment for an offence. Such punishment will always condition people's freedom as nondomination: removing the capacity for undominated choice (capital punishment); restricting the range over which such choice may be exercised (prison); or raising the costs of making certain undominated choices (fines). But it need not result in the person punished having their liberty compromised through subjection to the arbitrary will of another. This remark is not meant to make legal punishment seem any more tolerable, only to articulate a perhaps surprising corollary of the conception of freedom as nondomination.

inimical to freedom, constituting an arbitrary rule as distinct from a rule of law: an arbitrary rule as distinct from the republican vision of an 'empire of laws, and not of men' (Harrington 1992: 8). And the same view enabled Bentham and those friends of his who opposed the American cause in the 1770s to argue against the colonists' main complaint. This was that, since the British parliament was not constrained in the laws that it passed for the governance of the American colonies—since it was not constrained in the same way that it was constrained in Britain itself—those laws represented an arbitrary interference with Americans and compromised their liberty (Lind 1776). Hobbes could argue that Leviathan did no worse than commonwealths in respect of the liberty of its subjects, since all law compromises liberty. And Bentham and his friends could argue on the same grounds that, in regard to liberty, Americans fared no worse under the law imposed by the British parliament than those in Britain itself.

So much for the harder-to-lose-freedom effect of opposing freedom to nondomination, not noninterference. But what of the easier-to-lose-freedom effect of shifting the antonym?

THE EASIER-TO-LOSE-FREEDOM EFFECT

This effect comes of the fact that someone loses freedom, not just to the extent that another person interferes on an arbitrary basis in their choices, but to the extent that another agent has the capacity to do this. With freedom as nondomination, a person loses freedom to the extent that they live under the thumb of another, even if that thumb is never used against them. Suppose that, under the existing laws and mores, a wife may be abused on an arbitrary basis by her husband, at least in certain areas and in a certain measure. Even if her husband is a loving and caring individual, such a wife cannot count as fully free under the construal of freedom as nondomination. And neither can the employee who lives under the thumb of an employer, nor the member of a minority who lives under the thumb of a majority coalition, nor the debtor who lives under the thumb of a creditor, nor anyone in such a subservient position.

Where the first effect of shifting the antonym shows up particularly in the assessment of law and liberty, the second relates to the association between law and slavery. As it became a matter of common assumption after Bentham that law represents a compromise of liberty, albeit a compromise that may be for the good overall, so it became impossible to maintain that to be unfree is always, in some measure, to be enslaved (Patterson 1991); no one was prepared to say that the law makes slaves of those who live under it. But before Bentham, when freedom was opposed first and foremost to domination, the association between unfreedom and slavery was complete. To be unfree was to live at the mercy of another; and that was, to live under a condition of enslavement to them.

Thus, Algernon Sydney (1990: 17) could write in the 1680s: 'liberty solely consists in an independency upon the will of another, and by the name of slave we understand a man, who can neither dispose of his person nor goods, but enjoys all at the will of his master'. And in the following century, the authors of *Cato's Letters* could give a characteristically forceful statement to the theme. 'Liberty is, to live upon one's own Terms; Slavery is, to live at the mere Mercy of another; and a Life of Slavery is, to those who can bear it, a continual State of Uncertainty and Wretchedness, often an Apprehension of Violence, often the lingering Dread of a violent Death' (Trenchard and Gordon 1971, vol 2: 249–250).

The easier-to-lose-freedom effect of opposing liberty to domination connects with the slavery theme, because one of the striking things about a slave is that they remain a slave even if their master is entirely benign and never interferes with them. As Algernon Sydney (1990: 441) put it, 'he is a slave who serves the best and gentlest man in the world, as well as he who serves the worst'. Or as it was put by Richard Price (1991: 77–78) in the eighteenth century: 'Individuals in private life, while held under the power of masters, cannot be denominated free, however equitably and kindly they may be treated. This is strictly true of communities as well as of individuals'. There is domination, and there is unfreedom, even if no actual interference occurs.

I mentioned that the first effect of opposing freedom to domination provided an argument for the defenders of the American cause: while those in Britain were not made unfree by the law, given that the law could not be arbitrarily imposed there, those in America did not enjoy a similar status under the law. I should add that the second effect enabled them to sheet this argument home. They were in a position to argue that, even though the British parliament did not interfere much in American affairs—even though it levied only a small tax—still, because it could levy whatever tax it wished, without any serious restraint on its will, it related to the American colonists as master to slave.

Joseph Priestley (1993: 140) offers a nice example of this line of argument.

> Q. What *is* the great grievance that those people complain of? A. It is their being taxed by the parliament of Great Britain, the members of which are so far from taxing themselves, that they ease themselves at the same time. If this measure takes place, the colonists will be reduced to a state of as complete servitude, as any people of which there is an account in history. For by the same power, by which the people of England can compel them to *pay one penny,* they may compel them to pay the *last penny* they have. There will be nothing but arbitrary imposition on the one side, and humble petition on the other.

THREE FURTHER REMARKS

My comments on the two main differences associated with opposing freedom to domination rather than to interference should serve to make the notion intelligible. I want to add three further remarks, however, in order to underline some points that are important for understanding it fully.

First, although domination is constituted by one agent's having the capacity to interfere on an arbitrary basis in the affairs of another, some plausible empirical assumptions link it with a shared awareness on the part of the individuals or groups involved that this capacity exists. The question of whether you are undominated is bound to be of interest to anyone. The facts that make you undominated, if indeed you are such—the facts about your comparative resources, for example, and about the degree to which you are protected by legal and other means—are bound to be salient to all involved. Under standard assumptions as to people's inductive and inferential abilities, it follows that the fact of nondomination will be a matter of common recognition among the individuals in question (Lewis 1969: 56). And that is something of the greatest significance. For it means that under standard ways of achieving it, freedom as nondomination is intimately linked with the ability to look others in the eye, without having to defer to them or fear them. Montesquieu (1989: 157) emphasizes this theme when he writes: 'Political liberty in a citizen is that tranquillity of spirit which comes from the opinion each one has of his security, and in order for him to have this liberty the government must be such that one citizen cannot fear another citizen'.

The second remark that I want to make is also about domination. If someone is to enjoy freedom as nondomination, it is not enough that the other people are unlikely to exercise arbitrary interference; those other people must lack the capacity to interfere arbitrarily in that person's life, not just be unlikely to interfere. Suppose that you are subject to interference on an arbitrary basis from someone who, as it happens, really likes you and is extremely unlikely to interfere. If it still remains the case that, by the ordinary standards of free-will attribution, they have a capacity to interfere or not to interfere, and this on a more or less arbitrary basis, then you are dominated in some measure by them and are thus far unfree. This is not a hard line to take, since you clearly suffer to the extent that the person has the capacity to interfere arbitrarily with you: you suffer to the extent that such interference is accessible to them as an agent, however improbable it is that they will exercise it. Their capacity for arbitrary interference means, for example, that you lack grounds for the subjective state of mind that goes with freedom as nondomination; you have reason to defer to the person in question and to look for their continued favour.

The third and last point is the most important. When Bentham and his associates came to reject the notion of freedom as nondomination, freedom as nonslavery, one theme in their reflections was that this sort of freedom did not come in degrees and so, unlike the rival conception, lent itself to 'panegyric and careless declamation' (Paley 1825: 359–360; Long 1977: ch. 4). John Lind (1776: 25) expressed the criticism strongly in his attack on Richard Price's talk of the American colonists as slaves. 'Things must be always at the maximum or minimum; there are no intermediate gradations: what is not white must be black'. The third point I want to make is that this perception is mistaken. Freedom as nondomination is not an all-or-nothing matter.

The point should be obvious on a little reflection. Agents may have a more or less ready capacity to interfere. And the interference for which they have a capacity may be more or less serious, and may be available more or less without cost: say, without risk of retaliation. Thus the freedom as nondomination of those they are in a position to affect may be more or less intense; the weaker the agents, the greater the freedom of those they may affect.

Intensity, I should add, is only one dimension in which freedom as nondomination may vary. As it is more or less intense, so freedom as nondomination may also be of one or another extent: it may be available for a smaller or larger number of choices, for choices that are more or less costly, and for choices of intuitively lesser or greater significance. Even if we have attained the highest possible intensity of nondomination for people in a society, there may be room for improving the range of undominated choice that is available to them: we may make the range of choice larger, or less costly, or intuitively more significant. Even if we remove all compromising influences on freedom as nondomination, it may still be possible to remove conditioning influences as well.

Thus, freedom as nondomination may be increased in either of two broad dimensions, intensity or extent; and we must decide how those dimensions are to be weighed against one another (Pettit 1997: ch. 3). Indeed, a similar problem arises with freedom as noninterference: it increases in intensity so far as interference is blocked, and increases in extent so far as the range of unobstructed choice is expanded, say, by providing people with extra resources. But I can overlook such problems of weighting here, as I shall be concerned with the promotion of these values only in the dimension of intensity. The question I address in the next section bears only on what is required for maximizing equal nondomination in the dimension of intensity.

THE SIGNIFICANCE OF THE REPUBLICAN IDEAL

Why is the republican conception of liberty politically significant for the modern state? In a word, because it would recall the state to performing, in relation to citizens generally, the service that a republic—even a republic hidden under the form of a monarchy—was expected to perform for traditional elites. Many late-eighteenth-century reformers, such as Bentham and Paley, may have dropped the ideal of freedom as nondomination, because they balked at the radical implications of trying to ensure for the common run of people—their constituency of concern—the sort of standing that nondomination, as distinct from noninterference, would imply (Pettit 1997). We can easily understand why it may have been impossible for them to envisage a state that would in this rich sense liberate servants as well as masters, women as well as men. But this is no longer an obviously infeasible ideal, even if it is obviously unattained. The limits on what we can envisage the state doing, and the limits on what we can imagine civil society allowing the state to do, have shifted dramatically over the last couple of centuries or so. Republicanism went underground at the time when the state began to become inclusivist, thereby permitting the state to become simultaneously more or less minimalist.[5] It is high time that the doctrine was restored to prominence, allowing us to consider the direction that an inclusive republic—a republic dedicated to the general promotion of freedom as nondomination—would have to take.

I have tried to display the significance of the republican perspective elsewhere, examining the impact of the republican ideal on our notions of equality and community; on the policy-commitments that we prescribe for the modern state; on the way we conceive of constitutional and democratic values and institutions; on the approach that we take to issues of regulation and control; and on the image we have of how the state should relate to civil society (Pettit 1997). In order to illustrate the way in which the republican perspective can affect our thinking, I will concentrate here on its significance for issues of redistribution. This theme is particularly relevant, because it is at the centre of contemporary political discussions, and it also connects with the hostile reaction of Paley and others like him to the republican ideal.

FREEDOM AS NONINTERFERENCE, AND REDISTRIBUTION

How far is the maximal equal distribution of freedom as noninterference consistent with inequalities in other dimensions? How

---

[5] Liberalism can be identified as the movement that took freedom as the primary ideal and that construed it as noninterference. In this case, then, short of taking on a secondary ideal—something like the second principle of justice proposed by Rawls (1971)—or of insisting on making freedom more and more effective—see Van Parijs (1995)—it will tend to support a minimal state. Left-leaning liberals, of course, generally want to follow the sorts of lines represented by Rawls and Van Parijs. For more, see Pettit (1997, Introduction).

far is it consistent, for example, with different levels of provision in basic goods like food and shelter, modes of transport and media of reliable information; in basic services like medical care, legal counsel, and accident insurance; in human capital of the kind associated with training and education; in social capital of the sort that consists in being able to call with confidence on others; in political capital such as office and authority confer; and in the material capital that is necessary for production? How far is it likely to require putting inequalities in these matters right or at least alleviating their effects: in particular, coercively putting them right, or coercively alleviating their effects, under state initiatives? How far is it likely to require what I shall describe, in a word, as redistribution?

The common wisdom on this question is that the maximal equal distribution of freedom as noninterference would leave a lot to be desired in regard to redistribution: it would fall short, under most conceptions, of achieving distributive justice (Rawls 1971). I think that wisdom is well placed, and I wish to argue that, in this respect, freedom as nondomination represents a sharply contrasted ideal: the maximal equal distribution of such freedom requires a much more substantial commitment to redistribution.

Before coming to that argument, however, it will be useful to see why the connection between freedom as noninterference and distributive justice is so loose. Two questions arise from the viewpoint of freedom as noninterference, when any such issue of redistribution is considered. First, how far will redistribution entail interference in people's lives by the state? And second, how far will redistribution lower the probability of interference by other agents?

The answer to the first question is that redistribution always entails a degree of interference by the state. For even the most basic form of redistribution involves taxing some to give to others, and that in itself constitutes interference; it deprives those who are taxed of a choice in how to use their money. Besides tax, most forms of redistribution also require inspectors and other officials to oversee the operation. Thus the redistributive measures involve the creation of new possibilities of interference in people's lives.

The answer to the first question means that the onus of proof always lies, from the perspective of freedom as noninterference, with those who counsel redistribution. Whether redistribution in any area is to be supported, then, depends on whether the answer to the second question shows clearly that the margin whereby redistribution will reduce interference in a society is greater than the margin whereby it introduces interference itself. The margin of projected improvement will have to be large enough to ensure that even when we discount for the less-than-certain nature of the projection, the argument squarely favours redistribution.

Nevertheless, it is not easy to find grounds to defend the required answer to the second question. It is always possible for the opponent to argue that, so long as we do not think of the relatively advantaged as downright malicious, we must expect them not to be generally disposed to harm the disadvantaged, and not to be generally in need of curtailment by the redistributive state. Perhaps employers are in a position under the status quo to interfere in various ways with their employees. But why expect them to interfere rather than striving for good and productive relationships? Perhaps husbands are able, given their greater strength and greater cultural backing, to abuse their wives. But why expect them to practise such abuse rather than remaining faithful to their affections and commitments? Perhaps those who lack medical care and legal counsel are prey to the unscrupulous. But why expect doctors and lawyers to be unwilling to provide essential services pro bono, especially when they can make good publicity of providing such services?

I sympathize with the drift of these rhetorical questions, believing that it is a mistake to demonize the relatively advantaged and see them always as potential offenders (Pettit 1995). But the effect of the questions in the context of endorsing an ideal of freedom as noninterference is what concerns me now, not the propriety of raising them. The effect is to lead those who take the ideal as the only relevant yardstick of social performance not to require much in the way of redistribution: not to require much in the way of what we intuitively describe as distributive justice. It is quite possible to believe that the regime under which freedom as noninterference is equally distributed at maximal levels is a regime that allows great inequalities in other regards.

Freedom as Nondomination, and Redistribution

We can begin to recognize the significance of the republican ideal of freedom when we notice that its connection with redistribution is different from that of freedom as noninterference. We have seen that the project of equalizing freedom as noninterference at the maximal possible level is hostile to redistribution in two ways. First, it introduces a presumption against redistribution; it casts the onus on the side of anyone who wants to argue for redistribution. And second, it ensures that any argument for redistribution must be probabilistic in a manner that is bound to make it easy to resist. I wish to argue that the ideal of maximizing freedom as nondomination at the maximal level possible differs from the associated ideal of freedom as noninterference in both these respects.

Freedom as noninterference introduces a presumption against redistribution, because redistribution is itself a species of the evil of interference. But no corresponding argument is available with freedom as nondomination. For if the redistributive measures adopted can be pursued under a fair rule of law, and are so pursued, then they do not themselves introduce any form of domination. I assume that many of the redistributive measures contemplated in discussions of distributive justice can be pursued under a fair rule of law. Freedom as nondomination, then, does not introduce any presumption against redistribution of the kind associated with freedom as noninterference. If redistributive measures are used in the promotion of nondomination, the good at which they are directed does not have to be balanced against a violation of that very good in the process of production; the process of production need not itself represent a form of domination.

The process is not entirely innocent, of course. As we mentioned, any rule of law, and certainly any redistributive rule of law, is going to remove certain choices or raise the costs of pursuing them. But this way of restricting choice, this way of conditioning people's freedom as nondomination, falls far short of compromising such freedom on their part. If it succeeds in reducing the extent to which the poor or the sick or the needy have their freedom compromised, then this cost in the conditioning of the freedom of people generally is well worth paying.

Here is another way of thinking about the point. Redistribution under a fair rule of law counts in the republican ledger-book as a form of conditioning of liberty on a par with the conditioning affected by factors like poverty or disability or illness or whatever. Redistribution involves moving around the factors that serve as

conditioning influences on freedom: and this, without itself domi-
nating anyone; without itself compromising anyone's freedom as
nondomination. If that reshuffling of freedom-relevant factors
can itself increase the degree of equal freedom in the society, then
there is little or no question to raise about it. There is no reason
to have a presumption against it.

This argument, I hasten to emphasize, is advanced under the
assumption that the redistribution effected is achieved under a
fair rule of law. And that assumption remains plausible only up
to a certain level, and only under a certain kind, of redistribution
by a state. Suppose that the redistribution allowed involves the
exercise of unconstrained discretion by individual agents of the
state; the discretion may arise in the way goods are taken from
some, for example, or in the way goods are given to others. Or
suppose that the redistribution is so extensive, or subject to such
frequent adjustments, that people hardly know where they stand
relative to the state. Under any such suppositions, the prospect
of redistribution looks very unattractive from a republican point
of view.

The republican tradition of thinking has always put the state
under severe scrutiny, for fear that state authorities will ever
become, or ever support, relatively arbitrary powers. In arguing
that the ideal of freedom as nondomination is not hostile to redistribution, in particular not hostile in the manner of freedom
as noninterference, I do not mean to reject that tradition. I think
that, if we treasure freedom as nondomination, then we have to be
vigilant about not allowing the state certain sorts of power; we have
to be careful to see that it is subject to all sorts of constitutional
and other constraints. My point has been only that, provided a
state can be sufficiently constrained—and that may be a very big
proviso—there is nothing inherently objectionable about allowing
it to use redistributive means for promoting antipower.[6]

The second point that we noticed about the redistributive significance of equalizing noninterference was that the question of
whether any redistributive measure increased people's freedom

---

[6] Libertarians often say that they are against big government. Republicans are
also against big government, but in a different sense. They object, not necessarily
to government's having redistributive rights and responsibilities, but rather to the
government's having power to act arbitrarily in the pursuit of redistributive ends;
the pursuit must always be governed by a fair rule of law.

as noninterference remained inevitably a probabilistic matter. Perhaps we can interfere with employers to ensure that they do not interfere in certain ways with their employees. Perhaps we can interfere with husbands to ensure that they do not interfere in certain ways with their wives. But before we think of practising interference, we have to convince ourselves that some shaky arithmetic comes out right. We have to convince ourselves that there is a suitably high probability of a suitably large reduction in the practice of interference by employers and husbands. That thought may well give pause to any projects of redistribution that the ideal of freedom as noninterference is otherwise likely to sponsor.

Like the matter of the presumption against redistribution, however, the ideal of freedom as antipower, freedom as nondomination, has quite a different impact here. Suppose that an employer has the capacity in some measure to interfere arbitrarily in the affairs of an employee. Employment is so scarce and the prospect of unemployment so repellent, that the employer can alter agreed conditions of work, make life much tougher for employees, or even practise some illegal interference in their affairs, with relative ease. And suppose now that we contemplate introducing a system of unemployment benefits, or a set of health and safety regulations, or an arrangement for arbitrating workplace disputes, that would improve the lot of employees. Do we have to do a range of probabilistic sums before we can be sure of the benefits of such a redistributive regime?

Assuming that the regime is consistent with a fair rule of law, and does not itself introduce an independent source of domination—provided it does not have any dominational side effects—it should be clear that no such sums are necessary. Just the existence of reasonable unemployment benefits is bound to reduce the extent to which an employee is willing to tolerate arbitrary interference by an employer, and by the same token reduces the capacity of the employer to interfere at will and with impunity in the lives of employees. There is no uncertainty plaguing the connection. Or at least there is no uncertainty of the kind that makes the connection with freedom as noninterference so problematic.

Similar points go through on a number of fronts. The fact that people are poor or illiterate or ignorant or unable to get legal counsel or uninsured against illness or incapable of getting around—the fact that they lack basic capabilities in any of these regards (Sen 1985)—makes them subject to a certain sort of exploitation and manipulation. Other things being equal, then, any improvement in their lot is bound to reduce the capacity of others to interfere more or less arbitrarily in their lives. And that means that, other things being equal—dominational side effects being absent—any such improvement is bound to increase their freedom as nondomination.

The crucial difference in this second respect between the ideals of freedom as noninterference and freedom as nondomination comes of the fact that the first ideal is compromised only by actual interference, the second by the capacity for interference, in particular the capacity for arbitrary interference. It may be unclear whether a given measure will actually reduce the overall level of interference practised by the more advantaged, while it is absolutely certain that the measure will reduce their capacity for interference.

Suppose that the employer in our earlier example is actually benign, or actually committed to a smooth and productive workplace, and thus is unlikely ever to interfere in the affairs of employees. The introduction of employment benefits, or health and safety regulations, or arbitration procedures, will not significantly reduce the probability of interference in such a scenario; that probability is already negligible. But still, the introduction of any such scheme will certainly reduce the employer's capacity for arbitrary interference. For whether the employer interferes or not will no longer be dependent on their good grace; it will be substantially determined by factors outside the employer's will.

Some will retort at this point that there is no reason why we should want to reduce the capacity of an employer to interfere with employees, especially given the cost of doing so, when it is certain that no interference will actually occur. But that is to shift the issue from the matter of what the ideal of freedom as nondomination would require—and, in particular, from the observation that it would require, other things being equal, that the employer is constrained—to the issue of whether it is an attractive ideal. My aim here is not to argue that it is an attractive ideal (on this issue see Pettit 1997), only that it is a redistributively demanding one.

We saw earlier that freedom as noninterference may be maximized, and maximized under the constraint of more or less equal distribution, without any significant redistribution of resources being required. What we have now seen is that, in this respect, as in so many others, freedom as nondomination is quite different. The republican ideal, just in itself, may be capable of encoding the redistributive measures that many of us would think it reasonable to require of the modern state. While remaining an ideal of liberty, it may give adequate expression to the more demanding aspirations that the nonlibertarians amongst us find compelling.

REFERENCES

Bentham, Jeremy. 'Anarchical Fallacies', in *The Works of Jeremy Bentham*, ed. J. Bowring, vol. 2. (Edinburgh: W. Tait, 1843).

Berlin, Isaiah. *Two Concepts of Liberty.* (Oxford, UK: Oxford University Press, 1958).

Blackstone, William. *Commentaries on the Laws of England*, 9th ed. (New York: Garland 1978 [1783]).

Constant, Benjamin. *Constant: Political Writings*, ed. B. Fontana. (Cambridge, UK: Cambridge University Press, 1988).

Dworkin, Ronald. *Taking Rights Seriously.* (London: Duckworth, 1978).

Harrington, James. *The Commonwealth of Oceana, and a System of Politics*, ed. J. G. A. Pocock. (Cambridge, UK: Cambridge University Press, 1992).

Hobbes, Thomas. *Leviathan*, ed. C. B. MacPherson. (Harmondsworth, UK: Penguin, 1968).

Lewis, David. *Convention.* (Cambridge, MA: Harvard University Press, 1969).

Lind, John. *Three Letters to Dr Price.* (London: T. Payne, 1776).

Locke, John. *Two Treatises of Government*, ed. Peter Laslett. (New York: Mentor, 1965).

Long, Douglas C. *Bentham on Liberty.* (Toronto: University of Toronto Press, 1977).

Mill, J. S. *Essays on Ethics, Religion, and Society.* (Collected Works, vol. 10). (London: Routledge, 1969).

Miller, David. *Market, State and Community.* (Oxford: Oxford University Press, 1990).

Montesquieu, Charles de Secondat. *The Spirit of the Laws*, trans. and ed. A. M. Cohler, B. C. Miller, and H. S. Stone. (Cambridge, UK: Cambridge University Press, 1989).

Paine, Tom. *Political Writings*, ed. Bruce Kuklick. (Cambridge, UK: Cambridge University Press, 1989).

Paley, William. *The Principles of Moral and Political Philosophy.* (Collected Works, vol. 4). (London: C. and J. Rivington, 1825).

Patterson, Orlando. *Freedom in the Making of Western Culture*. (New York: Basic-Books, 1991).

Pettit, Philip. 'Institutional Design and Rational Choice', in R. E. Goodin, ed., *The Theory of Institutional Design*. (Cambridge, UK: Cambridge University Press, 1995).

——. 'Freedom as Anti-Power'. *Ethics* 106 (1996).

——. *Republicanism: A Theory of Freedom and Government*. (Oxford, UK: Oxford University Press, 1997).

Price, Richard. *Political Writings*, ed. D. O. Thomas. (Cambridge, UK: Cambridge University Press, 1991).

Priestley, Joseph. *Political Writings*, ed. P. N. Miller. (Cambridge, UK: Cambridge University Press, 1993).

Rawls, John. *A Theory of Justice*. (Oxford, UK: Oxford University Press, 1971).

Sen, Amartya. *Commodities and Capabilities*. (Amsterdam: North-Holland, 1985).

Skinner, Quentin. 'Machiavelli on the Maintenance of Liberty'. *Politics* 18 (1983).

Spitz, Jean-Fabien. *La Liberté Politique*. (Paris: Presses Universitaires de France, 1995).

Sydney, Algernon. *Discourses Concerning Government*, ed. T. G. West. (Indianapolis, IN: Liberty Classics, 1990).

——.*Court Maxims*, ed. H. W. Blom, E. H. Muller, and Ronald Janse. (Cambridge, UK: Cambridge University Press, 1996).

Trenchard, John, and Thomas Gordon. *Cato's Letters*. 6th ed. (New York: Da Capo, 1971 [1755]).

Van Parijs, Philippe. *Real Freedom for All*. (Oxford, UK: Oxford University Press, 1995).

TWELVE

A Third Concept of Liberty

Quentin Skinner

My starting point is one of the claims most widely accepted in current discussions about the theory of liberty. There is one over-arching formula, we are told, under which all intelligible locutions about freedom can be subsumed. The prevalence of this belief appears to be due in large part to the influence of a single classic article, Gerald MacCallum's 'Negative and Positive Freedom' (1967). Whenever the freedom of an agent is in question, Mac-Callum maintains, it will always be freedom from some element of constraint on doing or becoming (or not doing or becoming) something. Consequently, to speak of the presence of freedom is always to speak of an absence: absence of constraint on an agent from realising some goal or end. There is, in other words, only one concept of liberty.

These observations bring me to Isaiah Berlin, a thinker who devoted himself to many disparate themes, literary and historical as well as philosophical, but whose most important and influential work was on the theory of freedom. It is on that topic that I propose to concentrate. I shall focus in particular on Berlin's most celebrated contribution to the debate, his essay entitled 'Two Concepts of Liberty', recently republished in a handsome new collection.[1]

The abiding merit of Berlin's text is that, by contrast with the conventional wisdom I began by citing, Berlin succeeds in showing that a strong distinction needs to be marked between two rival

This essay was first presented as the inaugural Isaiah Berlin Memorial Lecture to the British Academy on November 21, 2001, and published as Quentin Skinner, 'A Third Concept of Liberty', *London Review of Books*. Reprinted by permission of the author and of the London Review of Books: www.lrb.co.uk.

[1] Isaiah Berlin, *Liberty*, ed. Henry Hardy (Oxford, UK: Oxford University Press, 2002).

and incommensurable concepts of liberty, which he, too, labels 'positive' and 'negative'. When he discusses negative liberty, he gives an account closely resembling the analysis that, according to MacCallum and his numerous followers, must be given of any claim about freedom if it is to be intelligible. To see, therefore, where Berlin has something challenging to add to the argument, we need to turn to his account of what he calls positive liberty.

Berlin's attempt to mark off this separate concept is admittedly dogged by several false starts. He begins by suggesting that, whereas negative liberty is freedom from constraint, positive liberty is freedom to follow a certain form of life. But this distinction cannot be used to disclose two different concepts of liberty, if only because all cases of negative liberty are at once cases in which I am free from constraint and in consequence free to act should I choose. Berlin next suggests that the positive sense of the word refers to the idea of being one's own master as opposed to being acted on by external forces. But this, too, fails to isolate a separate concept of positive liberty. For the situation in which I am free to act in virtue of not being hindered by external forces is, according to Berlin's own analysis, the situation of someone in possession of their liberty in the ordinary negative sense.

It soon emerges, however, that Berlin's concern is not with the idea of being your own master. Rather, he is interested in the very different notion (although he sometimes runs them together) of mastering your self. When he first employs this formula, he uses it to refer to the thought—equally familiar to students of Plato and of Freud—that the obstacles to your capacity to act freely may be internal rather than external, and that you will need to free yourself from these psychological constraints if you are to behave autonomously. But this, too, fails to capture a separate concept of positive liberty. For while the notion of an internal obstacle extends the range of things that can count as constraints, we are still speaking about the need to get rid of an element of constraint if we are to act freely, and are still speaking in consequence about the idea of negative liberty.

The principal claim, however, that Berlin wishes to make about self-mastery proves to be a different and more convincing one. According to those who have wished to give a positive content to the idea of liberty, he suggests, the freedom of human agents consists in their having managed most fully to become themselves.

Freedom is thus equated not with self-mastery but rather with self-realisation, and above all with self-perfection, with the idea (as Berlin expresses it) of my self at its best. The positive concept is thus that, as Berlin finally summarises, 'whatever is the true goal of man ... must be identical with his freedom'.

If there is any one philosopher whom Berlin had in mind in formulating this definition, I think it must have been Bernard Bosanquet. In *The Philosophical Theory of the State,* first published in 1899, Bosanquet speaks in so many words about the 'negative idea' of being 'free from constraint' and contrasts this juristic concept, as he calls it, with what he describes as the 'fuller' or 'positive' understanding of the term. Furthermore, when Bosanquet characterises the negative ideal as that of being preserved against trespass, and contrasts it with the positive view of the 'real' or 'ideal' self whose activity is identical with freedom, Berlin echoes his phraseology almost word for word.

Behind Bosanquet's analysis, however, lies the overwhelming influence of T. H. Green. As Bosanquet acknowledges in the chapter I have been quoting, he makes 'great use' of the analysis of freedom offered by Green in his *Principles of Political Obligation,* originally published in 1886. Green does not explicitly speak in that work (although he does elsewhere) of 'positive' liberty, but he provides a subtler and more careful analysis than Bosanquet does of what might be meant by giving a positive content to the ideal. 'Real freedom', according to Green, 'consists in the whole man having found his object'. To speak of the freedom of a man is thus to speak of 'the state in which he shall have realised his ideal of himself'. Freedom is, in short, the name of an end-state; as Green concludes, it is 'in some sense the goal of moral endeavour'.

It is hard nowadays to recapture how disquieting this analysis seemed to many Anglophone philosophers writing in the aftermath of the First World War. L. T. Hobhouse, for example, whose critique of Hegel, Green, and Bosanquet appeared in 1918, went so far as to assert that in the bombing of London he had witnessed 'the visible and tangible outcome' of this 'false and wicked doctrine'. To anyone of Berlin's generation, however, these anxieties about Hegelian philosophy remained remarkably acute, and these are the feelings that Berlin is registering, I think, in his account of positive liberty and the dangers to which it gives rise.

I do not wish, however, to press the historical point. My reason for quoting Green and Bosanquet is to lend further support to what seems to me Berlin's most important contention, and my reason for wishing to add this support is that Berlin seems to me to miss the force of his own argument. This becomes clear when he responds to MacCallum's insistence that all claims about freedom conform to the same triadic structure, since they are all claims about the need to be free from constraint to do or become something. Berlin merely returns the suggestion—which I have already shown to be confused—that some pleas for liberty reflect a simpler dyadic structure, since they are nothing more than pleas to be liberated. What Berlin should have retorted, it seems to me, is that the positive conception of liberty he rightly isolates cannot be made to conform to the triadic structure on which MacCallum and his followers insist. The crux of Green's and Bosanquet's argument is that the freedom of human agents consists in their having succeeded in realising an ideal of themselves. But this is not to speak of a condition in which someone is free to do or become something, as required by MacCallum's analysis. It is to speak of a condition in which someone has succeeded in becoming something. Freedom is not being viewed as absence of constraint on action; it is being viewed as a pattern of action of a certain kind.

Berlin's argument can be carried yet another step if we recognise that what underlies these theories of positive liberty is the belief that human nature has an essence, and that we are free if and only if we succeed in realising that essence in our lives. This enables us to see that there will be as many different interpretations of positive liberty as there are different views about the moral character of humankind. Suppose you accept the Christian view that the essence of our nature is religious, and thus that we attain our highest ends if and only if we consecrate our lives to God. Then you will believe that, in the words of Thomas Cranmer, the service of God 'is perfect freedom'. Or suppose you accept the Aristotelian argument that man is a political animal, the argument restated as a theory of freedom by Hannah Arendt in *Between Past and Future* (1961). Then you will believe that, as Arendt maintains, 'freedom ... and politics coincide' and that 'this freedom is primarily experienced in action'.

Faced with these equations between freedom and certain forms of life, how can MacCallum and his followers hope to rescue their contention that all intelligible claims about liberty must be claims about absence of constraint? As far as I can see, their only recourse will be to suggest that the arguments I have cited from Green and Bosanquet are not intelligible as claims about liberty; that they must either be muddled or be talking about something else. As Berlin excellently points out, however, there is no difficulty in seeing how the neo-Hegelians took their thesis, without any incoherence, to be one about human freedom. The claim they are advancing is that if, and only if, we actually follow the most fulfilling way of life shall we overcome the constraints and obstacles to our realisation of our full potential, and thereby realise our ideal of ourselves. The living of such a life alone frees us from such constraints and, by making us fully ourselves, makes us fully free.

As the title of his essay indicates, Berlin's main concern is to contrast this positive ideal of freedom with what he describes, following much precedent, as negative liberty. As we have seen, by negative liberty Berlin means absence of constraint, and the specific interpretation he believes must be given to the concept of constraint is that it must consist in some act of interference, by some external agency, with the capacity of another agent to pursue 'possible choices and activities'. These obstacles or hindrances need not be intentional, for Berlin allows that they may be the result of—as opposed to being deliberately caused by—the actions of others. But his fundamental contention is that the absence marking the presence of liberty must always be absence of interference.

While this is a familiar vision of human liberty, it is a matter of no small difficulty to state it with precision, and it is worth noting that Berlin's statement embodies a valuable qualification often omitted in more recent accounts. Berlin adds that I am unfree 'if I am prevented by others from doing what I could otherwise do'. I may be physically obstructed in such a way that an action within my powers becomes impossible to perform. Or I may be subjected to such a degree of coercion that the action is rendered, in Jeremy Bentham's phrase, ineligible. But in either case my loss of freedom stems from 'the deliberate interference of other human beings within the area in which I could otherwise act'.

Berlin's way of articulating this distinction is strongly reminiscent of Thomas Hobbes's analysis of free action in his *Leviathan* of 1651. Hobbes compares the predicament of two men who are unable to leave a room. One possesses the power to leave, but has been 'restrained with walls, or chains' and thereby disempowered; the other straightforwardly lacks the ability, because he is 'fastened to his bed by sickness'. According to Hobbes's analysis, the first man is unfree to leave, but the second is neither free nor unfree; he is simply unable. The reason, Hobbes explains, is that the idea of free action presupposes the idea of deliberating between alternatives. But it makes no sense to deliberate as to whether to perform an action we already know to be beyond our powers.

Contrast this understanding with the view, currently prevalent, that we need to distinguish between the formal and the effective possession of negative liberty. One of the examples Berlin gives in distinguishing lack of freedom from inability is the case of a man who cannot read because he is blind. If we apply the distinction between formal and effective freedom, we arrive at the view that the blind man is formally free to read, because no one is interfering with him in this pursuit. But he is not effectively free, since he is not in a position to make use of his formal liberty.

Berlin's Hobbesian approach enables us to see that this kind of analysis results at best in confusion and at worst in a kind of mockery of freedom. There are two contrasting points to be brought out here. One is that, on Berlin's account, the blind man is neither formally nor effectively free to read. As Berlin insists, I am free only if I am capable of exercising an ability, should I choose, without interference. But the predicament of the blind man is that he is incapable of exercising the ability to read under any circumstances. The contrasting point is that, on Berlin's account, the blind man is neither formally nor effectively unfree to read. To be unfree is to have been rendered incapable of exercising an ability I possess. But the blind man has not in this way been disempowered; he is simply not in possession of the relevant ability. Although Berlin's analysis of negative liberty is exceptionally acute and valuable, it nevertheless seems to me to suffer from a serious limitation of coverage. This weakness, moreover, is one that it shares with almost every other recent statement of the theory of negative liberty I have come across. This being so, the nature of the weakness seems to me well worth trying to identify and remedy, and this is the task to which I shall devote the rest of these remarks.

When Berlin first introduces his view of negative liberty, he rightly observes that 'this is what the classical English political philosophers meant' by freedom, and he specifically refers us to Hobbes's definition in *Leviathan*. What Berlin misses, however, is the fiercely polemical character of Hobbes's analysis. When Hobbes announces, in words that Berlin echoes closely, that our liberty consists of nothing more than absence of external impediments, he is attempting at the same time to discredit and supersede a rival and strongly contrasting understanding of negative liberty. This rival theory had risen to prominence in English public debate in the early decades of the seventeenth century, and it appeared to Hobbes to be extremely dangerous as well as hopelessly confused.

I can best bring out the significance of Hobbes's critique if I try to answer a question raised by Berlin in the introduction to his revised edition of 'Two Concepts of Liberty'. He asks when the idea of freedom as nothing other than noninterference was first explicitly formulated, and what prompted its rise to its present hegemonal prominence. I would answer that it is very hard to find an explicit statement of such a theory any earlier than Hobbes's in *Leviathan*, and that what prompted him to articulate it was his sense of the need to respond to the 'democratical gentlemen', as he called them, who had deployed their very different theory to promote the cause of Parliament against the Crown and to legitimise the execution of King Charles I in 1649.

Hobbes's counter-revolutionary challenge eventually won the day. To cite Berlin's own litany, we find his basic line of argument taken up by David Hume, Jeremy Bentham, to some degree by John Stuart Mill, and even more closely (Berlin might have added) by Henry Sidgwick. This great tradition of classical utilitarianism proved impressively successful at occupying the entire conceptual space, thereby managing to dismiss any rival interpretations as either pernicious or confused. As a result of this profound and enduring ideological success, the alternative vision of negative liberty that Hobbes originally set out to discredit has virtually sunk from sight. What I now want to do is to try to lift it back to the surface.

As I have indicated, the theory in question rose to prominence in Anglophone political theory in the course of the disputes between Crown and Parliament in seventeenth-century Britain. Critics of the royal prerogative began to argue that, to the extent that they were obliged to live in dependence on the power of the king, and obliged in consequence to rely on his goodwill for the continuation of their rights and liberties, they were living in a state of servitude. They insisted, in other words, that freedom is restricted not only by actual interference or the threat of it, but also by the mere knowledge that we are living in dependence on the goodwill of others. These writers are not making the obvious point that the possibility of arbitrary interference renders our liberty less robust or secure. They are arguing that our mere awareness of living under an arbitrary power—a power capable of interfering with our activities without having to consider our interests—serves in itself to limit our liberty. Knowing that we are free to do or forbear only because someone else has chosen not to stop us is what reduces us to servitude.

The immediate inspiration for this way of thinking appears to have stemmed from a number of medieval common-law texts, above all those of Bracton and Littleton. But the most striking feature of these discussions (although later common lawyers did their best to ignore the fact) is that they in turn owe their phraseology entirely to the analysis of freedom and slavery to be found in the *Digest of Roman Law*. There we are first informed that 'the fundamental division within the law of persons is that all men and women are either free or are slaves'. Next we are given a formal definition of slavery. 'Slavery is an institution of the law of nations by which someone is, contrary to nature, subjected to the dominion of someone else'. This in turn is held to yield a definition of individual liberty. If everyone in a civil association is either free or a slave, then a free citizen must be someone who is not under the dominion of anyone else, but is capable of acting in their own right.

By the time these distinctions were definitively summarised in Justinian's Codex, they had been the common coin of Roman political theory for generations. They had been popularised above all by the sequence of great historians—Sallust, Livy, Tacitus—who had traced the subversion of the republican constitution and its collapse into the servitude of the principate. If you turn to any of these authorities, you will find it argued once again that what it means to possess your liberty is, as Livy puts it, 'to be in your own power', not obliged to live at the mercy of anyone else.

It was this understanding of political liberty that a number of spokesmen in the English Parliament began to deploy in criticism of the Crown in the early decades of the seventeenth century. They were partly protesting against what they took to be straightforward violations of their fundamental rights. But they were also objecting to what they saw as a deeper affront to liberty. They were fearful of the underlying principle that, in times of necessity, the Crown possesses the discretionary power to override civil rights. The objection they developed was that, if the Crown is the bearer of any such prerogatives, this is as much as to say that our property and personal liberties are held not 'of right' but merely 'of grace', since the Crown can take them away without injustice at any time.

What troubled these critics was the view of rights implied by this understanding of the prerogative. To claim that our basic liberties are subject to being taken away with impunity is to declare that they do not have the status of rights; it is to say that they are mere licenses or privileges. This was the insight that prompted these critics to reach for their Bracton—and indeed their Livy and Tacitus. To accept that we hold our liberties at discretion, they retort, is to accept that we are living in dependence on the will of the king. But to admit that we are living in such a state of dependence is to admit that we are living not as free citizens but as slaves. The mere knowledge that the Crown possesses such prerogatives is what reduces us to servitude.

The moment at which these arguments provoked a fatal crisis came in 1642. When the House of Commons brought forward a proposal early in February to take control of the militia, Charles I made it clear that he would veto any such legislation by exercising his so-called prerogative of the Negative Voice. Parliament then took the revolutionary step of claiming that, at least in times of emergency, it must possess the right to legislate even in the absence of the royal assent. The reason why this must be so, a number of spokesmen now proclaimed, is that the alternative is national servitude. The most influential statement of the parliamentary case was furnished by Henry Parker in his *Observations* of July 1642. If the Crown can block any legislation with the Negative Voice, this will reduce the Parliament to a state of dependence on the will of the king. But if we permit the king 'to be the sole, supreme competent Judge in this case, we resign all into his hands, we give lives, liberties, Laws, Parliaments, all to be held at mere discretion' and thereby consign ourselves to slavery.

Parker was not the first to put forward this argument, but his *Observations* offered the most confident statement of the case, and did much to make it central to the rhetoric of the ensuing Civil War. We encounter the same argument in Parliament's call to arms of August 1642, and we encounter it yet again after the parliamentary victory, when it was used to justify not merely the regicide but the abolition of the monarchy. The charge against Charles I at his trial was that he had ruled by his arbitrary will, and hence tyrannically. The Act of March 1649 abolishing the office of king confirmed that monarchy is 'dangerous to the liberty, safety, and public interest of the people', and added that in England the effect of the prerogative has been 'to oppress and impoverish and enslave the subject'.

This neo-Roman analysis of what it means to possess our freedom carried with it a distinctive view of the relations between the liberty of citizens and the constitution of the state. The essence of the argument is that freedom is restricted by dependence. To be free as a citizen, therefore, requires that the actions of the state should reflect the will of all its citizens, for otherwise the excluded will remain dependent on those whose wills move the state to act. The outcome is the belief—crucial alike to the English Revolution of the seventeenth century and to the American and French Revolutions of a century later—that it is possible to enjoy our individual liberty if and only if we live as citizens of self-governing republics. To live as subjects of a monarch is to live as slaves.

It would be wrong to imply that Isaiah Berlin failed to recognise the existence of this tradition of thought. It is true that he never discusses it with the same historical specificity as he brings to bear on the other two traditions he examines, and that he never singles out any particular theorist or movement capable of being associated with this alternative standpoint. Given, however, that he was writing at the height of the debate about decolonialisation, he could scarcely have been unaware that nations as well as individuals often claim to be unfree when they are condemned to social or political dependence. He devotes considerable attention at the end of his essay to what he describes as the resulting 'search for status', and he explicitly asks himself whether it might not 'be natural or desirable to call the demand for recognition and status a demand for liberty in some third sense'.

Having raised the question, however, Berlin confidently answers that no such third concept of liberty can be coherently entertained. To speak of dependence as lack of liberty, he writes, would be to confound freedom with other concepts in a manner at once misleading and confused. Stating his grounds for this conclusion, Berlin goes on to enunciate his most general claim about the concept of liberty. He insists that it is true not merely of any coherent account of negative freedom, but of any concept of freedom whatever, that it must embody, at least as a minimum, the idea of absence of interference. If we are to speak of constraints on our liberty, we must be able to point to some visible act of hindrance, the aim or consequence of which was to impede us in the exercise of our powers.

It is precisely this assumption, however, that the writers I have been considering reject. The distinctive claim they defend is that a mere awareness of living in dependence on the goodwill of others serves in itself to restrict our options and thereby limits our liberty. The effect is to dispose us to make and avoid certain choices, and is thus to place clear constraints on our freedom of action, even though our rulers may never interfere with our activities or even show the least sign of threatening to interfere with them.

The exploration of this argument had been a leading preoccupation of the classical historians I have singled out. Tacitus in particular speaks with an unforgettable combination of agony and contempt about the psychological impact of living under tyranny. If you are subject to unaccountable power, you will find in the first place that there are many things you are not free to say or do. Above all, you will need to ensure that you avoid saying or doing anything that might be construed by your rulers as an act of challenge, emulation, or reproach. You will likewise find that you lack the freedom to abstain from saying and doing certain things. When required to advise your rulers or to comment on their behaviour, you will find yourself constrained to endorse whatever policies they already wish to pursue. Yet more serious is the long-term psychological damage inflicted by such forms of self-censorship. As Tacitus bitterly emphasises, servitude inevitably breeds servility. When a whole nation is inhibited from exercising its highest talents and virtues, these qualities will begin to atrophy and the people will gradually sink into an abject condition of torpor and sluggishness.

It was this analysis that exercised perhaps the most formative influence on the democratical gentlemen who challenged the government of Charles I and instituted the first and only British republic. So far. They, too, were deeply preoccupied by the dangerous implications of the fact that unaccountable rulers are inevitably surrounded by servile flatterers, and have little hope of hearing frank advice. As in the case of the classical historians, however, their principal anxiety was that, under such rulers, no one will perform any deeds requiring public spirit or courageous and great-hearted qualities. At first they lacked the vocabulary in which to express this Tacitean insight, but they gradually popularised a series of neologisms that enabled them to refer directly to the loss of spirit, courage, and great-heartedness that tyranny brings in its train. The final effect, as they put it, is that everyone becomes dispirited, discouraged, disheartened.

For all the power of this analysis, contemporary political theory has largely neglected it. Berlin's view that negative liberty must be construed as absence of interference remains the orthodoxy, and nowhere more so than in Great Britain and the United States. But this is deeply ironic, especially in the American case, for the United States was born out of the rival theory that negative liberty consists of absence of dependence. When Congress adopted Thomas Jefferson's *Declaration* in July 1776, what they decided to call it, no one needs reminding, was a *Declaration of Independence*. But do we ever pause long enough over that word? Independence from what? From living in dependence on the arbitrary power of the British Crown. And what made Congress believe that this justified revolution? Their acceptance of the classical contention that, if you depend on the goodwill of anyone else for the upholding of your rights, it follows that—even if your rights are in fact upheld—you will be living in servitude.

Given our current predicament, it is unfortunate that this way of thinking about freedom has become so widely discredited. We are again being urged to recognise that, in times of emergency, civil liberties must bow to national security. We are being urged, that is, to acknowledge that our liberties are held not as rights but by grace of our rulers, and that it is for them to tell us what counts as an emergency. These arguments are of course being put to us in the name of freedom and democracy. But it is worth recalling that, according to the American Founding Fathers, and to the democratical gentlemen by whom they were so greatly influenced, this is to speak the language of tyranny.

Selected Bibliography

Studies of the Concept of Liberty

Benn, S. I. *A Theory of Freedom* (Cambridge, UK: Cambridge University Press, 1988).

Benn, S. I., and W. L. Weinstein. 'Being Free to Act and Being a Free Man'. *Mind* 80 (1971): 194–211.

Brenkert, G. *Political Freedom* (London: Routledge, 1991).

Carter, I. *A Measure of Freedom* (Oxford, UK: Oxford University Press, 1999).

Connolly, W. E. *The Terms of Political Discourse* (Lexington, MA: D. C. Heath, 1974), chapter 4.

Crocker, L. *Positive Liberty* (The Hague: M. Nijhoff, 1980).

Day, J. P. *Liberty and Justice* (London: Croom Helm, 1987).

Dworkin, G. *The Theory and Practice of Autonomy* (Cambridge, UK: Cambridge University Press, 1988).

Feinberg, J. 'The Idea of a Free Man', in J. Feinberg, *Rights, Justice, and the Bounds of Liberty* (Princeton, NJ: Princeton University Press, 1980).

Flathman, R. E. *The Philosophy and Politics of Freedom* (Chicago, IL: University of Chicago Press, 1987).

Gray, J. N. 'On Liberty, Liberalism, and Essential Contestability'. *British Journal of Political Science* 8 (1978): 385–402.

——. *Liberalisms* (London: Routledge, 1989).

Gray, T. *Freedom* (Basingstoke, UK: Macmillan, 1991).

Griffiths, A. Phillips, ed. *Of Liberty* (Cambridge, UK: Cambridge University Press, 1983).

Kramer, M. *The Quality of Freedom* (Oxford, UK: Oxford University Press, 2003).

Lindley, R. *Autonomy* (London: Macmillan, 1986).

O'Neill, O. 'The Most Extensive Liberty'. *Proceedings of the Aristotelian Society* 80 (1979–1980): 45–59.

Oppenheim, F. E. *Dimensions of Freedom* (New York: St Martin's Press/London: Macmillan, 1961).

Pettit, P. *A Theory of Freedom* (Cambridge, UK: Polity Press, 2001).

Swift, A. *Political Philosophy: A Beginner's Guide for Students and Politicians* (Cambridge, UK: Polity Press, 2001), Part II.

Young, R. *Personal Autonomy: Beyond Negative and Positive Liberty* (London and Sydney: Croom Helm, 1986).

HISTORIES OF THE IDEA OF LIBERTY

No comprehensive study exists, but the following offer partial guidance.

Acton, Lord. *Essays in the History of Liberty,* ed. J. R. Frears (Indianapolis, IN: Liberty Classics, 1985).

Carlyle, A. J. *Political Liberty: A History of the Conception in the Middle Ages and Modern Times* (London: Frank Cass, 1963).

Lewis, C. S. *Studies in Words* (Cambridge, UK: Cambridge University Press, 1960), chapter 5.

Patterson, O. *Freedom,* vol 1: *Freedom in the Making of the Western World* (London: I. B. Tauris, 1991).

Skinner, Q. *Liberty before Liberalism* (Cambridge, UK: Cambridge University Press, 1998).

SOME APPLICATIONS OF THE CONCEPT TO ISSUES OF POLICY

Liberty and the Market Economy

Cohen, G. A. *Self-Ownership, Freedom, and Equality* (Cambridge, UK: Cambridge University Press, 1995), chapters 1–2.

Friedman, M. *Capitalism and Freedom* (Chicago, IL: University of Chicago Press, 1962).

Hayek, F. A. *The Constitution of Liberty* (London: Routledge and Kegan Paul, 1960).

——. *Law, Legislation, and Liberty* (London: Routledge and Kegan Paul, 1982).

Miller, D. *Market, State, and Community: Theoretical Foundations of Market Socialism* (Oxford, UK: Clarendon Press, 1989), chapter 1.

Nozick, R. *Anarchy, State, and Utopia* (Oxford, UK: Blackwell, 1974), Part II.

Olsaretti, S. *Liberty, Desert, and the Market: A Philosophical Study* (Cambridge, UK: Cambridge University Press, 2004), chapters 4–6.

Sen, A. 'Markets and Freedom', in A. Sen, ed., *Rationality and Freedom* (Cambridge, MA: Harvard University Press, 2002).

Liberty and Socialism

Gould, B. *Socialism and Freedom* (London: Macmillan, 1985).

Hayek, F. A. *The Road to Serfdom* (London: Routledge and Kegan Paul, 1944).

Levine, A. *Arguing for Socialism* (London: Verso, 1988).

Plant, R. 'Socialism, Markets, and End States', in J. Le Grand and S. Estrin, eds., *Market Socialism* (Oxford, UK: Clarendon Press, 1989).

Ryan, A. 'Liberty and Socialism', in B. Pimlott, ed., *Fabian Essays in Socialist Thought* (London: Heinemann, 1984).

Selucky, R. *Marxism, Socialism, Freedom* (London: Macmillan, 1979), chapter 5.

Freedom and Social Policy

Goodin, R. 'Freedom and the Welfare State: Theoretical Foundations'. *Journal of Social Policy* 11 (1982): 149–176. (A revised version appears as R. Goodin, *Reasons for Welfare* [Princeton, NJ: Princeton University Press, 1988], chapter 11.)

Jones, P. 'Freedom and the Redistribution of Resources'. *Journal of Social Policy* 11 (1982): 217–238.

Jordan, B. *Freedom and the Welfare State* (London: Routledge and Kegan Paul, 1976).

Van Parijs, P. *Real Freedom for All* (Oxford, UK: Clarendon Press, 1995), especially chapters 1–2.

Weale, A. *Political Theory and Social Policy* (London: Macmillan, 1989), chapters 3–4.

Freedom of Speech

Baker, C. E. *Human Liberty and Freedom of Speech* (New York: Oxford University Press, 1989).

Brison, S. 'The Autonomy Defense of Free Speech'. *Ethics* 108 (1997–1998): 312–339.

Cohen, J. 'Freedom of Expression'. *Philosophy and Public Affairs* 22 (1993): 173–225.

Fiss, O. *The Irony of Free Speech* (Cambridge, MA: Harvard University Press, 1998).

Scanlon, T. 'A Theory of Freedom of Expression', in T. Scanlon, *The Difficulty of Tolerance* (Cambridge, UK: Cambridge University Press, 2003).

Schauer, F. *Free Speech: A Philosophical Enquiry* (Cambridge, UK: Cambridge University Press, 1982).

The Limits of Liberty

Buchanan, J. *The Limits of Liberty: Between Anarchy and Leviathan* (Chicago, IL: University of Chicago Press, 1975).

Feinberg, J. *The Moral Limits of the Criminal Law*. 4 vols. (New York: Oxford University Press, 1984–1988).

Hart, H. L. A. *Law, Liberty, and Morality* (London: Oxford University Press, 1963).

Mendus, S. *Toleration and the Limits of Liberalism* (London: Macmillan, 1989).

Feminism and Freedom

Coole, D. 'Constructing and Deconstructing Liberty: A Feminist and Poststructuralist Analysis'. *Political Studies* 41 (1993): 83–95.

Di Stefano, C. 'Autonomy in the Light of Difference', in N. Hirschmann and C. Di Stefano, eds., *Revisioning the Political: Feminist Reconstructions of Traditional Concepts in Western Political Theory* (Boulder, CO: Westview Press, 1996).

Hirschmann, N. *The Subject of Liberty: Toward a Feminist Theory of Freedom* (Princeton, NJ: Princeton University Press, 2003).

Jamieson, B. *Real Choices: Feminism, Freedom, and the Limits of Law* (University Park: Pennsylvania State University Press, 2001).

Radcliffe Richards, J. *The Sceptical Feminist* (Harmondsworth, UK: Penguin, 1994), chapter 3.

IDEAS OF LIBERTY IN SOME MAJOR POLITICAL THEORISTS

The most useful general source is Z. Pelczynski and J. N. Gray, eds., *Conceptions of Liberty in Political Philosophy* (London: Athlone Press, 1984).

Niccolò Machiavelli (1469–1527)

Machiavelli, N. *The Discourses,* ed. B. Crick (Harmondsworth, UK: Penguin, 1970).

Coby, J. P. *Machiavelli's Romans: Liberty and Greatness in the Discourses on Livy* (Lanham, MD: Lexington Books, 1999).

Colish, M. L. 'The Idea of Liberty in Machiavelli'. *Journal of the History of Ideas* 32 (1971): 323–350.

Skinner, Q. 'Machiavelli on Virtue and the Maintenance of Liberty' and 'The Idea of Negative Liberty: Machiavellian and Modern Perspectives', in Q. Skinner, *Visions of Politics,* vol. II (Cambridge, UK: Cambridge University Press, 2002).

Thomas Hobbes (1588–1679)

Hobbes, T. *Leviathan,* ed. R. Tuck (Cambridge, UK: Cambridge University Press, 1996).

Kramer, M. 'On the Unavoidability of Actions: Quentin Skinner, Thomas Hobbes, and the Modern Doctrine of Negative Liberty'. *Inquiry* 44 (2001): 315–330.

Pennock, J. R. 'Hobbes's Confusing "Clarity"—The Case of "Liberty"', in K. C. Brown, ed., *Hobbes Studies* (Oxford, UK: Blackwell, 1965).

Raphael, D. D. 'Hobbes', in Z. Pelczynski and J. N. Gray, eds., *Conceptions of Liberty in Political Philosophy* (London: Athlone Press, 1984).

Skinner, Q. 'Hobbes on the Proper Signification of Liberty', in Q. Skinner, *Visions of Politics,* vol. III (Cambridge, UK: Cambridge University Press, 2002).

Van Mill, D. 'Hobbes's Theories of Freedom'. *Journal of Politics* 57 (1995): 443–459.

Von Leyden, W. *Hobbes and Locke* (London: Macmillan, 1981), chapters 1–2.

John Locke (1632–1704)

Locke, J. *Letter on Toleration*, ed. R. Klibansky and J. W. Gough (Oxford, UK: Clarendon Press, 1968).
——. *Two Treatises of Government*, ed. P. Laslett (Cambridge, UK: Cambridge University Press, 1988).
Parry, G. *John Locke* (London: Allen and Unwin, 1978).
Polin, R. 'John Locke's Conception of Freedom', in J. W. Yolton, ed., *John Locke: Problems and Perspectives* (Cambridge, UK: Cambridge University Press, 1969).
Simmons, A. J. *On the Edge of Anarchy: Locke, Consent and the Limits of Society* (Princeton, NJ: Princeton University Press, 1993).
Tully, J. 'Locke on Liberty', in Z. Pelczynski and J. N. Gray, eds., *Conceptions of Liberty in Political Philosophy* (London: Athlone Press, 1984).
Waldron, J. 'Locke, Toleration and the Rationality of Persecution', in J. Waldron, *Liberal Rights* (Cambridge, UK: Cambridge University Press, 1993).

Jean Jacques Rousseau (1712–1778)

Rousseau, J. J. *The Social Contract and Discourses,* trans. and ed. G. D. H. Cole, J. H. Brumfitt, and J. C. Hall (London: Dent, 1973).
Chapman, J. W. *Rousseau: Totalitarian or Liberal?* (New York: Columbia University Press, 1956).
Fetscher, I. 'Rousseau's Concepts of Freedom in the Light of His Philosophy of History', in C. J. Friedrich, ed., *Nomos IV: Liberty* (New York: Atherton Press, 1962).
Gardiner, P. 'Rousseau on Liberty', in Z. Pelczynski and J. N. Gray, eds., *Conceptions of Liberty in Political Philosophy* (London: Athlone Press, 1984).
Miller, J. *Rousseau: Dreamer of Democracy* (New Haven, CT: Yale University Press, 1984), chapter 7.
Neuhouser, F. 'Freedom, Dependence, and the General Will'. *Philosophical Review* 102 (1993): 363–395.
Plamenatz, J. P. 'Ce qui ne signifie autre chose sinon qu'on le forcera d'être libre', in M. Cranston and R. S. Peters, eds., *Hobbes and Rousseau: A Collection of Critical Essays* (New York: Doubleday, 1972).
Wokler, R., ed. *Rousseau and Liberty* (Manchester, UK: Manchester University Press, 1995).

Immanuel Kant (1724–1804)

Kant, I. *Kant's Political Writings,* ed. H. Reiss (Cambridge, UK: Cambridge University Press, 1971).
——. *Foundations of the Metaphysics of Morals,* trans. L. W. Beck (New York: Macmillan, 1986).

Bielefeldt, H. 'Autonomy and Republicanism: Immanuel Kant's Philosophy of Freedom'. *Political Theory* 25 (1997): 524–558.

Flikschuh, K. *Kant and Modern Political Philosophy* (Cambridge, UK: Cambridge University Press, 2000).

Murphy, J. G. *Kant: The Philosophy of Right* (London: Macmillan, 1970).

Taylor, C. 'Kant's Theory of Freedom', in Z. Pelczynski and J. N. Gray, eds., *Conceptions of Liberty in Political Philosophy* (London: Athlone Press, 1984).

Williams, H. *Kant's Political Philosophy* (Oxford, UK: Blackwell, 1983).

Benjamin Constant (1767–1830)

Constant, B. 'The Liberty of the Ancients Compared with That of the Moderns', in B. Constant, *Political Writings,* ed. B. Fontana (Cambridge, UK: Cambridge University Press, 1988).

Holmes, S. *Benjamin Constant and the Making of Modern Liberalism* (New Haven, CT: Yale University Press, 1984).

Georg Wilhelm Friedrich Hegel (1770–1831)

Hegel, G. W. F. *Philosophy of Right,* trans. T. M. Knox (Oxford, UK: Clarendon Press, 1952).

Neuhouser, F. *Foundations of Hegel's Social Theory: Actualizing Freedom* (Cambridge, MA: Harvard University Press, 2000).

Patten, A. *Hegel's Idea of Freedom* (Oxford, UK: Oxford University Press, 1999).

Pelczynski, Z. 'Freedom in Hegel', in Z. Pelczynski and J. N. Gray, eds., *Conceptions of Liberty in Political Philosophy* (London: Athlone Press, 1984).

Plamenatz, J. P. 'History as the Realization of Freedom', in Z. Pelczynski, ed., *Hegel's Political Philosophy: Problems and Perspectives* (Cambridge, UK: Cambridge University Press, 1970).

Schacht, R. L. 'Hegel on Freedom', in A. MacIntyre, ed., *Hegel: A Collection of Critical Essays* (Notre Dame, IN: University of Notre Dame Press, 1972).

Wood, A. *Hegel's Ethical Thought* (Cambridge, UK: Cambridge University Press, 1990), chapter 2.

John Stuart Mill (1806–1873)

Mill, J. S. 'On Liberty', in J. S. Mill, *Utilitarianism: On Liberty; Representative Government,* ed. A. D. Lindsay (London: Dent, 1964).

Friedman, R. B. 'A New Exploration of Mill's Essay *On Liberty*'. *Political Studies* 14 (1966): 281–304.

Gray, J. N. *Mill on Liberty: A Defence* (London: Routledge and Kegan Paul, 1983).

Hamburger, J. *John Stuart Mill on Liberty and Control* (Princeton, NJ: Princeton University Press, 1999).

Rees, J. C. *John Stuart Mill's* On Liberty (Oxford, UK: Clarendon Press, 1985).

Riley, J. *Mill on Liberty* (London: Routledge, 1998).

Skorupski, J. *John Stuart Mill* (London: Routledge, 1989), chapter 10.

Smith, G. W. 'J. S. Mill on Freedom', in Z. Pelczynski and J. N. Gray, eds., *Conceptions of Liberty in Political Philosophy* (London: Athlone Press, 1984).

Ten, C. L. *Mill on Liberty* (Oxford, UK: Clarendon Press, 1980).

Karl Marx *(1818–1883)*

Marx, K. *Selected Writings,* ed. D. McLellan (Oxford, UK: Oxford University Press, 1977).

Brenkert, G. G. *Marx's Ethics of Freedom* (London: Routledge and Kegan Paul, 1983), chapter 4.

Lukes, S. *Marxism and Morality* (Oxford, UK: Clarendon Press, 1985), chapter 5.

Plamenatz, J. P. *Karl Marx's Philosophy of Man* (Oxford, UK: Clarendon Press, 1975), chapters 12–13.

Smith, G. W. 'Marxian Metaphysics and Individual Freedom', in G. H. R. Parkinson, ed., *Marx and Marxisms* (Cambridge, UK: Cambridge University Press, 1982).

Wood, A. *Karl Marx* (London: Routledge, 1999), chapter 4.

John Rawls *(1921–2002)*

Rawls, J. *A Theory of Justice* (Cambridge, MA: Harvard University Press, 1971), chapter 4.

——. 'The Basic Liberties and Their Priority', in J. Rawls, *Political Liberalism* (New York: Columbia University Press, 1993).

Daniels, N. 'Equal Liberty and the Unequal Worth of Liberty', in N. Daniels, ed., *Reading Rawls* (Oxford, UK: Blackwell, 1975).

Hart, H. L. A. 'Rawls on Liberty and Its Priority', in N. Daniels, ed., *Reading Rawls* (Oxford, UK: Blackwell, 1975).

Nagel, T. 'Rawls and Liberalism', in S. Freeman, ed., *The Cambridge Companion to Rawls* (Cambridge, UK: Cambridge University Press, 2003).

Paul, J. 'Rawls on Liberty', in Z. Pelczynski and J. N. Gray, eds., *Conceptions of Liberty in Political Philosophy* (London: Athlone Press, 1984).

Michel Foucault *(1926–1984)*

Foucault, M. 'Two Lectures', in M. Foucault, *Power/Knowledge,* ed. C. Gordon (Hemel Hempstead, UK: Harvester, 1980).

——. *Discipline and Punish* (Harmondsworth, UK: Penguin, 1991).

Dumm, T. *Michel Foucault and the Politics of Freedom* (Thousand Oaks, CA: Sage, 1996).

262   *Selected Bibliography*

Rajchman, J. *Michel Foucault: The Freedom of Philosophy* (New York: Columbia University Press, 1985).

Taylor, C. 'Foucault on Freedom and Truth'. *Political Theory* 12 (1984): 152–183. (Reprinted in C. Taylor, *Philosophy and the Human Sciences* [Cambridge, UK: Cambridge University Press, 1985].)

ADDITIONAL READING RELEVANT TO THE ESSAYS REPRINTED IN THIS VOLUME

T. H. Green

Green, T. H. 'On the Different Senses of "Freedom" as Applied to Will and to the Moral Progress of Man', in P. Harris and J. Morrow, eds. *Lectures on the Principles of Political Obligation* (Cambridge, UK: Cambridge University Press, 1986).

Dimova-Cookson, M. 'A New Scheme of Positive and Negative Freedom: Reconstructing T. H. Green on Freedom'. *Political Theory* 31 (2003): 508–532.

Nicholls, D. 'Positive Liberty, 1880–1914'. *American Political Science Review* 56 (1962): 114–128.

Nicholson, P. *The Political Philosophy of the British Idealists* (Cambridge, UK: Cambridge University Press, 1990), Studies IV–V.

Norman, R. *Free and Equal* (Oxford, UK: Oxford University Press, 1987), chapters 2–3.

Simhony, A. 'Beyond Negative and Positive Freedom: T. H. Green's View of Freedom'. *Political Theory* 21 (1993): 28–54.

Weinstein, W. L. 'The Concept of Liberty in Nineteenth-Century English Political Thought'. *Political Studies* 13 (1965): 145–162.

Isaiah Berlin

Berlin, I. *Liberty,* ed. Henry Hardy (Oxford, UK: Oxford University Press, 2002).

Cohen, M. 'Berlin and the Liberal Tradition'. *Philosophical Quarterly* 10 (1960): 216–227.

Crowder, G. *Isaiah Berlin: Liberty and Pluralism* (Cambridge, UK: Polity Press, 2004), especially chapter 4.

Gray, J. *Berlin* (London: Fontana Press, 1995), chapter 1.

——. 'On Negative and Positive Liberty'. *Political Studies* 28, no. 4 (1980): 507–526. (Reprinted in Z. Pelczynski and J. N. Gray, eds., *Conceptions of Liberty in Political Philosophy* [London: Athlone Press, 1984], and in J. Gray, *Liberalisms* [London: Routledge, 1989].)

Hunt, I. 'Freedom and Its Conditions'. *Australasian Journal of Philosophy* 69 (1991): 288–301.

MacPherson, C. B. 'Berlin's Division of Liberty', in *Democratic Theory: Essays in Retrieval* (Oxford, UK: Clarendon Press, 1973).

Swift, A. *Political Philosophy: A Beginner's Guide for Students and Politicians* (Cambridge, UK: Polity Press, 2001), Part II.

Hannah Arendt

Arendt, H. *On Revolution* (Harmondsworth, UK: Penguin, 1973).

Beiner, R. 'Action, Natality, and Citizenship: Hannah Arendt's Concept of Freedom', in Z. Pelczynski and J. N. Gray, eds., *Conceptions of Liberty in Political Philosophy* (London: Athlone Press, 1984).

Canovan, M. *The Political Thought of Hannah Arendt* (London: Methuen, 1977).

Crick, B. 'Freedom as Politics', in P. Laslett and W. G. Runciman, eds., *Philosophy, Politics, and Society*, 3rd ser. (Oxford, UK: Blackwell, 1967).

Kateb, G. 'Freedom and Worldliness in the Thought of Hannah Arendt'. *Political Theory* 5 (1977): 141–182.

Keenan, A. 'Promises, Promises: The Abyss of Freedom and the Loss of the Political in the Work of Hannah Arendt'. *Political Theory* 22 (1994): 297–322.

F. A. Hayek

Barry, N. 'Hayek on Liberty', in Z. Pelczynski and J. N. Gray, eds., *Conceptions of Liberty in Political Philosophy* (London: Athlone Press, 1984).

Gray, J. N. *Hayek on Liberty* (Oxford, UK: Blackwell, 1984).

——. 'Hayek on Liberty, Rights, and Justice'. *Ethics* 92 (1981–1982): 73–84. (Reprinted in J. Gray, *Liberalisms* [London: Routledge, 1989].)

Hamowy, R. 'Freedom and the Rule of Law in F. A. Hayek'. *Il politico* 36 (1971): 349–377.

Kukathas, C. *Hayek and Modern Liberalism* (Oxford, UK: Clarendon Press, 1989), chapter 4.

Gerald C. MacCallum, Jr.

Baldwin, T. 'MacCallum and the Two Concepts of Freedom'. *Ratio* 26 (1984): 125–142.

Gray, J. 'On Positive and Negative Liberty'. *Political Studies* 28 (1980): 507–526. (Reprinted in Z. Pelczynski and J. N. Gray, eds., *Conceptions of Liberty in Political Philosophy* [London: Athlone Press, 1984], and in J. Gray, *Liberalisms* [London: Routledge, 1989].)

Hillel Steiner

Steiner, H. 'How Free: Computing Personal Liberty', in A. Phillips Griffiths, ed., *Of Liberty* (Cambridge, UK: Cambridge University Press, 1983).

Carter, I. *A Measure of Freedom* (Oxford, UK: Oxford University Press, 1999), chapter 6.

Gray, J. 'Liberalism and the Choice of Liberties', in J. Gray, *Liberalisms* (London: Routledge, 1989).

Kramer, M. *The Quality of Freedom* (Oxford, UK: Oxford University Press, 2003), chapter 5.

Taylor, M. *Community, Anarchy, and Liberty* (Cambridge, UK: Cambridge University Press, 1982), chapter 4.

Charles Taylor

Megone, C. 'One Concept of Liberty'. *Political Studies* 35 (1987): 611–622.

Steiner, H. 'How Free: Computing Personal Liberty', in A. Phillips Griffiths, ed., *Of Liberty* (Cambridge, UK: Cambridge University Press, 1983).

G. A. Cohen

Cohen, G. A. 'The Structure of Proletarian Unfreedom', in *History, Labour, and Freedom: Themes from Marx* (Oxford, UK: Clarendon Press, 1988).

——. 'Illusions about Private Property and Freedom', in J. Mepham and D.-H. Ruben, eds., *Issues in Marxist Philosophy,* vol. IV (Brighton, UK: Harvester Press, 1981).

Brenkert, G. G. 'Cohen on Proletarian Unfreedom'. *Philosophy and Public Affairs* 14 (1985): 91–98.

Gray, J. N. 'Against Cohen on Proletarian Unfreedom'. *Social Philosophy and Policy* 6 (1988–1989): 77–112. Also available as E. F. Paul et al., eds., *Capitalism* (Oxford, UK: Blackwell, 1989).

David Miller

Carter, I. *A Measure of Freedom* (Oxford, UK: Oxford University Press, 1999), chapter 8.

Kristjansson, K. *Social Freedom: The Responsibility View* (Cambridge, UK: Cambridge University Press, 1996), chapters 2–4.

Nancy J. Hirschmann

Hirschmann, N. *The Subject of Liberty: Toward a Feminist Theory of Freedom* (Princeton, NJ: Princeton University Press, 2003).

Philip Pettit

Pettit, P. 'Freedom as Anti-Power'. *Ethics* 106 (1996): 576–604.

——. *Republicanism: A Theory of Freedom and Government* (Oxford, UK: Oxford University Press, 1997).

Gaus, G. 'Backwards into the Future: Neorepublicanism as a Postsocialist Critique of Market Society'. *Social Philosophy and Policy* 20 (2003): 59–91, section II.

Maddox, G. 'The Limits of Neo-Roman Liberty'. *History of Political Thought* 23 (2002): 418–431.

Quentin Skinner

Skinner, Q. 'The Idea of Negative Liberty: Philosophical and Historical Perspectives', in R. Rorty, J. B. Schneewind, and Q. Skinner, eds., *Philosophy in History* (Cambridge, UK: Cambridge University Press, 1984).

——. 'The Paradoxes of Political Liberty', in *The Tanner Lectures on Human Values*, vol. VII (Salt Lake City: University of Utah Press, 1986. Reprinted in D. Miller, ed., *Liberty* [Oxford, UK: Oxford University Press, 1991]).

Kelly, P. 'Classical Utilitarianism and the Concept of Freedom: A Response to the Republican Critique'. *Journal of Political Ideologies* 6 (2001): 13–31.

Kramer, M. *The Quality of Freedom* (Oxford, UK: Oxford University Press, 2003), chapter 2.

Patten, A. 'The Republican Critique of Liberalism'. *British Journal of Political Science* 26 (1996): 25–44.

Pettit, P. 'Keeping Republican Freedom Simple'. *Political Theory* 30 (2002): 339–356.

INDEX

About the Editor and Contributors

Hannah Arendt (1906–1975) was born and educated in Germany before immigrating to the United States in 1941. She taught at the New School of Social Research and at the Universities of California, Princeton, Columbia, and Chicago. Her major works were *The Human Condition* (1958), *On Revolution* (1963), and *The Life of the Mind* (1978).

Isaiah Berlin (1909–1997) was a Fellow of All Souls College, Oxford, and from 1957 to 1967, Chichele Professor of Social and Political Theory. His publications include *Karl Marx* (1939), *Concepts and Categories* (1978), *The Crooked Timber of Humanity* (1990), and *Liberty* (2002).

G. A. Cohen was educated at McGill University and taught at University College, London, before becoming Chichele Professor of Social and Political Theory at Oxford. He has published *Karl Marx's Theory of History* (1978), *Self-ownership, Freedom, and Equality* (1995), and *If You're an Egalitarian, How Come You're So Rich?* (2000).

T. H. Green (1836–1882) was a Fellow of Balliol College and Whyte's Professor of Moral Philosophy at Oxford. His most important works were *Lectures on the Principles of Political Obligation* (1879–1880) and *Prolegomena to Ethics* (1883).

F. A. Hayek (1899–1992) studied in Vienna and held professorships at the London School of Economics and the Universities of Chicago and Freiburg. He was awarded a Nobel Prize for economics in 1974. His works include *The Road to Serfdom* (1944), *The Constitution of Liberty* (1960), and *Law, Legislation, and Liberty* (1982).

Nancy J. Hirschmann taught at Cornell University before becoming a professor of Political Science at the University of Pennsylvania. Her publications include *Rethinking Obligation: A Feminist Method for Political Theory* (1992) and *The Structure of Liberty* (2003).

Gerald C. MacCallum, Jr. (1925–1987) was educated at the University of California at Berkeley, and became a professor of Philosophy at the University

279

of Wisconsin. He published *Political Philosophy* (1987), and some of his articles in legal and political philosophy were collected in *Legislative Intent and Other Essays on Law, Politics, and Morality* (1993).

David Miller is a professor of Political Theory and a Fellow of Nuffield College, Oxford. His books include *On Nationality* (1995), *Principles of Social Justice* (1999), and *Political Philosophy: A Very Short Introduction* (2003).

Philip Pettit was born in Ireland and held professorships at the University of Bradford and the Australian National University before taking up his present post as professor of Politics and Philosophy at Princeton University. Among his more recent books are *The Common Mind* (1993), *Republicanism* (1997), and *A Theory of Freedom* (2001).

Quentin Skinner was formerly professor of Political Science at Cambridge University and now holds the Regius Chair in Modern History. His many books include *Meaning and Context,* edited with J. Tully (1988), *The Foundations of Modern Political Thought* (1978), *Liberty before Liberalism* (1998), and *Visions of Politics* (2002).

Hillel Steiner is professor of Political Philosophy in the Department of Government, International Politics, and Philosophy at Manchester University. He has published many papers on the issues of liberty, rights, and distributive justice as well as *An Essay on Rights* (1994).

Charles Taylor was formerly Chichele Professor of Social and Political Theory at Oxford and professor of Philosophy and Political Science at McGill University; he is now professor of Philosophy at Northwestern University. His books include *Hegel* (1975), *Sources of the Self* (1989), and *Modern Social Imaginaries* (2004).